Selected Teachings of James Allen

By James Allen

As a Man Thinketh
The Way of Peace
Above Life's Turmoil
Byways to Blessedness
The Path of Prosperity

Start Publishing PD LLC
Copyright © 2024 by Start Publishing PD LLC

All rights reserved, including the right to reproduce this book or portions thereof in any form whatsoever.

Start Publishing PD is a registered trademark of Start Publishing PD LLC
Manufactured in the United States of America

Cover art: Shutterstock/Taisiya Kozorez

Cover design: Jennifer Do

10 9 8 7 6 5 4 3 2 1

ISBN 979-8-8809-1128-8

As a Man Thinketh

Mind is the Master power that moulds and makes,
And Man is Mind, and evermore he takes
The tool of Thought, and, shaping what he wills,
Brings forth a thousand joys, a thousand ills:—
He thinks in secret, and it comes to pass:
Environment is but his looking-glass.

Foreword

This little volume (the result of meditation and experience) is not intended as an exhaustive treatise on the much-written-upon subject of the power of thought. It is suggestive rather than explanatory, its object being to stimulate men and women to the discovery and perception of the truth that—

"They themselves are makers of themselves."

by virtue of the thoughts, which they choose and encourage; that mind is the master-weaver, both of the inner garment of character and the outer garment of circumstance, and that, as they may have hitherto woven in ignorance and pain they may now weave in enlightenment and happiness.

James Allen.
Broad Park Avenue,
Ilfracombe,
England

Thought and Character

The aphorism, "As a man thinketh in his heart so is he," not only embraces the whole of a man's being, but is so comprehensive as to reach out to every condition and circumstance of his life. A man is literally *what he thinks*, his character being the complete sum of all his thoughts.

As the plant springs from, and could not be without, the seed, so every act of a man springs from the hidden seeds of thought, and could not have appeared without them. This applies equally to those acts called "spontaneous" and "unpremeditated" as to those, which are deliberately executed.

Act is the blossom of thought, and joy and suffering are its fruits; thus does a man garner in the sweet and bitter fruitage of his own husbandry.

"Thought in the mind hath made us, What we are By thought was wrought and built. If a man's mind Hath evil thoughts, pain comes on him as comes The wheel the ox behind....

...If one endure In purity of thought, joy follows him As his own shadow—sure."

Man is a growth by law, and not a creation by artifice, and cause and effect is as absolute and undeviating in the hidden realm of thought as in the world of visible and material things. A noble and Godlike character is not a thing of favor or chance, but is the natural result of continued effort in right thinking, the effect of long-cherished association with Godlike thoughts. An ignoble and bestial character, by the same process, is the result of the continued harboring of groveling thoughts.

Man is made or unmade by himself; in the armory of thought he forges the weapons by which he destroys himself; he also fashions the tools with which he builds for himself heavenly mansions of joy and strength and peace. By the right choice and true application of thought, man ascends to the Divine Perfection; by the abuse and wrong application of thought, he descends below the level of the beast. Between these two extremes are all the grades of character, and man is their maker and master.

Of all the beautiful truths pertaining to the soul which have been restored and brought to light in this age, none is more gladdening or fruitful of divine promise and confidence than this—that man is the master of thought, the molder of character, and the maker and shaper of condition, environment, and destiny.

As a being of Power, Intelligence, and Love, and the lord of his own thoughts, man holds the key to every situation, and contains within himself that transforming and regenerative agency by which he may make himself what he wills.

Man is always the master, even in his weaker and most abandoned state; but in his weakness and degradation he is the foolish master who misgoverns his "household." When he begins to reflect upon his condition, and to search diligently for the Law upon which his being is established, he then becomes the wise master, directing his energies with intelligence, and fashioning his thoughts to fruitful issues. Such is the *conscious* master, and man can only thus become by discovering *within himself* the laws of thought; which discovery is totally a matter of application, self analysis, and experience.

Only by much searching and mining, are gold and diamonds obtained, and man can find every truth connected with his being, if he will dig deep into the mine of his soul; and that he is the maker of his character, the molder of his life, and the builder of his destiny, he may unerringly prove, if he will watch, control, and alter his thoughts, tracing their effects upon himself, upon others, and upon his life and circumstances, linking cause and effect by patient practice and investigation, and utilizing his every experience, even to the most trivial, everyday occurrence, as a means of obtaining that knowledge of himself which is Understanding, Wisdom, Power. In this direction, as in no other, is the law absolute that "He that seeketh findeth; and to him that knocketh it shall be opened;" for only by patience, practice, and ceaseless importunity can a man enter the Door of the Temple of Knowledge.

Effect of Thought on Circumstances

Man's mind may be likened to a garden, which may be intelligently cultivated or allowed to run wild; but whether cultivated or neglected, it must, and will, *bring forth*. If no useful seeds are *put* into it, then an abundance of useless weed-seeds will *fall* therein, and will continue to produce their kind.

Just as a gardener cultivates his plot, keeping it free from weeds, and growing the flowers and fruits which he requires, so may a man tend the garden of his mind, weeding out all the wrong, useless, and impure thoughts, and cultivating toward perfection the flowers and fruits of right, useful, and pure thoughts. By pursuing this process, a man sooner or later discovers that he is the master-gardener of his soul, the director of his life. He also reveals, within himself, the laws of thought, and understands, with ever-increasing accuracy, how the thought-forces and mind elements operate in the shaping of his character, circumstances, and destiny.

Thought and character are one, and as character can only manifest and discover itself through environment and circumstance, the outer conditions of a person's life will always be found to be harmoniously related to his inner state. This does not mean that a man's circumstances at any given time are an indication of his *entire* character, but that those circumstances are so intimately connected with some vital thought-element within himself that, for the time being, they are indispensable to his development.

Every man is where he is by the law of his being; the thoughts which he has built into his character have brought him there, and in the arrangement of his life there is no element of chance, but all is the result of a law which cannot err. This is just as true of those who feel "out of harmony" with their surroundings as of those who are contented with them.

As a progressive and evolving being, man is where he is that he may learn that he may grow; and as he learns the spiritual lesson which any circumstance contains for him, it passes away and gives place to other circumstances.

Man is buffeted by circumstances so long as he believes himself to be the creature of outside conditions, but when he realizes that he is a creative power, and that he may command the hidden soil and seeds of his being out of which circumstances grow, he then becomes the rightful master of himself.

That circumstances grow out of thought every man knows who has for any length of time practiced self-control and self-purification, for he will have noticed that the alteration in his circumstances has been in exact ratio with his altered mental condition. So true is this that when a man earnestly applies himself to remedy the defects in his character, and makes swift and marked progress, he passes rapidly through a succession of vicissitudes.

The soul attracts that which it secretly harbors; that which it loves, and also that which it fears; it reaches the height of its cherished aspirations; it falls to the level of its unchastened desires,—and circumstances are the means by which the soul receives its own.

Every thought-seed sown or allowed to fall into the mind, and to take root there, produces its own, blossoming sooner or later into act, and bearing its own fruitage of opportunity and circumstance. Good thoughts bear good fruit, bad thoughts bad fruit.

The outer world of circumstance shapes itself to the inner world of thought, and both pleasant and unpleasant external conditions are factors, which make for the ultimate good of the individual. As the reaper of his own harvest, man learns both by suffering and bliss.

Following the inmost desires, aspirations, thoughts, by which he allows himself to be dominated, (pursuing the will-o'-the-wisps of impure imaginings or steadfastly walking the highway of strong and high endeavor), a man at last arrives at their fruition and fulfilment in the outer conditions of his life. The laws of growth and adjustment everywhere obtains.

A man does not come to the almshouse or the jail by the tyranny of fate or circumstance, but by the pathway of groveling thoughts and base desires. Nor does a pure-minded man fall suddenly into crime by stress of any mere external force; the criminal thought had long been secretly fostered in the heart, and the hour of opportunity revealed its gathered power. Circumstance does not make the man; it reveals him to himself No such conditions can exist as descending into vice and its attendant sufferings apart from vicious inclinations, or ascending into virtue and its pure happiness without the continued cultivation of virtuous aspirations; and man, therefore, as the lord and master of thought, is the maker of himself the shaper and author of environment. Even at birth the soul comes to its own and through every step of its earthly pilgrimage it attracts those combinations of conditions which reveal itself, which are the reflections of its own purity and, impurity, its strength and weakness.

Men do not attract that which they *want*, but that which they *are*. Their whims, fancies, and ambitions are thwarted at every step, but their inmost thoughts and desires are fed with their own food, be it foul or clean. The "divinity that shapes our ends" is in ourselves; it is our very self. Only himself manacles man: thought and action are the gaolers of Fate—they imprison, being base; they are also the angels of Freedom—they liberate, being noble. Not what he wishes and prays for does a man get, but what he justly earns. His wishes and prayers are only gratified and answered when they harmonize with his thoughts and actions.

In the light of this truth, what, then, is the meaning of "fighting against circumstances?" It means that a man is continually revolting against an *effect* without, while all the time he is nourishing and preserving its *cause* in his heart. That cause may take the form of a conscious vice or an unconscious weakness; but whatever it is, it stubbornly retards the efforts of its possessor, and thus calls aloud for remedy.

Men are anxious to improve their circumstances, but are unwilling to improve themselves; they therefore remain bound. The man who does not shrink from self-crucifixion can never fail to accomplish the object upon which his heart is set. This is as true of earthly as of heavenly things. Even the man whose sole object is to acquire wealth must be prepared to make great personal sacrifices before he can accomplish his object; and how much more so he who would realize a strong and well-poised life?

Here is a man who is wretchedly poor. He is extremely anxious that his surroundings and home comforts should be improved, yet all the time he shirks his work, and considers he is justified in trying to deceive his employer on the ground of the insufficiency of his wages. Such a man does not understand the simplest rudiments of those principles which are the basis of true prosperity, and is not only totally unfitted to rise out of his wretchedness, but is actually attracting to himself a still deeper wretchedness by dwelling in, and acting out, indolent, deceptive, and unmanly thoughts.

Here is a rich man who is the victim of a painful and persistent disease as the result of gluttony. He is willing to give large sums of money to get rid of it, but he will not sacrifice his gluttonous desires. He wants to gratify his taste for rich and unnatural viands and have his health as well. Such a man is totally unfit to have health, because he has not yet learned the first principles of a healthy life.

Here is an employer of labor who adopts crooked measures to avoid paying the regulation wage, and, in the hope of making larger profits, reduces the wages of his workpeople. Such a man is altogether unfitted for prosperity, and when he finds himself bankrupt, both as regards reputation and riches, he blames circumstances, not knowing that he is the sole author of his condition.

I have introduced these three cases merely as illustrative of the truth that man is the causer (though nearly always is unconsciously) of his circumstances, and that, whilst aiming at a good end, he is continually frustrating its accomplishment by encouraging thoughts and desires which cannot possibly harmonize with that end. Such cases could be multiplied and varied almost indefinitely, but this is not necessary, as the reader can, if he so resolves, trace the action of the laws of thought in his own mind and life, and until this is done, mere external facts cannot serve as a ground of reasoning.

Circumstances, however, are so complicated, thought is so deeply rooted, and the conditions of happiness vary so, vastly with individuals, that a man's entire soul-condition (although it may be known to himself) cannot be judged by another from the external aspect of his life alone. A man may be honest in certain directions, yet suffer privations; a man may be dishonest in certain directions, yet acquire wealth; but the conclusion usually formed that the one man fails *because of his particular honesty*, and that the other *prospers because of his particular dishonesty*, is the result of a superficial judgment, which assumes that the dishonest man is almost totally corrupt, and the honest man almost entirely virtuous. In the light of a deeper knowledge and wider experience such judgment is found to be erroneous. The dishonest man may have some admirable virtues, which the other does, not possess; and the honest man obnoxious vices which are absent in the other. The honest man reaps the good results of his honest thoughts and acts; he also brings upon himself the sufferings, which his vices produce. The dishonest man likewise garners his own suffering and happiness.

It is pleasing to human vanity to believe that one suffers because of one's virtue; but not until a man has extirpated every sickly, bitter, and impure thought from his mind, and washed every sinful stain from his soul, can he be in a position to know and declare that his sufferings are the result of his good, and not of his bad qualities; and on the way to, yet long before he has reached, that supreme perfection, he will have found, working in his mind and life, the Great Law which is absolutely just, and which cannot, therefore, give good for evil, evil for good. Possessed of such knowledge, he will then know, looking back upon his past ignorance and blindness, that his life is, and always was, justly ordered, and that all his past experiences, good and bad, were the equitable outworking of his evolving, yet unevolved self.

Good thoughts and actions can never produce bad results; bad thoughts and actions can never produce good results. This is but saying that nothing can come from corn but corn, nothing from nettles but nettles. Men understand this law in the natural world, and work with it; but few understand it in the mental and moral world (though its operation there is just as simple and undeviating), and they, therefore, do not co-operate with it.

Suffering is *always* the effect of wrong thought in some direction. It is an indication that the individual is out of harmony with himself, with the Law of his being. The sole and supreme use of suffering is to purify, to burn out all that is useless and impure. Suffering ceases for him who is pure. There could be no object in burning gold after the dross had been removed, and a perfectly pure and enlightened being could not suffer.

The circumstances, which a man encounters with suffering, are the result of his own mental in harmony. The circumstances, which a man encounters with blessedness, are the result of his own mental harmony. Blessedness, not material possessions, is the measure of right thought; wretchedness, not lack of material possessions, is the measure of wrong thought. A man may be cursed and rich; he may be blessed and poor. Blessedness and riches are only joined together when the riches are rightly and wisely used; and the poor man only descends into wretchedness when he regards his lot as a burden unjustly imposed.

Indigence and indulgence are the two extremes of wretchedness. They are both equally unnatural and the result of mental disorder. A man is not rightly conditioned until he is a happy, healthy, and prosperous being; and happiness, health, and prosperity are the result of a harmonious adjustment of the inner with the outer, of the man with his surroundings.

A man only begins to be a man when he ceases to whine and revile, and commences to search for the hidden justice which regulates his life. And as he adapts his mind to that regulating factor, he ceases to accuse others as the cause of his condition, and builds himself up in strong and noble thoughts; ceases to kick against circumstances, but begins to *use* them as aids to his more rapid progress, and as a means of discovering the hidden powers and possibilities within himself.

Law, not confusion, is the dominating principle in the universe; justice, not injustice, is the soul and substance of life; and righteousness, not corruption, is the molding and moving force in the spiritual government of the world. This being so, man has but to right himself to find that the universe is right; and during the process of putting himself right he will find that as he alters his thoughts towards things and other people, things and other people will alter towards him.

The proof of this truth is in every person, and it therefore admits of easy investigation by systematic introspection and self-analysis. Let a man radically alter his thoughts, and he will be astonished at the rapid transformation it will effect in the material conditions of his life. Men imagine that thought can be kept secret, but it cannot; it rapidly crystallizes into habit, and habit solidifies into circumstance. Bestial thoughts crystallize into habits of drunkenness and sensuality, which solidify into circumstances of destitution and disease: impure thoughts of every kind crystallize into enervating and confusing habits, which solidify into distracting and adverse circumstances: thoughts of fear, doubt, and indecision crystallize into weak, unmanly, and irresolute habits, which solidify into circumstances of failure, indigence, and slavish dependence: lazy thoughts crystallize into habits of uncleanliness and dishonesty, which solidify into circumstances of foulness and beggary: hateful and condemnatory thoughts crystallize into habits of accusation and violence, which solidify into circumstances of injury and persecution: selfish thoughts of all kinds crystallize into habits of self-seeking, which solidify into circumstances more or less distressing. On the other hand, beautiful thoughts of all kinds crystallize into habits of grace and kindliness, which solidify into genial and sunny circumstances: pure thoughts crystallize into habits of temperance and self-control, which solidify into circumstances of repose and peace: thoughts of courage, self-reliance, and decision crystallize into manly habits, which solidify into circumstances of success, plenty, and freedom: energetic thoughts crystallize into habits of cleanliness and industry, which solidify into circumstances of pleasantness: gentle and forgiving thoughts crystallize into habits of gentleness, which solidify into protective and preservative circumstances: loving and unselfish thoughts crystallize into habits of self-forgetfulness for others, which solidify into circumstances of sure and abiding prosperity and true riches.

A particular train of thought persisted in, be it good or bad, cannot fail to produce its results on the character and circumstances. A man cannot *directly* choose his circumstances, but he can choose his thoughts, and so indirectly, yet surely, shape his circumstances.

Nature helps every man to the gratification of the thoughts, which he most encourages, and opportunities are presented which will most speedily bring to the surface both the good and evil thoughts.

Let a man cease from his sinful thoughts, and all the world will soften towards him, and be ready to help him; let him put away his weakly and sickly thoughts, and lo, opportunities will spring up on every hand to aid his strong resolves; let him encourage good thoughts, and no hard fate shall bind him down to wretchedness and shame. The world is your kaleidoscope, and the varying combinations of colors, which at every succeeding moment it presents to you are the exquisitely adjusted pictures of your ever-moving thoughts.

"So You will be what you will to be;
Let failure find its false content
In that poor word, 'environment,'
But spirit scorns it, and is free.

"It masters time, it conquers space;
It cowes that boastful trickster, Chance,
And bids the tyrant Circumstance
Uncrown, and fill a servant's place.

"The human Will, that force unseen,
The offspring of a deathless Soul,
Can hew a way to any goal,
Though walls of granite intervene.
"Be not impatient in delays
But wait as one who understands;
When spirit rises and commands
The gods are ready to obey."

Effect of Thought on Health and the Body

The body is the servant of the mind. It obeys the operations of the mind, whether they be deliberately chosen or automatically expressed. At the bidding of unlawful thoughts the body sinks rapidly into disease and decay; at the command of glad and beautiful thoughts it becomes clothed with youthfulness and beauty.

Disease and health, like circumstances, are rooted in thought. Sickly thoughts will express themselves through a sickly body. Thoughts of fear have been known to kill a man as speedily as a bullet, and they are continually killing thousands of people just as surely though less rapidly. The people who live in fear of disease are the people who get it. Anxiety quickly demoralizes the whole body, and lays it open to the, entrance of disease; while impure thoughts, even if not physically indulged, will soon shatter the nervous system.

Strong, pure, and happy thoughts build up the body in vigor and grace. The body is a delicate and plastic instrument, which responds readily to the thoughts by which it is impressed, and habits of thought will produce their own effects, good or bad, upon it.

Men will continue to have impure and poisoned blood, so long as they propagate unclean thoughts. Out of a clean heart comes a clean life and a clean body. Out of a defiled mind proceeds a defiled life and a corrupt body. Thought is the fount of action, life, and manifestation; make the fountain pure, and all will be pure.

Change of diet will not help a man who will not change his thoughts. When a man makes his thoughts pure, he no longer desires impure food.

Clean thoughts make clean habits. The so-called saint who does not wash his body is not a saint. He who has strengthened and purified his thoughts does not need to consider the malevolent microbe.

If you would protect your body, guard your mind. If you would renew your body, beautify your mind. Thoughts of malice, envy, disappointment, despondency, rob the body of its health and grace. A sour face does not come by chance; it is made by sour thoughts. Wrinkles that mar are drawn by folly, passion, and pride.

I know a woman of ninety-six who has the bright, innocent face of a girl. I know a man well under middle age whose face is drawn into inharmonious contours. The one is the result of a sweet and sunny disposition; the other is the outcome of passion and discontent.

As you cannot have a sweet and wholesome abode unless you admit the air and sunshine freely into your rooms, so a strong body and a bright, happy, or serene countenance can only result from the free admittance into the mind of thoughts of joy and goodwill and serenity.

On the faces of the aged there are wrinkles made by sympathy, others by strong and pure thought, and others are carved by passion: who cannot distinguish them? With those who have lived righteously, age is calm, peaceful, and softly mellowed, like the setting sun. I have recently seen a philosopher on his deathbed. He was not old except in years. He died as sweetly and peacefully as he had lived.

There is no physician like cheerful thought for dissipating the ills of the body; there is no comforter to compare with goodwill for dispersing the shadows of grief and sorrow. To live continually in thoughts of ill will, cynicism, suspicion, and envy, is to be confined in a self made prison-hole. But to think well of all, to be cheerful with all, to patiently learn to find the good in all—such unselfish thoughts are the very portals of heaven; and to dwell day by day in thoughts of peace toward every creature will bring abounding peace to their possessor.

Thought and Purpose

Until thought is linked with purpose there is no intelligent accomplishment. With the majority the bark of thought is allowed to "drift" upon the ocean of life. Aimlessness is a vice, and such drifting must not continue for him who would steer clear of catastrophe and destruction.

They who have no central purpose in their life fall an easy prey to petty worries, fears, troubles, and self-pityings, all of which are indications of weakness, which lead, just as surely as deliberately planned sins (though by a different route), to failure, unhappiness, and loss, for weakness cannot persist in a power evolving universe.

A man should conceive of a legitimate purpose in his heart, and set out to accomplish it. He should make this purpose the centralizing point of his thoughts. It may take the form of a spiritual ideal, or it may be a worldly object, according to his nature at the time being; but whichever it is, he should steadily focus his thought-forces upon the object, which he has set before him. He should make this purpose his supreme duty, and should devote himself to its attainment, not allowing his thoughts to wander away into ephemeral fancies, longings, and imaginings. This is the royal road to self-control and true concentration of thought. Even if he fails again and again to accomplish his purpose (as he necessarily must until weakness is overcome), the *strength of character gained* will be the measure of *his true* success, and this will form a new starting-point for future power and triumph.

Those who are not prepared for the apprehension of a *great* purpose should fix the thoughts upon the faultless performance of their duty, no matter how insignificant their task may appear. Only in this way can the thoughts be gathered and focused, and resolution and energy be developed, which being done, there is nothing which may not be accomplished.

The weakest soul, knowing its own weakness, and believing this truth *that strength can only be developed by effort and practice*, will, thus believing, at once begin to exert itself, and, adding effort to effort, patience to patience, and strength to strength, will never cease to develop, and will at last grow divinely strong.

As the physically weak man can make himself strong by careful and patient training, so the man of weak thoughts can make them strong by exercising himself in right thinking.

To put away aimlessness and weakness, and to begin to think with purpose, is to enter the ranks of those strong ones who only recognize failure as one of the pathways to attainment; who make all conditions serve them, and who think strongly, attempt fearlessly, and accomplish masterfully.

Having conceived of his purpose, a man should mentally mark out a *straight* pathway to its achievement, looking neither to the right nor the left. Doubts and fears should be rigorously excluded; they are disintegrating elements, which break up the straight line of effort, rendering it crooked, ineffectual, useless. Thoughts of doubt and fear never accomplished anything, and never can. They always lead to failure. Purpose, energy, power to do, and all strong thoughts cease when doubt and fear creep in.

The will to do springs from the knowledge that we *can* do. Doubt and fear are the great enemies of knowledge, and he who encourages them, who does not slay them. thwarts himself at every step.

He who has conquered doubt and fear has conquered failure. His every, thought is allied with power, and all difficulties are bravely met and wisely overcome. His purposes are seasonably planted, and they bloom and bring forth fruit, which does not fall prematurely to the ground.

Thought allied fearlessly to purpose becomes creative force: he who *knows* this is ready to become something higher and stronger than a mere bundle of wavering thoughts and fluctuating sensations; he who *does* this has become the conscious and intelligent wielder of his mental powers.

The Thought-factor in Achievement

All that a man achieves and all that he fails to achieve is the direct result of his own thoughts. In a justly ordered universe, where loss of equipoise would mean total destruction, individual responsibility must be absolute. A man's weakness and strength, purity and impurity, are his own, and not another man's; they are brought about by himself, and not by another; and they can only be altered by himself, never by another. His condition is also his own, and not another man's. His suffering and his happiness are evolved from within. As he thinks, so he is; as he continues to think, so he remains.

A strong man cannot help a weaker unless that weaker is *willing* to be helped, and even then the weak man must become strong of himself; he must, by his own efforts, develop the strength which he admires in another. None but himself can alter his condition.

It has been usual for men to think and to say, "Many men are slaves because one is an oppressor; let us hate the oppressor." Now, however, there is amongst an increasing few a tendency to reverse this judgment, and to say, "One man is an oppressor because many are slaves; let us despise the slaves."

The truth is that oppressor and slave are co-operators in ignorance, and, while seeming to afflict each other, are in reality afflicting themselves. A perfect Knowledge perceives the action of law in the weakness of the oppressed and the misapplied power of the oppressor; a perfect Love, seeing the suffering, which both states entail, condemns neither; a perfect Compassion embraces both oppressor and oppressed.

He who has conquered weakness, and has put away all selfish thoughts, belongs neither to oppressor nor oppressed. He is free.

A man can only rise, conquer, and achieve by lifting up his thoughts. He can only remain weak, and abject, and miserable by refusing to lift up his thoughts.

Before a man can achieve anything, even in worldly things, he must lift his thoughts above slavish animal indulgence. He may not, in order to succeed, give up all animality and selfishness, by any means; but a portion of it must, at least, be sacrificed. A man whose first thought is bestial indulgence could neither think clearly nor plan methodically; he could not find and develop his latent resources, and would fail in any undertaking. Not having commenced to manfully control his thoughts, he is not in a position to control affairs and to adopt serious responsibilities. He is not fit to act independently and stand alone. But he is limited only by the thoughts, which he chooses.

There can be no progress, no achievement without sacrifice, and a man's worldly success will be in the measure that he sacrifices his confused animal thoughts, and fixes his mind on the development of his plans, and the strengthening of his resolution and self-reliance. And the higher he lifts his thoughts, the more manly, upright, and righteous he becomes, the greater will be his success, the more blessed and enduring will be his achievements.

The universe does not favor the greedy, the dishonest, the vicious, although on the mere surface it may sometimes appear to do so; it helps the honest, the magnanimous, the virtuous. All the great Teachers of the ages have declared this in varying forms, and to prove and know it a man has but to persist in making himself more and more virtuous by lifting up his thoughts.

Intellectual achievements are the result of thought consecrated to the search for knowledge, or for the beautiful and true in life and nature. Such achievements may be sometimes connected with vanity and ambition, but they are not the outcome of those characteristics; they are the natural outgrowth of long and arduous effort, and of pure and unselfish thoughts.

Spiritual achievements are the consummation of holy aspirations. He who lives constantly in the conception of noble and lofty thoughts, who dwells upon all that is pure and unselfish, will, as surely as the sun reaches its zenith and the moon its full, become wise and noble in character, and rise into a position of influence and blessedness.

Achievement, of whatever kind, is the crown of effort, the diadem of thought. By the aid of self-control, resolution, purity, righteousness, and well-directed thought a man ascends; by the aid of animality, indolence, impurity, corruption, and confusion of thought a man descends.

A man may rise to high success in the world, and even to lofty altitudes in the spiritual realm, and again descend into weakness and wretchedness by allowing arrogant, selfish, and corrupt thoughts to take possession of him.

Victories attained by right thought can only be maintained by watchfulness. Many give way when success is assured, and rapidly fall back into failure.

All achievements, whether in the business, intellectual, or spiritual world, are the result of definitely directed thought, are governed by the same law and are of the same method; the only difference lies in *the object of attainment.*

He who would accomplish little must sacrifice little; he who would achieve much must sacrifice much; he who would attain highly must sacrifice greatly.

Visions and Ideals

The dreamers are the saviors of the world. As the visible world is sustained by the invisible, so men, through all their trials and sins and sordid vocations, are nourished by the beautiful visions of their solitary dreamers. Humanity cannot forget its dreamers; it cannot let their ideals fade and die; it lives in them; it knows them as they *realities* which it shall one day see and know.

Composer, sculptor, painter, poet, prophet, sage, these are the makers of the after-world, the architects of heaven. The world is beautiful because they have lived; without them, laboring humanity would perish.

He who cherishes a beautiful vision, a lofty ideal in his heart, will one day realize it. Columbus cherished a vision of another world, and he discovered it; Copernicus fostered the vision of a multiplicity of worlds and a wider universe, and he revealed it; Buddha beheld the vision of a spiritual world of stainless beauty and perfect peace, and he entered into it.

Cherish your visions; cherish your ideals; cherish the music that stirs in your heart, the beauty that forms in your mind, the loveliness that drapes your purest thoughts, for out of them will grow all delightful conditions, all, heavenly environment; of these, if you but remain true to them, your world will at last be built.

To desire is to obtain; to aspire is to, achieve. Shall man's basest desires receive the fullest measure of gratification, and his purest aspirations starve for lack of sustenance? Such is not the Law: such a condition of things can never obtain: "ask and receive."

Dream lofty dreams, and as you dream, so shall you become. Your Vision is the promise of what you shall one day be; your Ideal is the prophecy of what you shall at last unveil.

The greatest achievement was at first and for a time a dream. The oak sleeps in the acorn; the bird waits in the egg; and in the highest vision of the soul a waking angel stirs. Dreams are the seedlings of realities.

Your circumstances may be uncongenial, but they shall not long remain so if you but perceive an Ideal and strive to reach it. You cannot travel *within* and stand still *without*. Here is a youth hard pressed by poverty and labor; confined long hours in an unhealthy workshop; unschooled, and lacking all the arts of refinement. But he dreams of better things; he thinks of intelligence, of refinement, of grace and beauty. He conceives of, mentally builds up, an ideal condition of life; the vision of a wider liberty and a larger scope takes possession of him; unrest urges him to action, and he utilizes all his spare time and means, small though they are, to the development of his latent powers and resources. Very soon so altered has his mind become that the workshop can no longer hold him. It has become so out of harmony with his mentality that it falls out of his life as a garment is cast aside, and, with the growth of opportunities, which fit the scope of his expanding powers, he passes out of it forever. Years later we see this youth as a full-grown man. We find him a master of certain forces of the mind, which he wields with worldwide influence and almost unequaled power. In his hands he holds the cords of gigantic responsibilities; he speaks, and lo, lives are changed; men and women hang upon his words and remold their characters, and, sunlike, he becomes the fixed and luminous center round which innumerable destinies revolve. He has realized the Vision of his youth. He has become one with his Ideal.

And you, too, youthful reader, will realize the Vision (not the idle wish) of your heart, be it base or beautiful, or a mixture of both, for you will always gravitate toward that which you, secretly, most love. Into your hands will be placed the exact results of your own thoughts; you will receive that which you earn; no more, no less. Whatever your present environment may be, you will fall, remain, or rise with your thoughts, your Vision, your Ideal. You will become as small as your controlling desire; as great as your dominant aspiration: in the beautiful words of Stanton Kirkham Davis, "You may be keeping accounts, and presently you shall walk out of the door that for so long has seemed to you the barrier of your ideals, and shall find yourself before an audience—the pen still behind your ear, the ink stains on your fingers and then and there shall pour out the torrent of your inspiration. You may be driving sheep, and you shall wander to the city-bucolic and open-mouthed; shall wander under the intrepid guidance of the spirit into the studio of the master, and after a time he shall say, 'I have nothing more to teach you.' And now you have become the master, who did so recently dream of great things while driving sheep. You shall lay down the saw and the plane to take upon yourself the regeneration of the world."

The thoughtless, the ignorant, and the indolent, seeing only the apparent effects of things and not the things themselves, talk of luck, of fortune, and chance. Seeing a man grow rich, they say, "How lucky he is!" Observing another become intellectual, they exclaim, "How highly favored he is!" And noting the saintly character and wide influence of another, they remark, "How chance aids him at every turn!" They do not see the trials and failures and struggles which these men have voluntarily encountered in order to gain their experience; have no knowledge of the sacrifices they have made, of the undaunted efforts they have put forth, of the faith they have exercised, that they might overcome the apparently insurmountable, and realize the Vision of their heart. They do not know the darkness and the heartaches; they only see the light and joy, and call it "luck". They do not see the long and arduous journey, but only behold the pleasant goal, and call it "good fortune," do not understand the process, but only perceive the result, and call it chance.

In all human affairs there are *efforts*, and there are *results*, and the strength of the effort is the measure of the result. Chance is not. Gifts, powers, material, intellectual, and spiritual possessions are the fruits of effort; they are thoughts completed, objects accomplished, visions realized.

The Vision that you glorify in your mind, the Ideal that you enthrone in your heart—this you will build your life by, this you will become.

Serenity

Calmness of mind is one of the beautiful jewels of wisdom. It is the result of long and patient effort in self-control. Its presence is an indication of ripened experience, and of a more than ordinary knowledge of the laws and operations of thought.

A man becomes calm in the measure that he understands himself as a thought evolved being, for such knowledge necessitates the understanding of others as the result of thought, and as he develops a right understanding, and sees more and more clearly the internal relations of things by the action of cause and effect he ceases to fuss and fume and worry and grieve, and remains poised, steadfast, serene.

The calm man, having learned how to govern himself, knows how to adapt himself to others; and they, in turn, reverence his spiritual strength, and feel that they can learn of him and rely upon him. The more tranquil a man becomes, the greater is his success, his influence, his power for good. Even the ordinary trader will find his business prosperity increase as he develops a greater self-control and equanimity, for people will always prefer to deal with a man whose demeanor is strongly equable.

The strong, calm man is always loved and revered. He is like a shade-giving tree in a thirsty land, or a sheltering rock in a storm. "Who does not love a tranquil heart, a sweet-tempered, balanced life? It does not matter whether it rains or shines, or what changes come to those possessing these blessings, for they are always sweet, serene, and calm. That exquisite poise of character, which we call serenity is the last lesson of culture, the fruitage of the soul. It is precious as wisdom, more to be desired than gold—yea, than even fine gold.

How insignificant mere money seeking looks in comparison with a serene life—a life that dwells in the ocean of Truth, beneath the waves, beyond the reach of tempests, in the Eternal Calm!

"How many people we know who sour their lives, who ruin all that is sweet and beautiful by explosive tempers, who destroy their poise of character, and make bad blood! It is a question whether the great majority of people do not ruin their lives and mar their happiness by lack of self-control. How few people we meet in life who are well balanced, who have that exquisite poise which is characteristic of the finished character!

Yes, humanity surges with uncontrolled passion, is tumultuous with ungoverned grief, is blown about by anxiety and doubt only the wise man, only he whose thoughts are controlled and purified, makes the winds and the storms of the soul obey him.

Tempest-tossed souls, wherever ye may be, under whatsoever conditions ye may live, know this in the ocean of life the isles of Blessedness are smiling, and the sunny shore of your ideal awaits your coming. Keep your hand firmly upon the helm of thought. In the bark of your soul reclines the commanding Master; He does but sleep: wake Him. Self-control is strength; Right Thought is mastery; Calmness is power. Say unto your heart, "Peace, be still!"

The Way of Peace

The Power of Meditation

Spiritual meditation is the pathway to Divinity. It is the mystic ladder which reaches from earth to heaven, from error to Truth, from pain to peace. Every saint has climbed it; every sinner must sooner or later come to it, and every weary pilgrim that turns his back upon self and the world, and sets his face resolutely toward the Father's Home, must plant his feet upon its golden rounds. Without its aid you cannot grow into the divine state, the divine likeness, the divine peace, and the fadeless glories and unpolluting joys of Truth will remain hidden from you.

Meditation is the intense dwelling, in thought, upon an idea or theme, with the object of thoroughly comprehending it, and whatsoever you constantly meditate upon you will not only come to understand, but will grow more and more into its likeness, for it will become incorporated into your very being, will become, in fact, your very self. If, therefore, you constantly dwell upon that which is selfish and debasing, you will ultimately become selfish and debased; if you ceaselessly think upon that which is pure and unselfish you will surely become pure and unselfish.

Tell me what that is upon which you most frequently and intensely think, that to which, in your silent hours, your soul most naturally turns, and I will tell you to what place of pain or peace you are traveling, and whether you are growing into the likeness of the divine or the bestial.

There is an unavoidable tendency to become literally the embodiment of that quality upon which one most constantly thinks. Let, therefore, the object of your meditation be above and not below, so that every time you revert to it in thought you will be lifted up; let it be pure and unmixed with any selfish element; so shall your heart become purified and drawn nearer to Truth, and not defiled and dragged more hopelessly into error.

Meditation, in the spiritual sense in which I am now using it, is the secret of all growth in spiritual life and knowledge. Every prophet, sage, and savior became such by the power of meditation. Buddha meditated upon the Truth until he could say, "I am the Truth." Jesus brooded upon the Divine immanence until at last he could declare, "I and my Father are One."

Meditation centered upon divine realities is the very essence and soul of prayer. It is the silent reaching of the soul toward the Eternal. Mere petitionary prayer without meditation is a body without a soul, and is powerless to lift the mind and heart above sin and affliction. If you are daily praying for wisdom, for peace, for loftier purity and a fuller realization of Truth, and that for which you pray is still far from you, it means that you are praying for one thing while living out in thought and act another. If you will cease from such waywardness, taking your mind off those things the selfish clinging to which debars you from the possession of the stainless realities for which you pray: if you will no longer ask God to grant you that which you do not deserve, or to bestow upon you that love and compassion which you refuse to bestow upon others, but will commence to think and act in the spirit of Truth, you will day by day be growing into those realities, so that ultimately you will become one with them.

He who would secure any worldly advantage must be willing to work vigorously for it, and he would be foolish indeed who, waiting with folded hands, expected it to come to him for the mere asking. Do not then vainly imagine that you can obtain the heavenly possessions without making an effort. Only when you commence to work earnestly in the Kingdom of Truth will you be allowed to partake of the Bread of Life, and when you have, by patient and uncomplaining effort, earned the spiritual wages for which you ask, they will not be withheld from you.

If you really seek Truth, and not merely your own gratification; if you love it above all worldly pleasures and gains; more, even, than happiness itself, you will be willing to make the effort necessary for its achievement.

If you would be freed from sin and sorrow; if you would taste of that spotless purity for which you sigh and pray; if you would realize wisdom and knowledge, and would enter into the possession of profound and abiding peace, come now and enter the path of meditation, and let the supreme object of your meditation be Truth.

At the outset, meditation must be distinguished from *idle reverie*. There is nothing dreamy and unpractical about it. It is *a process of searching and uncompromising thought which allows nothing to remain but the simple and naked truth*. Thus meditating you will no longer strive to build yourself up in your prejudices, but, forgetting self, you will remember only that you are seeking the Truth. And so you will remove, one by one, the errors which you have built around yourself in the past, and will patiently wait for the revelation of Truth which will come when your errors have been sufficiently removed. In the silent humility of your heart you will realize that

> "There is an inmost center in us all
> Where Truth abides in fulness; and around,
> Wall upon wall, the gross flesh hems it in;
> This perfect, clear perception, which is Truth,
> A baffling and perverting carnal mesh
> Blinds it, and makes all error; and to know,
> Rather consists in opening out a way
> Whence the imprisoned splendor may escape,
> Than in effecting entry for a light
> Supposed to be without."

Select some portion of the day in which to meditate, and keep that period sacred to your purpose. The best time is the very early morning when the spirit of repose is upon everything. All natural conditions will then be in your favor; the passions, after the long bodily fast of the night, will be subdued, the excitements and worries of the previous day will have died away, and the mind, strong and yet restful, will be receptive to spiritual instruction. Indeed, one of the first efforts you will be called upon to make will be to shake off lethargy and indulgence, and if you refuse you will be unable to advance, for the demands of the spirit are imperative.

To be spiritually awakened is also to be mentally and physically awakened. The sluggard and the self-indulgent can have no knowledge of Truth. He who, possessed of health and strength, wastes the calm, precious hours of the silent morning in drowsy indulgence is totally unfit to climb the heavenly heights.

He whose awakening consciousness has become alive to its lofty possibilities, who is beginning to shake off the darkness of ignorance in which the world is enveloped, rises before the stars have ceased their vigil, and, grappling with the darkness within his soul, strives, by holy aspiration, to perceive the light of Truth while the unawakened world dreams on.

> "The heights by great men reached and kept,
> Were not attained by sudden flight,
> But they, while their companions slept,
> Were toiling upward in the night."

No saint, no holy man, no teacher of Truth ever lived who did not rise early in the morning. Jesus habitually rose early, and climbed the solitary mountains to engage in holy communion. Buddha always rose an hour before sunrise and engaged in meditation, and all his disciples were enjoined to do the same.

If you have to commence your daily duties at a very early hour, and are thus debarred from giving the early morning to systematic meditation, try to give an hour at night, and should this, by the length and laboriousness of your daily task be denied you, you need not despair, for you may turn your thoughts upward in holy meditation in the intervals of your work, or in those few idle minutes which you now waste in aimlessness; and should your work be of that kind which becomes by practice automatic, you may meditate while engaged upon it. That eminent Christian saint and philosopher, Jacob Boehme, realized his vast knowledge of divine things whilst working long hours as a shoemaker. In every life there is time to think, and the busiest, the most laborious is not shut out from aspiration and meditation.

Spiritual meditation and self-discipline are inseparable; you will, therefore, commence to meditate upon yourself so as to try and understand yourself, for, remember, the great object you will have in view will be the complete removal of all your errors in order that you may realize Truth. You will begin to question your motives, thoughts, and acts, comparing them with your ideal, and endeavoring to look upon them with a calm and impartial eye. In this manner you will be continually gaining more of that mental and spiritual equilibrium without which men are but helpless straws upon the ocean of life. If you are given to hatred or anger you will meditate upon gentleness and forgiveness, so as to become acutely alive to a sense of your harsh and foolish conduct. You will then begin to dwell in thoughts of love, of gentleness, of abounding forgiveness; and as you overcome the lower by the higher, there will gradually, silently steal into your heart a knowledge of the divine Law of Love with an understanding of its bearing upon all the intricacies of life and conduct. And in applying this knowledge to your every thought, word, and act, you will grow more and more gentle, more and more loving, more and more divine. And thus with every error, every selfish desire, every human weakness; by the power of meditation is it overcome, and as each sin, each error is thrust out, a fuller and clearer measure of the Light of Truth illumines the pilgrim soul.

Thus meditating, you will be ceaselessly fortifying yourself against your only *real* enemy, your selfish, perishable self, and will be establishing yourself more and more firmly in the divine and imperishable self that is inseparable from Truth. The direct outcome of your meditations will be a calm, spiritual strength which will be your stay and resting-place in the struggle of life. Great is the overcoming power of holy thought, and the strength and knowledge gained in the hour of silent meditation will enrich the soul with saving remembrance in the hour of strife, of sorrow, or of temptation.

As, by the power of meditation, you grow in wisdom, you will relinquish, more and more, your selfish desires which are fickle, impermanent, and productive of sorrow and pain; and will take your stand, with increasing steadfastness and trust, upon unchangeable principles, and will realize heavenly rest.

The use of meditation is the acquirement of a knowledge of eternal principles, and the power which results from meditation is the ability to rest upon and trust those principles, and so become one with the Eternal. The end of meditation is, therefore, direct knowledge of Truth, God, and the realization of divine and profound peace.

Let your meditations take their rise from the ethical ground which you now occupy. Remember that you are to *grow* into Truth by steady perseverance. If you are an orthodox Christian, meditate ceaselessly upon the spotless purity and divine excellence of the character of Jesus, and apply his every precept to your inner life and outward conduct, so as to approximate more and more toward his perfection. Do not be as those religious ones, who, refusing to meditate upon the Law of Truth, and to put into practice the precepts given to them by their Master, are content to formally worship, to cling to their particular creeds, and to continue in the ceaseless round of sin and suffering. Strive to rise, by the power of meditation, above all selfish clinging to partial gods or party creeds; above dead formalities and lifeless ignorance. Thus walking the high way of wisdom, with mind fixed upon the spotless Truth, you shall know no halting-place short of the realization of Truth.

He who earnestly meditates first perceives a truth, as it were, afar off, and then realizes it by daily practice. It is only the doer of the Word of Truth that can know of the doctrine of Truth, for though by pure thought the Truth is perceived, it is only actualized by practice.

Said the divine Gautama, the Buddha, "He who gives himself up to vanity, and does not give himself up to meditation, forgetting the real aim of life and grasping at pleasure, will in time envy him who has exerted himself in meditation," and he instructed his disciples in the following "Five Great Meditations":—

"The first meditation is the meditation of love, in which you so adjust your heart that you long for the weal and welfare of all beings, including the happiness of your enemies.

"The second meditation is the meditation of pity, in which you think of all beings in distress, vividly representing in your imagination their sorrows and anxieties so as to arouse a deep compassion for them in your soul.

"The third meditation is the meditation of joy, in which you think of the prosperity of others, and rejoice with their rejoicings.

"The fourth meditation is the meditation of impurity, in which you consider the evil consequences of corruption, the effects of sin and diseases. How trivial often the pleasure of the moment, and how fatal its consequences.

"The fifth meditation is the meditation on serenity, in which you rise above love and hate, tyranny and oppression, wealth and want, and regard your own fate with impartial calmness and perfect tranquillity."

By engaging in these meditations the disciples of the Buddha arrived at a knowledge of the Truth. But whether you engage in these particular meditations or not matters little so long as your object is Truth, so long as you hunger and thirst for that righteousness which is a holy heart and a blameless life. In your meditations, therefore, let your heart grow and expand with ever-broadening love, until, freed from all hatred, and passion, and condemnation, it embraces the whole universe with thoughtful tenderness. As the flower opens its petals to receive the morning light, so open your soul more and more to the glorious light of Truth. Soar upward upon the wings of aspiration; be fearless, and believe in the loftiest possibilities. Believe that a life of absolute meekness is possible; believe that a life of stainless purity is possible; believe that a life of perfect holiness is possible; believe that the realization of the highest truth is possible. He who so believes, climbs rapidly the heavenly hills, whilst the unbelievers continue to grope darkly and painfully in the fog-bound valleys.

So believing, so aspiring, so meditating, divinely sweet and beautiful will be your spiritual experiences, and glorious the revelations that will enrapture your inward vision. As you realize the divine Love, the divine Justice, the divine Purity, the Perfect Law of Good, or God, great will be your bliss and deep your peace. Old things will pass away, and all things will become new. The veil of the material universe, so dense and impenetrable to the eye of error, so thin and gauzy to the eye of Truth, will be lifted and the spiritual universe will be revealed. Time will cease, and you will live only in Eternity. Change and mortality will no more cause you anxiety and sorrow, for you will become established in the unchangeable, and will dwell in the very heart of immortality.

Star of Wisdom

Star that of the birth of Vishnu,
Birth of Krishna, Buddha, Jesus,
Told the wise ones, Heavenward looking,
Waiting, watching for thy gleaming
In the darkness of the night-time,
In the starless gloom of midnight;
Shining Herald of the coming
Of the kingdom of the righteous;
Teller of the Mystic story
Of the lowly birth of Godhead
In the stable of the passions,
In the manger of the mind-soul;
Silent singer of the secret
Of compassion deep and holy
To the heart with sorrow burdened,
To the soul with waiting weary:—
Star of all-surpassing brightness,
Thou again dost deck the midnight;
Thou again dost cheer the wise ones
Watching in the creedal darkness,
Weary of the endless battle
With the grinding blades of error;
Tired of lifeless, useless idols,
Of the dead forms of religions;
Spent with watching for thy shining;
Thou hast ended their despairing;
Thou hast lighted up their pathway;
Thou hast brought again the old Truths
To the hearts of all thy Watchers;
To the souls of them that love thee
Thou dost speak of Joy and Gladness,
Of the peace that comes of Sorrow.
Blessed are they that can see thee,

Weary wanderers in the Night-time;
Blessed they who feel the throbbing,
In their bosoms feel the pulsing
Of a deep Love stirred within them
By the great power of thy shining.
Let us learn thy lesson truly;
Learn it faithfully and humbly;
Learn it meekly, wisely, gladly,
Ancient Star of holy Vishnu,
Light of Krishna, Buddha, Jesus.

The Two Masters, Self and Truth

Upon the battlefield of the human soul two masters are ever contending for the crown of supremacy, for the kingship and dominion of the heart; the master of self, called also the "Prince of this world," and the master of Truth, called also the Father God. The master self is that rebellious one whose weapons are passion, pride, avarice, vanity, self-will, implements of darkness; the master Truth is that meek and lowly one whose weapons are gentleness, patience, purity, sacrifice, humility, love, instruments of Light.

In every soul the battle is waged, and as a soldier cannot engage at once in two opposing armies, so every heart is enlisted either in the ranks of self or of Truth. There is no half-and-half course; "There is self and there is Truth; where self is, Truth is not, where Truth is, self is not." Thus spake Buddha, the teacher of Truth, and Jesus, the manifested Christ, declared that "No man can serve two masters; for either he will hate the one and love the other; or else he will hold to the one, and despise the other. Ye cannot serve God and Mammon."

Truth is so simple, so absolutely undeviating and uncompromising that it admits of no complexity, no turning, no qualification. Self is ingenious, crooked, and, governed by subtle and snaky desire, admits of endless turnings and qualifications, and the deluded worshipers of self vainly imagine that they can gratify every worldly desire, and at the same time possess the Truth. But the lovers of Truth worship Truth with the sacrifice of self, and ceaselessly guard themselves against worldliness and self-seeking.

Do you seek to know and to realize Truth? Then you must be prepared to sacrifice, to renounce to the uttermost, for Truth in all its glory can only be perceived and known when the last vestige of self has disappeared.

The eternal Christ declared that he who would be His disciple must "deny himself daily." Are you willing to deny yourself, to give up your lusts, your prejudices, your opinions? If so, you may enter the narrow way of Truth, and find that peace from which the world is shut out. The absolute denial, the utter extinction, of self is the perfect state of Truth, and all religions and philosophies are but so many aids to this supreme attainment.

Self is the denial of Truth. Truth is the denial of self. As you let self die, you will be reborn in Truth. As you cling to self, Truth will be hidden from you.

Whilst you cling to self, your path will be beset with difficulties, and repeated pains, sorrows, and disappointments will be your lot. There are no difficulties in Truth, and coming to Truth, you will be freed from all sorrow and disappointment.

Truth in itself is not hidden and dark. It is always revealed and is perfectly transparent. But the blind and wayward self cannot perceive it. The light of day is not hidden except to the blind, and the Light of Truth is not hidden except to those who are blinded by self.

Truth is the one Reality in the universe, the inward Harmony, the perfect Justice, the eternal Love. Nothing can be added to it, nor taken from it. It does not depend upon any man, but all men depend upon it. You cannot perceive the beauty of Truth while you are looking out through the eyes of self. If you are vain, you will color everything with your own vanities. If lustful, your heart and mind will be so clouded with the smoke and flames of passion, that everything will appear distorted through them. If proud and opinionative, you will see nothing in the whole universe except the magnitude and importance of your own opinions.

There is one quality which pre-eminently distinguishes the man of Truth from the man of self, and that is *humility*. To be not only free from vanity, stubbornness and egotism, but to regard one's own opinions as of no value, this indeed is true humility.

He who is immersed in self regards his own opinions as Truth, and the opinions of other men as error. But that humble Truth-lover who has learned to distinguish between opinion and Truth, regards all men with the eye of charity, and does not seek to defend his opinions against theirs, but sacrifices those opinions that he may love the more, that he may manifest the spirit of Truth, for Truth in its very nature is ineffable and can only be lived. He who has most of charity has most of Truth.

Men engage in heated controversies, and foolishly imagine they are defending the Truth, when in reality they are merely defending their own petty interests and perishable opinions. The follower of self takes up arms against others. The follower of Truth takes up arms against himself. Truth, being unchangeable and eternal, is independent of your opinion and of mine. We may enter into it, or we may stay outside; but both our defense and our attack are superfluous, and are hurled back upon ourselves.

Men, enslaved by self, passionate, proud, and condemnatory, believe their particular creed or religion to be the Truth, and all other religions to be error; and they proselytize with passionate ardor. There is but one religion, the religion of Truth. There is but one error, the error of self. Truth is not a formal belief; it is an unselfish, holy, and aspiring heart, and he who has Truth is at peace with all, and cherishes all with thoughts of love.

You may easily know whether you are a child of Truth or a worshiper of self, if you will silently examine your mind, heart, and conduct. Do you harbor thoughts of suspicion, enmity, envy, lust, pride, or do you strenuously fight against these? If the former, you are chained to self, no matter what religion you may profess; if the latter, you are a candidate for Truth, even though outwardly you may profess no religion. Are you passionate, self-willed, ever seeking to gain your own ends, self-indulgent, and self-centered; or are you gentle, mild, unselfish, quit of every form of self-indulgence, and are ever ready to give up your own? If the former, self is your master; if the latter, Truth is the object of your affection. Do you strive for riches? Do you fight, with passion, for your party? Do you lust for power and leadership? Are you given to ostentation and self-praise? Or have you given up the love of riches? Have you relinquished all strife? Are you content to take the lowest place, and to be passed by unnoticed? And have you ceased to talk about yourself and to regard yourself with self-complacent pride? If the former, even though you may imagine you worship God, the god of your heart is self. If the latter, even though you may withhold your lips from worship, you are dwelling with the Most High.

The signs by which the Truth-lover is known are unmistakable. Hear the Holy Krishna declare them, in Sir Edwin Arnold's beautiful rendering of the "Bhagavad Gita":—

"Fearlessness, singleness of soul, the will
Always to strive for wisdom; opened hand
And governed appetites; and piety,
And love of lonely study; humbleness,
Uprightness, heed to injure nought which lives
Truthfulness, slowness unto wrath, a mind
That lightly letteth go what others prize;
And equanimity, and charity
Which spieth no man's faults; and tenderness
Towards all that suffer; a contented heart,
Fluttered by no desires; a bearing mild,
Modest and grave, with manhood nobly mixed,
With patience, fortitude and purity;
An unrevengeful spirit, never given
To rate itself too high—such be the signs,
O Indian Prince! of him whose feet are set
On that fair path which leads to heavenly birth!"

When men, lost in the devious ways of error and self, have forgotten the "heavenly birth," the state of holiness and Truth, they set up artificial standards by which to judge one another, and make acceptance of, and adherence to, their own particular theology, the test of Truth; and so men are divided one against another, and there is ceaseless enmity and strife, and unending sorrow and suffering.

Reader, do you seek to realize the birth into Truth? There is only one way: *Let self die.* All those lusts, appetites, desires, opinions, limited conceptions and prejudices to which you have hitherto so tenaciously clung, let them fall from you. Let them no longer hold you in bondage, and Truth will be yours. Cease to look upon your own religion as superior to all others, and strive humbly to learn the supreme lesson of charity. No longer cling to the idea, so productive of strife and sorrow, that the Savior whom you worship is the only Savior, and that the Savior whom your brother worships with equal sincerity and ardor, is an impostor; but seek diligently the path of holiness, and then you will realize that every holy man is a savior of mankind.

The giving up of self is not merely the renunciation of outward things. It consists of the renunciation of the inward sin, the inward error. Not by giving up vain clothing; not by relinquishing riches; not by abstaining from certain foods; not by speaking smooth words; not by merely doing these things is the Truth found; but by giving up the spirit of vanity; by relinquishing the desire for riches; by abstaining from the lust of self-indulgence; by giving up all hatred, strife, condemnation, and self-seeking, and becoming gentle and pure at heart; by doing these things is the Truth found. To do the former, and not to do the latter, is pharisaism and hypocrisy, whereas the latter includes the former. You may renounce the outward world, and isolate yourself in a cave or in the depths of a forest, but you will take all your selfishness with you, and unless you renounce that, great indeed will be your wretchedness and deep your delusion. You may remain just where you are, performing all your duties, and yet renounce the world, the inward enemy. To be in the world and yet not of the world is the highest perfection, the most blessed peace, is to achieve the greatest victory. The renunciation of self is the way of Truth, therefore,

> "Enter the Path; there is no grief like hate,
> No pain like passion, no deceit like sense;
> Enter the Path; far hath he gone whose foot
> Treads down one fond offense."

As you succeed in overcoming self you will begin to see things in their right relations. He who is swayed by any passion, prejudice, like or dislike, adjusts everything to that particular bias, and sees only his own delusions. He who is absolutely free from all passion, prejudice, preference, and partiality, sees himself as he is; sees others as they are; sees all things in their proper proportions and right relations. Having nothing to attack, nothing to defend, nothing to conceal, and no interests to guard, he is at peace. He has realized the profound simplicity of Truth, for this unbiased, tranquil, blessed state of mind and heart is the state of Truth. He who attains to it dwells with the angels, and sits at the footstool of the Supreme. Knowing the Great Law; knowing the origin of sorrow; knowing the secret of suffering; knowing the way of emancipation in Truth, how can such a one engage in strife or condemnation; for though he knows that the blind, self-seeking world, surrounded with the clouds of its own illusions, and enveloped in the darkness of error and self, cannot perceive the steadfast Light of Truth, and is utterly incapable of comprehending the profound simplicity of the heart that has died, or is dying, to self, yet he also knows that when the suffering ages have piled up mountains of sorrow, the crushed and burdened soul of the world will fly to its final refuge, and that when the ages are completed, every prodigal will come back to the fold of Truth. And so he dwells in goodwill toward all, and regards all with that tender compassion which a father bestows upon his wayward children.

Men cannot understand Truth because they cling to self, because they believe in and love self, because they believe self to be the only reality, whereas it is the one delusion.

When you cease to believe in and love self you will desert it, and will fly to Truth, and will find the eternal Reality.

When men are intoxicated with the wines of luxury, and pleasure, and vanity, the thirst of life grows and deepens within them, and they delude themselves with dreams of fleshly immortality, but when they come to reap the harvest of their own sowing, and pain and sorrow supervene, then, crushed and humiliated, relinquishing self and all the intoxications of self, they come, with aching hearts to the one immortality, the immortality that destroys all delusions, the spiritual immortality in Truth.

Men pass from evil to good, from self to Truth, through the dark gate of sorrow, for sorrow and self are inseparable. Only in the peace and bliss of Truth is all sorrow vanquished. If you suffer disappointment because your cherished plans have been thwarted, or because someone has not come up to your anticipations, it is because you are clinging to self. If you suffer remorse for your conduct, it is because you have given way to self. If you are overwhelmed with chagrin and regret because of the attitude of someone else toward you, it is because you have been cherishing self. If you are wounded on account of what has been done to you or said of you, it is because you are walking in the painful way of self. All suffering is of self. All suffering ends in Truth. When you have entered into and realized Truth, you will no longer suffer disappointment, remorse, and regret, and sorrow will flee from you.

> "Self is the only prison that can ever bind the soul;
> Truth is the only angel that can bid the gates unroll;
> And when he comes to call thee, arise and follow fast;
> His way may lie through darkness, but it leads to light at last."

The woe of the world is of its own making. Sorrow purifies and deepens the soul, and the extremity of sorrow is the prelude to Truth.

Have you suffered much? Have you sorrowed deeply? Have you pondered seriously upon the problem of life? If so, you are prepared to wage war against self, and to become a disciple of Truth.

The intellectual who do not see the necessity for giving up self, frame endless theories about the universe, and call them Truth; but do thou pursue that direct line of conduct which is the practice of righteousness, and thou wilt realize the Truth which has no place in theory, and which never changes. Cultivate your heart. Water it continually with unselfish love and deep-felt pity, and strive to shut out from it all thoughts and feelings which are not in accordance with Love. Return good for evil, love for hatred, gentleness for ill-treatment, and remain silent when attacked. So shall you transmute all your selfish desires into the pure gold of Love, and self will disappear in Truth. So will you walk blamelessly among men, yoked with the easy yoke of lowliness, and clothed with the divine garment of humility.

> O come, weary brother! thy struggling and striving
> End thou in the heart of the Master of ruth;
> Across self's drear desert why wilt thou be driving,
> Athirst for the quickening waters of Truth
>
> When here, by the path of thy searching and sinning,

Flows Life's gladsome stream, lies Love's oasis green?
Come, turn thou and rest; know the end and beginning,
The sought and the searcher, the seer and seen.

Thy Master sits not in the unapproached mountains,
Nor dwells in the mirage which floats on the air,
Nor shalt thou discover His magical fountains
In pathways of sand that encircle despair.
In selfhood's dark desert cease wearily seeking
The odorous tracks of the feet of thy King;
And if thou wouldst hear the sweet sound of His speaking,
Be deaf to all voices that emptily sing.

Flee the vanishing places; renounce all thou hast;
Leave all that thou lovest, and, naked and bare,
Thyself at the shrine of the *Innermost* cast;
The Highest, the Holiest, the Changeless is there.

Within, in the heart of the Silence He dwelleth;
Leave sorrow and sin, leave thy wanderings sore;
Come bathe in His Joy, whilst He, whispering, telleth
Thy soul what it seeketh, and wander no more.

Then cease, weary brother, thy struggling and striving;
Find peace in the heart of the Master of ruth.
Across self's dark desert cease wearily driving;
Come; drink at the beautiful waters of Truth.

The Acquirement of Spiritual Power

The world is filled with men and women seeking pleasure, excitement, novelty; seeking ever to be moved to laughter or tears; not seeking strength, stability, and power; but courting weakness, and eagerly engaged in dispersing what power they have.

Men and women of real power and influence are few, because few are prepared to make the sacrifice necessary to the acquirement of power, and fewer still are ready to patiently build up character.

To be swayed by your fluctuating thoughts and impulses is to be weak and powerless; to rightly control and direct those forces is to be strong and powerful. Men of strong animal passions have much of the ferocity of the beast, but this is not power. The elements of power are there; but it is only when this ferocity is tamed and subdued by the higher intelligence that real power begins; and men can only grow in power by awakening themselves to higher and ever higher states of intelligence and consciousness.

The difference between a man of weakness and one of power lies not in the strength of the personal will (for the stubborn man is usually weak and foolish), but in that focus of consciousness which represents their states of knowledge.

The pleasure-seekers, the lovers of excitement, the hunters after novelty, and the victims of impulse and hysterical emotion lack that knowledge of principles which gives balance, stability, and influence.

A man commences to develop power when, checking his impulses and selfish inclinations, he falls back upon the higher and calmer consciousness within him, and begins to steady himself upon a principle. The realization of unchanging principles in consciousness is at once the source and secret of the highest power.

When, after much searching, and suffering, and sacrificing, the light of an eternal principle dawns upon the soul, a divine calm ensues and joy unspeakable gladdens the heart.

He who has realized such a principle ceases to wander, and remains poised and self-possessed. He ceases to be "passion's slave," and becomes a master-builder in the Temple of Destiny.

The man that is governed by self, and not by a principle, changes his front when his selfish comforts are threatened. Deeply intent upon defending and guarding his own interests, he regards all means as lawful that will subserve that end. He is continually scheming as to how he may protect himself against his enemies, being too self-centered to perceive that he is his own enemy. Such a man's work crumbles away, for it is divorced from Truth and power. All effort that is grounded upon self, perishes; only that work endures that is built upon an indestructible principle.

The man that stands upon a principle is the same calm, dauntless, self-possessed man under all circumstances. When the hour of trial comes, and he has to decide between his personal comforts and Truth, he gives up his comforts and remains firm. Even the prospect of torture and death cannot alter or deter him. The man of self regards the loss of his wealth, his comforts, or his life as the greatest calamities which can befall him. The man of principle looks upon these incidents as comparatively insignificant, and not to be weighed with loss of character, loss of Truth. To desert Truth is, to him, the only happening which can really be called a calamity.

It is the hour of crisis which decides who are the minions of darkness, and who the children of Light. It is the epoch of threatening disaster, ruin, and persecution which divides the sheep from the goats, and reveals to the reverential gaze of succeeding ages the men and women of power.

It is easy for a man, so long as he is left in the enjoyment of his possessions, to persuade himself that he believes in and adheres to the principles of Peace, Brotherhood, and Universal Love; but if, when his enjoyments are threatened, or he imagines they are threatened, he begins to clamor loudly for war, he shows that he believes in and stands upon, not Peace, Brotherhood, and Love, but strife, selfishness, and hatred.

He who does not desert his principles when threatened with the loss of every earthly thing, even to the loss of reputation and life, is the man of power; is the man whose every word and work endures; is the man whom the afterworld honors, reveres, and worships. Rather than desert that principle of Divine Love on which he rested, and in which all his trust was placed, Jesus endured the utmost extremity of agony and deprivation; and today the world prostrates itself at his pierced feet in rapt adoration.

There is no way to the acquirement of spiritual power except by that inward illumination and enlightenment which is the realization of spiritual principles; and those principles can only be realized by constant practice and application.

Take the principle of divine Love, and quietly and diligently meditate upon it with the object of arriving at a thorough understanding of it. Bring its searching light to bear upon all your habits, your actions, your speech and intercourse with others, your every secret thought and desire. As you persevere in this course, the divine Love will become more and more perfectly revealed to you, and your own shortcomings will stand out in more and more vivid contrast, spurring you on to renewed endeavor; and having once caught a glimpse of the incomparable majesty of that imperishable principle, you will never again rest in your weakness, your selfishness, your imperfection, but will pursue that Love until you have relinquished every discordant element, and have brought yourself into perfect harmony with it. And that state of inward harmony is spiritual power. Take also other spiritual principles, such as Purity and Compassion, and apply them in the same way, and, so exacting is Truth, you will be able to make no stay, no resting-place until the inmost garment of your soul is bereft of every stain, and your heart has become incapable of any hard, condemnatory, and pitiless impulse.

Only in so far as you understand, realize, and rely upon, these principles, will you acquire spiritual power, and that power will be manifested in and through you in the form of increasing dispassion, patience and equanimity.

Dispassion argues superior self-control; sublime patience is the very hall-mark of divine knowledge, and to retain an unbroken calm amid all the duties and distractions of life, marks off the man of power. "It is easy in the world to live after the world's opinion; it is easy in solitude to live after our own; but the great man is he who in the midst of the crowd keeps with perfect sweetness the independence of solitude."

Some mystics hold that perfection in dispassion is the source of that power by which miracles (so-called) are performed, and truly he who has gained such perfect control of all his interior forces that no shock, however great, can for one moment unbalance him, must be capable of guiding and directing those forces with a master-hand.

To grow in self-control, in patience, in equanimity, is to grow in strength and power; and you can only thus grow by focusing your consciousness upon a principle. As a child, after making many and vigorous attempts to walk unaided, at last succeeds, after numerous falls, in accomplishing this, so you must enter the way of power by first attempting to stand alone. Break away from the tyranny of custom, tradition, conventionality, and the opinions of others, until you succeed in walking lonely and erect among men. Rely upon your own judgment; be true to your own conscience; follow the Light that is within you; all outward lights are so many will-o'-the-wisps. There will be those who will tell you that you are foolish; that your judgment is faulty; that your conscience is all awry, and that the Light within you is darkness; but heed them not. If what they say is true the sooner you, as a searcher for wisdom, find it out the better, and you can only make the discovery by bringing your powers to the test. Therefore, pursue your course bravely. Your conscience is at least your own, and to follow it is to be a man; to follow the conscience of another is to be a slave. You will have many falls, will suffer many wounds, will endure many buffetings for a time, but press on in faith, believing that sure and certain victory lies ahead. Search for a rock, a principle, and having found it cling to it; get it under your feet and stand erect upon it, until at last, immovably fixed upon it, you succeed in defying the fury of the waves and storms of selfishness.

For selfishness in any and every form is dissipation, weakness, death; unselfishness in its spiritual aspect is conservation, power, life. As you grow in spiritual life, and become established upon principles, you will become as beautiful and as unchangeable as those principles, will taste of the sweetness of their immortal essence, and will realize the eternal and indestructible nature of the God within.

> No harmful shaft can reach the righteous man,
> Standing erect amid the storms of hate,
> Defying hurt and injury and ban,
> Surrounded by the trembling slaves of Fate.
>
> Majestic in the strength of silent power,
> Serene he stands, nor changes not nor turns;

Patient and firm in suffering's darkest hour,
Time bends to him, and death and doom he spurns.

Wrath's lurid lightnings round about him play,
And hell's deep thunders roll about his head;
Yet heeds he not, for him they cannot slay
Who stands whence earth and time and space are fled.

Sheltered by deathless love, what fear hath he?
Armored in changeless Truth, what can he know
Of loss and gain? Knowing eternity,
He moves not whilst the shadows come and go.

Call him immortal, call him Truth and Light
And splendor of prophetic majesty
Who bideth thus amid the powers of night,
Clothed with the glory of divinity.

The Realization of Selfless Love

It is said that Michael Angelo saw in every rough block of stone a thing of beauty awaiting the master-hand to bring it into reality. Even so, within each there reposes the Divine Image awaiting the master-hand of Faith and the chisel of Patience to bring it into manifestation. And that Divine Image is revealed and realized as stainless, selfless Love.

Hidden deep in every human heart, though frequently covered up with a mass of hard and almost impenetrable accretions, is the spirit of Divine Love, whose holy and spotless essence is undying and eternal. It is the Truth in man; it is that which belongs to the Supreme: that which is real and immortal. All else changes and passes away; this alone is permanent and imperishable; and to realize this Love by ceaseless diligence in the practice of the highest righteousness, to live in it and to become fully conscious in it, is to enter into immortality here and now, is to become one with Truth, one with God, one with the central Heart of all things, and to know our own divine and eternal nature.

To reach this Love, to understand and experience it, one must work with great persistency and diligence upon his heart and mind, must ever renew his patience and keep strong his faith, for there will be much to remove, much to accomplish before the Divine Image is revealed in all its glorious beauty.

He who strives to reach and to accomplish the divine will be tried to the very uttermost; and this is absolutely necessary, for how else could one acquire that sublime patience without which there is no real wisdom, no divinity? Ever and anon, as he proceeds, all his work will seem to be futile, and his efforts appear to be thrown away. Now and then a hasty touch will mar his image, and perhaps when he imagines his work is almost completed he will find what he imagined to be the beautiful form of Divine Love utterly destroyed, and he must begin again with his past bitter experience to guide and help him. But he who has resolutely set himself to realize the Highest recognizes no such thing as defeat. All failures are apparent, not real. Every slip, every fall, every return to selfishness is a lesson learned, an experience gained, from which a golden grain of wisdom is extracted, helping the striver toward the accomplishment of his lofty object. To recognize

> "That of our vices we can frame
> A ladder if we will but tread
> Beneath our feet each deed of shame,"

is to enter the way that leads unmistakably toward the Divine, and the failings of one who thus recognizes are so many dead selves, upon which he rises, as upon stepping-stones, to higher things.

Once come to regard your failings, your sorrows and sufferings as so many voices telling you plainly where you are weak and faulty, where you fall below the true and the divine, you will then begin to ceaselessly watch yourself, and every slip, every pang of pain will show you where you are to set to work, and what you have to remove out of your heart in order to bring it nearer to the likeness of the Divine, nearer to the Perfect Love. And as you proceed, day by day detaching yourself more and more from the inward selfishness the Love that is selfless will gradually become revealed to you. And when you are growing patient and calm, when your petulances, tempers, and irritabilities are passing away from you, and the more powerful lusts and prejudices cease to dominate and enslave you, then you will know that the divine is awakening within you, that you are drawing near to the eternal Heart, that you are not far from that selfless Love, the possession of which is peace and immortality.

Divine Love is distinguished from human loves in this supremely important particular, *it is free from partiality*. Human loves cling to a particular object to the exclusion of all else, and when that object is removed, great and deep is the resultant suffering to the one who loves. Divine Love embraces the whole universe, and, without clinging to any part, yet contains within itself the whole, and he who comes to it by gradually purifying and broadening his human loves until all the selfish and impure elements are burnt out of them, ceases from suffering. It is because human loves are narrow and confined and mingled with selfishness that they cause suffering. No suffering can result from that Love which is so absolutely pure that it seeks nothing for itself. Nevertheless, human loves are absolutely necessary as steps toward the Divine, and no soul is prepared to partake of Divine Love until it has become capable of the deepest and most intense human love. It is only by passing through human loves and human sufferings that Divine Love is reached and realized.

All human loves are perishable like the forms to which they cling; but there is a Love that is imperishable, and that does not cling to appearances.

All human loves are counterbalanced by human hates; but there is a Love that admits of no opposite or reaction; divine and free from all taint of self, that sheds its fragrance on all alike.

Human loves are reflections of the Divine Love, and draw the soul nearer to the reality, the Love that knows neither sorrow nor change.

It is well that the mother, clinging with passionate tenderness to the little helpless form of flesh that lies on her bosom, should be overwhelmed with the dark waters of sorrow when she sees it laid in the cold earth. It is well that her tears should flow and her heart ache, for only thus can she be reminded of the evanescent nature of the joys and objects of sense, and be drawn nearer to the eternal and imperishable Reality.

It is well that lover, brother, sister, husband, wife should suffer deep anguish, and be enveloped in gloom when the visible object of their affections is torn from them, so that they may learn to turn their affections toward the invisible Source of all, where alone abiding satisfaction is to be found.

It is well that the proud, the ambitious, the self-seeking, should suffer defeat, humiliation, and misfortune; that they should pass through the scorching fires of affliction; for only thus can the wayward soul be brought to reflect upon the enigma of life; only thus can the heart be softened and purified, and prepared to receive the Truth.

When the sting of anguish penetrates the heart of human love; when gloom and loneliness and desertion cloud the soul of friendship and trust, then it is that the heart turns toward the sheltering love of the Eternal, and finds rest in its silent peace. And whosoever comes to this Love is not turned away comfortless, is not pierced with anguish nor surrounded with gloom; and is never deserted in the dark hour of trial.

The glory of Divine Love can only be revealed in the heart that is chastened by sorrow, and the image of the heavenly state can only be perceived and realized when the lifeless, formless accretions of ignorance and self are hewn away.

Only that Love that seeks no personal gratification or reward, that does not make distinctions, and that leaves behind no heartaches, can be called divine.

Men, clinging to self and to the comfortless shadows of evil, are in the habit of thinking of divine Love as something belonging to a God who is out of reach; as something outside themselves, and that must for ever remain outside. Truly, the Love of God is ever beyond the reach of self, but when the heart and mind are emptied of self then the selfless Love, the supreme Love, the Love that is of God or Good becomes an inward and abiding reality.

And this inward realization of holy Love is none other than the Love of Christ that is so much talked about and so little comprehended. The Love that not only saves the soul from sin, but lifts it also above the power of temptation.

But how may one attain to this sublime realization? The answer which Truth has always given, and will ever give to this question is,—"Empty thyself, and I will fill thee." Divine Love cannot be known until self is dead, for self is the denial of Love, and how can that which is known be also denied? Not until the stone of self is rolled away from the sepulcher of the soul does the immortal Christ, the pure Spirit of Love, hitherto crucified, dead and buried, cast off the bands of ignorance, and come forth in all the majesty of His resurrection.

You believe that the Christ of Nazareth was put to death and rose again. I do not say you err in that belief; but if you refuse to believe that the gentle spirit of Love is crucified daily upon the dark cross of your selfish desires, then, I say, you err in this unbelief, and have not yet perceived, even afar off, the Love of Christ.

You say that you have tasted of salvation in the Love of Christ. Are you saved from your temper, your irritability, your vanity, your personal dislikes, your judgment and condemnation of others? If not, from what are you saved, and wherein have you realized the transforming Love of Christ?

He who has realized the Love that is divine has become a new man, and has ceased to be swayed and dominated by the old elements of self. He is known for his patience, his purity, his self-control, his deep charity of heart, and his unalterable sweetness.

Divine or selfless Love is not a mere sentiment or emotion; it is a state of knowledge which destroys the dominion of evil and the belief in evil, and lifts the soul into the joyful realization of the supreme Good. To the divinely wise, knowledge and Love are one and inseparable.

It is toward the complete realization of this divine Love that the whole world is moving; it was for this purpose that the universe came into existence, and every grasping at happiness, every reaching out of the soul toward objects, ideas and ideals, is an effort to realize it. But the world does not realize this Love at present because it is grasping at the fleeting shadow and ignoring, in its blindness, the substance. And so suffering and sorrow continue, and must continue until the world, taught by its self-inflicted pains, discovers the Love that is selfless, the wisdom that is calm and full of peace.

And this Love, this Wisdom, this Peace, this tranquil state of mind and heart may be attained to, may be realized by all who are willing and ready to yield up self, and who are prepared to humbly enter into a comprehension of all that the giving up of self involves. There is no arbitrary power in the universe, and the strongest chains of fate by which men are bound are self-forged. Men are chained to that which causes suffering because they desire to be so, because they love their chains, because they think their little dark prison of self is sweet and beautiful, and they are afraid that if they desert that prison they will lose all that is real and worth having.

"Ye suffer from yourselves, none else compels,
None other holds ye that ye live and die."

And the indwelling power which forged the chains and built around itself the dark and narrow prison, can break away when it desires and wills to do so, and the soul does will to do so when it has discovered the worthlessness of its prison, when long suffering has prepared it for the reception of the boundless Light and Love.

As the shadow follows the form, and as smoke comes after fire, so effect follows cause, and suffering and bliss follow the thoughts and deeds of men. There is no effect in the world around us but has its hidden or revealed cause, and that cause is in accordance with absolute justice. Men reap a harvest of suffering because in the near or distant past they have sown the seeds of evil; they reap a harvest of bliss also as a result of their own sowing of the seeds of good. Let a man meditate upon this, let him strive to understand it, and he will then begin to sow only seeds of good, and will burn up the tares and weeds which he has formerly grown in the garden of his heart.

The world does not understand the Love that is selfless because it is engrossed in the pursuit of its own pleasures, and cramped within the narrow limits of perishable interests mistaking, in its ignorance, those pleasures and interests for real and abiding things. Caught in the flames of fleshly lusts, and burning with anguish, it sees not the pure and peaceful beauty of Truth. Feeding upon the swinish husks of error and self-delusion, it is shut out from the mansion of all-seeing Love.

Not having this Love, not understanding it, men institute innumerable reforms which involve no inward sacrifice, and each imagines that his reform is going to right the world for ever, while he himself continues to propagate evil by engaging it in his own heart. That only can be called reform which tends to reform the human heart, for all evil has its rise there, and not until the world, ceasing from selfishness and party strife, has learned the lesson of divine Love, will it realize the Golden Age of universal blessedness.

Let the rich cease to despise the poor, and the poor to condemn the rich; let the greedy learn how to give, and the lustful how to grow pure; let the partisan cease from strife, and the uncharitable begin to forgive; let the envious endeavor to rejoice with others, and the slanderers grow ashamed of their conduct. Let men and women take this course, and, lo! the Golden Age is at hand. He, therefore, who purifies his own heart is the world's greatest benefactor.

Yet, though the world is, and will be for many ages to come, shut out from that Age of Gold, which is the realization of selfless Love, you, if you are willing, may enter it now, by rising above your selfish self; if you will pass from prejudice, hatred, and condemnation, to gentle and forgiving love.

Where hatred, dislike, and condemnation are, selfless Love does not abide. It resides only in the heart that has ceased from all condemnation.

You say, "How can I love the drunkard, the hypocrite, the sneak, the murderer? I am compelled to dislike and condemn such men." It is true you cannot love such men *emotionally*, but when you say that you must perforce dislike and condemn them you show that you are not acquainted with the Great over-ruling Love; for it is possible to attain to such a state of interior enlightenment as will enable you to perceive the train of causes by which these men have become as they are, to enter into their intense sufferings, and to know the certainty of their ultimate purification. Possessed of such knowledge it will be utterly impossible for you any longer to dislike or condemn them, and you will always think of them with perfect calmness and deep compassion.

If you love people and speak of them with praise until they in some way thwart you, or do something of which you disapprove, and then you dislike them and speak of them with dispraise, you are not governed by the Love which is of God. If, in your heart, you are continually arraigning and condemning others, selfless Love is hidden from you.

He who knows that Love is at the heart of all things, and has realized the all-sufficing power of that Love, has no room in his heart for condemnation.

Men, not knowing this Love, constitute themselves judge and executioner of their fellows, forgetting that there is the Eternal Judge and Executioner, and in so far as men deviate from them in their own views, their particular reforms and methods, they brand them as fanatical, unbalanced, lacking judgment, sincerity, and honesty; in so far as others approximate to their own standard do they look upon them as being everything that is admirable. Such are the men who are centered in self. But he whose heart is centered in the supreme Love does not so brand and classify men; does not seek to convert men to his own views, not to convince them of the superiority of his methods. Knowing the Law of Love, he lives it, and maintains the same calm attitude of mind and sweetness of heart toward all. The debased and the virtuous, the foolish and the wise, the learned and the unlearned, the selfish and the unselfish receive alike the benediction of his tranquil thought.

You can only attain to this supreme knowledge, this divine Love by unremitting endeavor in self-discipline, and by gaining victory after victory over yourself. Only the pure in heart see God, and when your heart is sufficiently purified you will enter into the New Birth, and the Love that does not die, nor change, nor end in pain and sorrow will be awakened within you, and you will be at peace.

He who strives for the attainment of divine Love is ever seeking to overcome the spirit of condemnation, for where there is pure spiritual knowledge, condemnation cannot exist, and only in the heart that has become incapable of condemnation is Love perfected and fully realized.

The Christian condemns the Atheist; the Atheist satirizes the Christian; the Catholic and Protestant are ceaselessly engaged in wordy warfare, and the spirit of strife and hatred rules where peace and love should be.

"He that hateth his brother is a murderer," a crucifier of the divine Spirit of Love; and until you can regard men of all religions and of no religion with the same impartial spirit, with all freedom from dislike, and with perfect equanimity, you have yet to strive for that Love which bestows upon its possessor freedom and salvation.

The realization of divine knowledge, selfless Love, utterly destroys the spirit of condemnation, disperses all evil, and lifts the consciousness to that height of pure vision where Love, Goodness, Justice are seen to be universal, supreme, all-conquering, indestructible.

Train your mind in strong, impartial, and gentle thought; train your heart in purity and compassion; train your tongue to silence and to true and stainless speech; so shall you enter the way of holiness and peace, and shall ultimately realize the immortal Love. So living, without seeking to convert, you will convince; without arguing, you will teach; not cherishing ambition, the wise will find you out; and without striving to gain men's opinions, you will subdue their hearts. For Love is all-conquering, all-powerful; and the thoughts, and deeds, and words of Love can never perish.

To know that Love is universal, supreme, all-sufficing; to be freed from the trammels of evil; to be quit of the inward unrest; to know that all men are striving to realize the Truth each in his own way; to be satisfied, sorrowless, serene; this is peace; this is gladness; this is immortality; this is Divinity; this is the realization of selfless Love.

> I stood upon the shore, and saw the rocks
> Resist the onslaught of the mighty sea,
> And when I thought how all the countless shocks
> They had withstood through an eternity,
> I said, "To wear away this solid main
> The ceaseless efforts of the waves are vain."
>
> But when I thought how they the rocks had rent,
> And saw the sand and shingles at my feet
> (Poor passive remnants of resistance spent)

Tumbled and tossed where they the waters meet,
Then saw I ancient landmarks 'neath the waves,
And knew the waters held the stones their slaves.

I saw the mighty work the waters wrought
By patient softness and unceasing flow;
How they the proudest promontory brought
Unto their feet, and massy hills laid low;
How the soft drops the adamantine wall
Conquered at last, and brought it to its fall.

And then I knew that hard, resisting sin
Should yield at last to Love's soft ceaseless roll
Coming and going, ever flowing in
Upon the proud rocks of the human soul;
That all resistance should be spent and past,
And every heart yield unto it at last.

Entering into the Infinite

From the beginning of time, man, in spite of his bodily appetites and desires, in the midst of all his clinging to earthly and impermanent things, has ever been intuitively conscious of the limited, transient, and illusionary nature of his material existence, and in his sane and silent moments has tried to reach out into a comprehension of the Infinite, and has turned with tearful aspiration toward the restful Reality of the Eternal Heart.

While vainly imagining that the pleasures of earth are real and satisfying, pain and sorrow continually remind him of their unreal and unsatisfying nature. Ever striving to believe that complete satisfaction is to be found in material things, he is conscious of an inward and persistent revolt against this belief, which revolt is at once a refutation of his essential mortality, and an inherent and imperishable proof that only in the immortal, the eternal, the infinite can he find abiding satisfaction and unbroken peace.

And here is the common ground of faith; here the root and spring of all religion; here the soul of Brotherhood and the heart of Love,—that man is essentially and spiritually divine and eternal, and that, immersed in mortality and troubled with unrest, he is ever striving to enter into a consciousness of his real nature.

The spirit of man is inseparable from the Infinite, and can be satisfied with nothing short of the Infinite, and the burden of pain will continue to weigh upon man's heart, and the shadows of sorrow to darken his pathway until, ceasing from his wanderings in the dream-world of matter, he comes back to his home in the reality of the Eternal.

As the smallest drop of water detached from the ocean contains all the qualities of the ocean, so man, detached in consciousness from the Infinite, contains within him its likeness; and as the drop of water must, by the law of its nature, ultimately find its way back to the ocean and lose itself in its silent depths, so must man, by the unfailing law of his nature, at last return to his source, and lose himself in the great ocean of the Infinite.

To re-become one with the Infinite is the goal of man. To enter into perfect harmony with the Eternal Law is Wisdom, Love and Peace. But this divine state is, and must ever be, incomprehensible to the merely personal. Personality, separateness, selfishness are one and the same, and are the antithesis of wisdom and divinity. By the unqualified surrender of the personality, separateness and selfishness cease, and man enters into the possession of his divine heritage of immortality and infinity.

Such surrender of the personality is regarded by the worldly and selfish mind as the most grievous of all calamities, the most irreparable loss, yet it is the one supreme and incomparable blessing, the only real and lasting gain. The mind unenlightened upon the inner laws of being, and upon the nature and destiny of its own life, clings to transient appearances, things which have in them no enduring substantiality, and so clinging, perishes, for the time being, amid the shattered wreckage of its own illusions.

Men cling to and gratify the flesh as though it were going to last for ever, and though they try to forget the nearness and inevitability of its dissolution, the dread of death and of the loss of all that they cling to clouds their happiest hours, and the chilling shadow of their own selfishness follows them like a remorseless specter.

And with the accumulation of temporal comforts and luxuries, the divinity within men is drugged, and they sink deeper and deeper into materiality, into the perishable life of the senses, and where there is sufficient intellect, theories concerning the immortality of the flesh come to be regarded as infallible truths. When a man's soul is clouded with selfishness in any or every form, he loses the power of spiritual discrimination, and confuses the temporal with the eternal, the perishable with the permanent, mortality with immortality, and error with Truth. It is thus that the world has come to be filled with theories and speculations having no foundation in human experience. Every body of flesh contains within itself, from the hour of birth, the elements of its own destruction, and by the unalterable law of its own nature must it pass away.

The perishable in the universe can never become permanent; the permanent can never pass away; the mortal can never become immortal; the immortal can never die; the temporal cannot become eternal nor the eternal become temporal; appearance can never become reality, nor reality fade into appearance; error can never become Truth, nor can Truth become error. Man cannot immortalize the flesh, but, by overcoming the flesh, by relinquishing all its inclinations, he can enter the region of immortality. "God alone hath immortality," and only by realizing the God state of consciousness does man enter into immortality.

All nature in its myriad forms of life is changeable, impermanent, unenduring. Only the informing Principle of nature endures. Nature is many, and is marked by separation. The informing Principle is One, and is marked by unity. By overcoming the senses and the selfishness within, which is the overcoming of nature, man emerges from the chrysalis of the personal and illusory, and wings himself into the glorious light of the impersonal, the region of universal Truth, out of which all perishable forms come.

Let men, therefore, practice self-denial; let them conquer their animal inclinations; let them refuse to be enslaved by luxury and pleasure; let them practice virtue, and grow daily into high and ever higher virtue, until at last they grow into the Divine, and enter into both the practice and the comprehension of humility, meekness, forgiveness, compassion, and love, which practice and comprehension constitute Divinity.

"Good-will gives insight," and only he who has so conquered his personality that he has but one attitude of mind, that of good-will, toward all creatures, is possessed of divine insight, and is capable of distinguishing the true from the false. The supremely good man is, therefore, the wise man, the divine man, the enlightened seer, the knower of the Eternal. Where you find unbroken gentleness, enduring patience, sublime lowliness, graciousness of speech, self-control, self-forgetfulness, and deep and abounding sympathy, look there for the highest wisdom, seek the company of such a one, for he has realized the Divine, he lives with the Eternal, he has become one with the Infinite. Believe not him that is impatient, given to anger, boastful, who clings to pleasure and refuses to renounce his selfish gratifications, and who practices not good-will and far-reaching compassion, for such a one hath not wisdom, vain is all his knowledge, and his works and words will perish, for they are grounded on that which passes away.

Let a man abandon self, let him overcome the world, let him deny the personal; by this pathway only can he enter into the heart of the Infinite.

The world, the body, the personality are mirages upon the desert of time; transitory dreams in the dark night of spiritual slumber, and those who have crossed the desert, those who are spiritually awakened, have alone comprehended the Universal Reality where all appearances are dispersed and dreaming and delusion are destroyed.

There is one Great Law which exacts unconditional obedience, one unifying principle which is the basis of all diversity, one eternal Truth wherein all the problems of earth pass away like shadows. To realize this Law, this

Unity, this Truth, is to enter into the Infinite, is to become one with the Eternal.

To center one's life in the Great Law of Love is to enter into rest, harmony, peace. To refrain from all participation in evil and discord; to cease from all resistance to evil, and from the omission of that which is good, and to fall back upon unswerving obedience to the holy calm within, is to enter into the inmost heart of things, is to attain to a living, conscious experience of that eternal and infinite principle which must ever remain a hidden mystery to the merely perceptive intellect. Until this principle is realized, the soul is not established in peace, and he who so realizes is truly wise; not wise with the wisdom of the learned, but with the simplicity of a blameless heart and of a divine manhood.

To enter into a realization of the Infinite and Eternal is to rise superior to time, and the world, and the body, which comprise the kingdom of darkness; and is to become established in immortality, Heaven, and the Spirit, which make up the Empire of Light.

Entering into the Infinite is not a mere theory or sentiment. It is a vital experience which is the result of assiduous practice in inward purification. When the body is no longer believed to be, even remotely, the real man; when all appetites and desires are thoroughly subdued and purified; when the emotions are rested and calm, and when the oscillation of the intellect ceases and perfect poise is secured, then, and not till then, does consciousness become one with the Infinite; not until then is childlike wisdom and profound peace secured.

Men grow weary and gray over the dark problems of life, and finally pass away and leave them unsolved because they cannot see their way out of the darkness of the personality, being too much engrossed in its limitations. Seeking to save his personal life, man forfeits the greater impersonal Life in Truth; clinging to the perishable, he is shut out from a knowledge of the Eternal.

By the surrender of self all difficulties are overcome, and there is no error in the universe but the fire of inward sacrifice will burn it up like chaff; no problem, however great, but will disappear like a shadow under the searching light of self-abnegation. Problems exist only in our own self-created illusions, and they vanish away when self is yielded up. Self and error are synonymous. Error is involved in the darkness of unfathomable complexity, but eternal simplicity is the glory of Truth.

Love of self shuts men out from Truth, and seeking their own personal happiness they lose the deeper, purer, and more abiding bliss. Says Carlyle—"There is in man a higher than love of happiness. He can do without happiness, and instead thereof find blessedness.

... Love not pleasure, love God. This is the Everlasting Yea, wherein all contradiction is solved; wherein whoso walks and works, it is well with him."

He who has yielded up that self, that personality that men most love, and to which they cling with such fierce tenacity, has left behind him all perplexity, and has entered into a simplicity so profoundly simple as to be looked upon by the world, involved as it is in a network of error, as foolishness. Yet such a one has realized the highest wisdom, and is at rest in the Infinite. He "accomplishes without striving," and all problems melt before him, for he has entered the region of reality, and deals, not with changing effects, but with the unchanging principles of things. He is enlightened with a wisdom which is as superior to ratiocination, as reason is to animality. Having yielded up his lusts, his errors, his opinions and prejudices, he has entered into possession of the knowledge of God, having slain the selfish desire for heaven, and along with it the ignorant fear of hell; having relinquished even the love of life itself, he has gained supreme bliss and Life Eternal, the Life which bridges life and death, and knows its own immortality. Having yielded up all without reservation, he has gained all, and rests in peace on the bosom of the Infinite.

Only he who has become so free from self as to be equally content to be annihilated as to live, or to live as to be annihilated, is fit to enter into the Infinite. Only he who, ceasing to trust his perishable self, has learned to trust in boundless measure the Great Law, the Supreme Good, is prepared to partake of undying bliss.

For such a one there is no more regret, nor disappointment, nor remorse, for where all selfishness has ceased these sufferings cannot be; and whatever happens to him he knows that it is for his own good, and he is content, being no longer the servant of self, but the servant of the Supreme. He is no longer affected by the changes of earth, and when he hears of wars and rumors of wars his peace is not disturbed, and where men grow angry and cynical and quarrelsome, he bestows compassion and love. Though appearances may contradict it, he knows that the world is progressing, and that

"Through its laughing and its weeping,
Through its living and its keeping,
Through its follies and its labors, weaving in and out of sight,
To the end from the beginning,
Through all virtue and all sinning,
Reeled from God's great spool of Progress, runs the golden thread of light."

When a fierce storm is raging none are angered about it, because they know it will quickly pass away, and when the storms of contention are devastating the world, the wise man, looking with the eye of Truth and pity, knows that it will pass away, and that out of the wreckage of broken hearts which it leaves behind the immortal Temple of Wisdom will be built.

Sublimely patient; infinitely compassionate; deep, silent, and pure, his very presence is a benediction; and when he speaks men ponder his words in their hearts, and by them rise to higher levels of attainment. Such is he who has entered into the Infinite, who by the power of utmost sacrifice has solved the sacred mystery of life.

Questioning Life and Destiny and Truth,
I sought the dark and labyrinthine Sphinx,
Who spake to me this strange and wondrous thing:—
"Concealment only lies in blinded eyes,
And God alone can see the Form of God."
I sought to solve this hidden mystery
Vainly by paths of blindness and of pain,
But when I found the Way of Love and Peace,
Concealment ceased, and I was blind no more:
Then saw I God e'en with the eyes of God.

Saints, Sages, and Saviors: the Law of Service

The spirit of Love which is manifested as a perfect and rounded life, is the crown of being and the supreme end of knowledge upon this earth.

The measure of a man's truth is the measure of his love, and Truth is far removed from him whose life is not governed by Love. The intolerant and condemnatory, even though they profess the highest religion, have the smallest measure of Truth; while those who exercise patience, and who listen calmly and dispassionately to all sides, and both arrive themselves at, and incline others to, thoughtful and unbiased conclusions upon all problems and issues, have Truth in fullest measure. The final test of wisdom is this,—how does a man live? What spirit does he manifest? How does he act under trial and temptation? Many men boast of being in possession of Truth who are continually swayed by grief, disappointment, and passion, and who sink under the first little trial that comes along. Truth is nothing if not unchangeable, and in so far as a man takes his stand upon Truth does he become steadfast in virtue, does he rise superior to his passions and emotions and changeable personality.

Men formulate perishable dogmas, and call them Truth. Truth cannot be formulated; it is ineffable, and ever beyond the reach of intellect. It can only be experienced by practice; it can only be manifested as a stainless heart and a perfect life.

Who, then, in the midst of the ceaseless pandemonium of schools and creeds and parties, has the Truth? He who lives it. He who practices it. He who, having risen above that pandemonium by overcoming himself, no longer engages in it, but sits apart, quiet, subdued, calm, and self-possessed, freed from all strife, all bias, all condemnation, and bestows upon all the glad and unselfish love of the divinity within him.

He who is patient, calm, gentle, and forgiving under all circumstances, manifests the Truth. Truth will never be proved by wordy arguments and learned treatises, for if men do not perceive the Truth in infinite patience, undying forgiveness, and all-embracing compassion, no words can ever prove it to them.

It is an easy matter for the passionate to be calm and patient when they are alone, or are in the midst of calmness. It is equally easy for the uncharitable to be gentle and kind when they are dealt kindly with, but he who retains his patience and calmness under all trial, who remains sublimely meek and gentle under the most trying circumstances, he, and he alone, is possessed of the spotless Truth. And this is so because such lofty virtues belong to the Divine, and can only be manifested by one who has attained to the highest wisdom, who has relinquished his passionate and self-seeking nature, who has realized the supreme and unchangeable Law, and has brought himself into harmony with it.

Let men, therefore, cease from vain and passionate arguments about Truth, and let them think and say and do those things which make for harmony, peace, love, and good-will. Let them practice heart-virtue, and search humbly and diligently for the Truth which frees the soul from all error and sin, from all that blights the human heart, and that darkens, as with unending night, the pathway of the wandering souls of earth.

There is one great all-embracing Law which is the foundation and cause of the universe, the Law of Love. It has been called by many names in various countries and at various times, but behind all its names the same unalterable Law may be discovered by the eye of Truth. Names, religions, personalities pass away, but the Law of Love remains. To become possessed of a knowledge of this Law, to enter into conscious harmony with it, is to become immortal, invincible, indestructible.

It is because of the effort of the soul to realize this Law that men come again and again to live, to suffer, and to die; and when realized, suffering ceases, personality is dispersed, and the fleshly life and death are destroyed, for consciousness becomes one with the Eternal.

The Law is absolutely impersonal, and its highest manifested expression is that of Service. When the purified heart has realized Truth it is then called upon to make the last, the greatest and holiest sacrifice, the sacrifice of the well-earned enjoyment of Truth. It is by virtue of this sacrifice that the divinely-emancipated soul comes to dwell among men, clothed with a body of flesh, content to dwell among the lowliest and least, and to be esteemed the servant of all mankind. That sublime humility which is manifested by the world's saviors is the seal of Godhead, and he who has annihilated the personality, and has become a living, visible manifestation of the impersonal, eternal, boundless Spirit of Love, is alone singled out as worthy to receive the unstinted worship of posterity. He only who succeeds in humbling himself with that divine humility which is not only the extinction of self, but is also the pouring out upon all the spirit of unselfish love, is exalted above measure, and given spiritual dominion in the hearts of mankind.

All the great spiritual teachers have denied themselves personal luxuries, comforts, and rewards, have abjured temporal power, and have lived and taught the limitless and impersonal Truth. Compare their lives and teachings, and you will find the same simplicity, the same self-sacrifice, the same humility, love, and peace both lived and preached by them. They taught the same eternal Principles, the realization of which destroys all evil. Those who have been hailed and worshiped as the saviors of mankind are manifestations of the Great impersonal Law, and being such, were free from passion and prejudice, and having no opinions, and no special letter of doctrine to preach and defend, they never sought to convert and to proselytize. Living in the highest Goodness, the supreme Perfection, their sole object was to uplift mankind by manifesting that Goodness in thought, word, and deed. They stand between man the personal and God the impersonal, and serve as exemplary types for the salvation of self-enslaved mankind.

Men who are immersed in self, and who cannot comprehend the Goodness that is absolutely impersonal, deny divinity to all saviors except their own, and thus introduce personal hatred and doctrinal controversy, and, while defending their own particular views with passion, look upon each other as being heathens or infidels, and so render null and void, as far as their lives are concerned, the unselfish beauty and holy grandeur of the lives and teachings of their own Masters. Truth cannot be limited; it can never be the special prerogative of any man, school, or nation, and when personality steps in, Truth is lost.

The glory alike of the saint, the sage, and the savior is this,—that he has realized the most profound lowliness, the most sublime unselfishness; having given up all, even his own personality, all his works are holy and enduring, for they are freed from every taint of self. He gives, yet never thinks of receiving; he works without regretting the past or anticipating the future, and never looks for reward.

When the farmer has tilled and dressed his land and put in the seed, he knows that he has done all that he can possibly do, and that now he must trust to the elements, and wait patiently for the course of time to bring about the harvest, and that no amount of expectancy on his part will affect the result. Even so, he who has realized Truth goes forth as a sower of the seeds of goodness, purity, love and peace, without expectancy, and never looking for results, knowing that there is the Great Over-ruling Law which brings about its own harvest in due time, and which is alike the source of preservation and destruction.

Men, not understanding the divine simplicity of a profoundly unselfish heart, look upon their particular savior as the manifestation of a special miracle, as being something entirely apart and distinct from the nature of things, and as being, in his ethical excellence, eternally unapproachable by the whole of mankind. This attitude of unbelief (for such it is) in the divine perfectibility of man, paralyzes effort, and binds the souls of men as with strong ropes to sin and suffering. Jesus "grew in wisdom" and was "perfected by suffering." What Jesus was, he became such; what Buddha was, he became such; and every holy man became such by unremitting perseverance in self-sacrifice. Once recognize this, once realize that by watchful effort and hopeful perseverance you can rise above your lower nature, and great and glorious will be the vistas of attainment that will open out before you. Buddha vowed that he would not relax his efforts until he arrived at the state of perfection, and he accomplished his purpose.

What the saints, sages, and saviors have accomplished, you likewise may accomplish if you will only tread the way which they trod and pointed out, the way of self-sacrifice, of self-denying service.

Truth is very simple. It says, "Give up self," "Come unto Me" (away from all that defiles) "and I will give you rest." All the mountains of commentary that have been piled upon it cannot hide it from the heart that is earnestly seeking for Righteousness. It does not require learning; it can be known in spite of learning. Disguised under many forms by erring self-seeking man, the beautiful simplicity and clear transparency of Truth remains unaltered and undimmed, and the unselfish heart enters into and partakes of its shining radiance. Not by weaving complex theories, not by building up speculative philosophies is Truth realized; but by weaving the web of inward purity, by building up the Temple of a stainless life is Truth realized.

He who enters upon this holy way begins by restraining his passions. This is virtue, and is the beginning of saintship, and saintship is the beginning of holiness. The entirely worldly man gratifies all his desires, and practices no more restraint than the law of the land in which he lives demands; the virtuous man restrains his passions; the saint attacks the enemy of Truth in its stronghold within his own heart, and restrains all selfish and impure thoughts; while the holy man is he who is free from passion and all impure thought, and to whom goodness and purity have become as natural as scent and color are to the flower. The holy man is divinely wise; he alone knows Truth in its fullness, and has entered into abiding rest and peace. For him evil has ceased; it has disappeared in the universal light of the All-Good. Holiness is the badge of wisdom. Said Krishna to the Prince Arjuna—

> "Humbleness, truthfulness, and harmlessness,
> Patience and honor, reverence for the wise,
> Purity, constancy, control of self,
> Contempt of sense-delights, self-sacrifice,
> Perception of the certitude of ill
> In birth, death, age, disease, suffering and sin;
> An ever tranquil heart in fortunes good
> And fortunes evil,...
> ...Endeavors resolute
> To reach perception of the utmost soul,
> And grace to understand what gain it were
> So to attain—this is true wisdom, Prince!
> And what is otherwise is ignorance!"

Whoever fights ceaselessly against his own selfishness, and strives to supplant it with all-embracing love, is a saint, whether he live in a cottage or in the midst of riches and influence; or whether he preaches or remains obscure.

To the worldling, who is beginning to aspire towards higher things, the saint, such as a sweet St. Francis of Assisi, or a conquering St. Anthony, is a glorious and inspiring spectacle; to the saint, an equally enrapturing sight is that of the sage, sitting serene and holy, the conqueror of sin and sorrow, no more tormented by regret and remorse, and whom even temptation can never reach; and yet even the sage is drawn on by a still more glorious vision, that of the savior actively manifesting his knowledge in selfless works, and rendering his divinity more potent for good by sinking himself in the throbbing, sorrowing, aspiring heart of mankind.

And this only is true service—to forget oneself in love towards all, to lose oneself in working for the whole. O thou vain and foolish man, who thinkest that thy many works can save thee; who, chained to all error, talkest loudly of thyself, thy work, and thy many sacrifices, and magnifiest thine own importance; know this, that though thy fame fill the whole earth, all thy work shall come to dust, and thou thyself be reckoned lower than the least in the Kingdom of Truth!

Only the work that is impersonal can live; the works of self are both powerless and perishable. Where duties, howsoever humble, are done without self-interest, and with joyful sacrifice, there is true service and enduring work. Where deeds, however brilliant and apparently successful, are done from love of self, there is ignorance of the Law of Service, and the work perishes.

It is given to the world to learn one great and divine lesson, the lesson of absolute unselfishness. The saints, sages, and saviors of all time are they who have submitted themselves to this task, and have learned and lived it. All the Scriptures of the world are framed to teach this one lesson; all the great teachers reiterate it.

It is too simple for the world which, scorning it, stumbles along in the complex ways of selfishness.

A pure heart is the end of all religion and the beginning of divinity. To search for this Righteousness is to walk the Way of Truth and Peace, and he who enters this Way will soon perceive that Immortality which is independent of birth and death, and will realize that in the Divine economy of the universe the humblest effort is not lost.

The divinity of a Krishna, a Gautama, or a Jesus is the crowning glory of self-abnegation, the end of the soul's pilgrimage in matter and mortality, and the world will not have finished its long journey until every soul has become as these, and has entered into the blissful realization of its own divinity.

   Great glory crowns the heights of hope by arduous struggle won;
   Bright honor rounds the hoary head that mighty works hath done;
   Fair riches come to him who strives in ways of golden gain.
   And fame enshrines his name who works with genius-glowing brain;
   But greater glory waits for him who, in the bloodless strife
   'Gainst self and wrong, adopts, in love, the sacrificial life;
   And brighter honor rounds the brow of him who, 'mid the scorns
   Of blind idolaters of self, accepts the crown of thorns;
   And fairer purer riches come to him who greatly strives
   To walk in ways of love and truth to sweeten human lives;
   And he who serveth well mankind exchanges fleeting fame
   For Light eternal, Joy and Peace, and robes of heavenly flame.

The Realization of Perfect Peace

In the external universe there is ceaseless turmoil, change, and unrest; at the heart of all things there is undisturbed repose; in this deep silence dwelleth the Eternal.

Man partakes of this duality, and both the surface change and disquietude, and the deep-seated eternal abode of Peace, are contained within him.

As there are silent depths in the ocean which the fiercest storm cannot reach, so there are silent, holy depths in the heart of man which the storms of sin and sorrow can never disturb. To reach this silence and to live consciously in it is peace.

Discord is rife in the outward world, but unbroken harmony holds sway at the heart of the universe. The human soul, torn by discordant passion and grief, reaches blindly toward the harmony of the sinless state, and to reach this state and to live consciously in it is peace.

Hatred severs human lives, fosters persecution, and hurls nations into ruthless war, yet men, though they do not understand why, retain some measure of faith in the overshadowing of a Perfect Love; and to reach this Love and to live consciously in it is peace.

And this inward peace, this silence, this harmony, this Love, is the Kingdom of Heaven, which is so difficult to reach because few are willing to give up themselves and to become as little children.

> "Heaven's gate is very narrow and minute,
> It cannot be perceived by foolish men
> Blinded by vain illusions of the world;
> E'en the clear-sighted who discern the way,
> And seek to enter, find the portal barred,
> And hard to be unlocked. Its massive bolts

Are pride and passion, avarice and lust."

Men cry peace! peace! where there is no peace, but on the contrary, discord, disquietude and strife. Apart from that Wisdom which is inseparable from self-renunciation, there can be no real and abiding peace.

The peace which results from social comfort, passing gratification, or worldly victory is transitory in its nature, and is burnt up in the heat of fiery trial. Only the Peace of Heaven endures through all trial, and only the selfless heart can know the Peace of Heaven.

Holiness alone is undying peace. Self-control leads to it, and the ever-increasing Light of Wisdom guides the pilgrim on his way. It is partaken of in a measure as soon as the path of virtue is entered upon, but it is only realized in its fullness when self disappears in the consummation of a stainless life.

"This is peace,
To conquer love of self and lust of life,
To tear deep-rooted passion from the heart
To still the inward strife."

If, O reader! you would realize the Light that never fades, the Joy that never ends, and the tranquillity that cannot be disturbed; if you would leave behind for ever your sins, your sorrows, your anxieties and perplexities; if, I say, you would partake of this salvation, this supremely glorious Life, then conquer yourself. Bring every thought, every impulse, every desire into perfect obedience to the divine power resident within you. There is no other way to peace but this, and if you refuse to walk it, your much praying and your strict adherence to ritual will be fruitless and unavailing, and neither gods nor angels can help you. Only to him that overcometh is given the white stone of the regenerate life, on which is written the New and Ineffable Name.

Come away, for awhile, from external things, from the pleasures of the senses, from the arguments of the intellect, from the noise and the excitements of the world, and withdraw yourself into the inmost chamber of your heart, and there, free from the sacrilegious intrusion of all selfish desires, you will find a deep silence, a holy calm, a blissful repose, and if you will rest awhile in that holy place, and will meditate there, the faultless eye of Truth will open within you, and you will see things as they really are. This holy place within you is your real and eternal self; it is the divine within you; and only when you identify yourself with it can you be said to be "clothed and in your right mind." It is the abode of peace, the temple of wisdom, the dwelling-place of immortality. Apart from this inward resting-place, this Mount of Vision, there can be no true peace, no knowledge of the Divine, and if you can remain there for one minute, one hour, or one day, it is possible for you to remain there always. All your sins and sorrows, your fears and anxieties are your own, and you can cling to them or you can give them up. Of your own accord you cling to your unrest; of your own accord you can come to abiding peace. No one else can give up sin for you; you must give it up yourself. The greatest teacher can do no more than walk the way of Truth for himself, and point it out to you; you yourself must walk it for yourself. You can obtain freedom and peace alone by your own efforts, by yielding up that which binds the soul, and which is destructive of peace.

    The angels of divine peace and joy are always at hand, and if you do not see them, and hear them, and dwell with them, it is because you shut yourself out from them, and prefer the company of the spirits of evil within you. You are what you will to be, what you wish to be, what you prefer to be. You can commence to purify yourself, and by so doing can arrive at peace, or you can refuse to purify yourself, and so remain with suffering.

    Step aside, then; come out of the fret and the fever of life; away from the scorching heat of self, and enter the inward resting-place where the cooling airs of peace will calm, renew, and restore you.

Come out of the storms of sin and anguish. Why be troubled and tempest-tossed when the haven of Peace of God is yours!

Give up all self-seeking; give up self, and lo! the Peace of God is yours!

Subdue the animal within you; conquer every selfish uprising, every discordant voice; transmute the base metals of your selfish nature into the unalloyed gold of Love, and you shall realize the Life of Perfect Peace. Thus subduing, thus conquering, thus transmuting, you will, O reader! while living in the flesh, cross the dark waters of mortality, and will reach that Shore upon which the storms of sorrow never beat, and where sin and suffering and dark uncertainty cannot come. Standing upon that Shore, holy, compassionate, awakened, and self-possessed and glad with unending gladness, you will realize that

"Never the Spirit was born, the Spirit will cease to be never;
Never was time it was not, end and beginning are dreams;
Birthless and deathless and changeless remaineth the Spirit for ever;
Death hath not touched it at all, dead though the house of it seems."

You will then know the meaning of Sin, of Sorrow, of Suffering, and that the end thereof is Wisdom; will know the cause and the issue of existence.

And with this realization you will enter into rest, for this is the bliss of immortality, this the unchangeable gladness, this the untrammeled knowledge, undefiled Wisdom, and undying Love; this, and this only, is the realization of Perfect Peace.

O thou who wouldst teach men of Truth!
Hast thou passed through the desert of doubt?
Art thou purged by the fires of sorrow? hath ruth
The fiends of opinion cast out
Of thy human heart? Is thy soul so fair
That no false thought can ever harbor there?
O thou who wouldst teach men of Love!
Hast thou passed through the place of despair?
Hast thou wept through the dark night of grief? does it move
   (Now freed from its sorrow and care)
Thy human heart to pitying gentleness,
Looking on wrong, and hate, and ceaseless stress?
O thou who wouldst teach men of Peace!
Hast thou crossed the wide ocean of strife?
Hast thou found on the Shores of the Silence,
Release from all the wild unrest of life?
From thy human heart hath all striving gone,
Leaving but Truth, and Love, and Peace alone?

Above Life's Turmoil

Foreword

We cannot alter external things, nor shape other people to our liking, nor could the world to our wishes but we can alter internal things,-our desires, passions, thoughts,-we can shape our liking to other people, and we can could the inner world of our own mind in accordance with wisdom, and so reconcile it to the outer world if men and things. The turmoil of the world we cannot avoid, but the disturbances of mind we can overcome. The duties and difficulties of life claim our attention, but we can rise above all anxiety concerning them. Surrounded by noise, we can yet have a quiet mind; involved in responsibilities, the heart can be at rest; in the midst of strife, we can know the abiding peace. The twenty pieces which comprise this book, unrelated as some of them are in the letter, will be found to be harmonious in the spirit, in that they point the reader towards those heights of self-knowledge and self-conquest which, rising above the turbulence of the world, lift their peaks where the Heavenly Silence reigns.

James Allen

True Happiness

To maintain an unchangeable sweetness of disposition, to think only thoughts that are pure and gentle, and to be happy under all circumstances,— such blessed conditions and such beauty of character and life should be the aim of all, and particularly so of those who wish to lessen the misery of the world. If anyone has failed to lift himself above ungentleness, impurity, and unhappiness, he is greatly deluded if he imagines he can make the world happier by the propagation of any theory or theology. He who is daily living in harshness, impurity, or unhappiness is day by day adding to the sum of the world's misery; whereas he who continually lives in goodwill, and does not depart from happiness, is day by day increasing the sum of the world's happiness, and this independently of any religious beliefs which these may or may not hold.

He who has not learned how to be gentle, or giving, loving and happy, has learned very little, great though his book-learning and profound his acquaintance which the letter of Scripture may be, for it is in the process of becoming gentle, pure, and happy that the deep, real and enduring lessons of life are learned. Unbroken sweetness of conduct in the face of all outward antagonism is the infallible indication of a self-conquered soul, the witness of wisdom, and the proof of the possession of Truth.

A sweet and happy soul is the ripened fruit of experience and wisdom, and it sheds abroad the invisible yet powerful aroma of its influence, gladdening the hearts of others, and purifying the world. And all who will, and who have not yet commenced, may begin this day, if they will so resolve, to live sweetly and happily, as becomes the dignity of a true manhood or womanhood. Do not say that your surroundings are against you. A man's surroundings are never against him; they are there to aid him, and all those outward occurrences over which you lose sweetness and peace of mind are the very conditions necessary to your development, and it is only by meeting and overcoming them that you can learn, and grow, and ripen. The fault is in yourself.

Pure happiness is the rightful and healthy condition of the soul, and all may possess it if they will live purely and unselfish.

"Have goodwill
To all that lives, letting unkindness die,
And greed and wrath, so that your lives be made
Like soft airs passing by."

Is this too difficult for you? Then unrest and unhappiness will continue to dwell with you. Your belief and aspiration and resolve are all that are necessary to make it easy, to render it in the near future a thing accomplished, a blessed state realized.

Despondency, irritability, anxiety and complaining, condemning and grumbling— all these are thought-cankers, mind-diseases; they are the indications of a wrong mental condition, and those who suffer from would do well to remedy their thinking and conduct. It is true there is much sin and misery in the world, so that all our love and compassion are needed, but our misery is not needed— there is already too much of that. No, it is our cheerfulness and happiness that are needed for there is too little of that. We can give nothing better to the world than beauty of life and character; without this, all other things are vain; this is pre-eminently excellent; it is enduring, real, and not to be overthrown, and it includes all joy and blessedness.

Cease to dwell pessimistically upon the wrongs around you; dwell no more in complaints about, and revolt against, the evil in others, and commence to live free from all wrong and evil yourself. Peace of mind, pure religion, and true reform lie this way. If you would have others true, be true; if you would have the world emancipated from misery and sin, emancipate yourself; if you would have your home and your surroundings happy, be happy. You can transform everything around you if you will transform yourself.

"Don't bewail and bemoan.....
Don't waste yourself in rejection, nor bark against the bad,
but chant the beauties of the good."

And this you will naturally and spontaneously do as you realize the good in yourself.

The Immortal Man

Immortality is here and now, and is not a speculative something beyond the grave. It is a lucid state of consciousness in which the sensations of the body, the varying and unfruitful states of mind, and the circumstances and events of life are seen to be of a fleeting and therefore of an illusory character.

Immortality does not belong to time, and will never be found in time; it belongs to Eternity; and just as time is here and now, so is Eternity here and now, and a man may find that Eternity and establish in it, if he will overcome the self that derives its life from the unsatisfying and perishable things of time.

Whilst a man remains immersed in sensation, desire, and the passing events of his day-by-day existence, and regards those sensations, desires, and passing events as of the essence of himself, he can have no knowledge of immortality. The thing which such a man desires, and which he mistakes for immortality, is persistence; that is, a continuous succession of sensations and events in time. Living in, loving and clinging to, the things which stimulate and minister to his immediate gratification, and realizing no state of consciousness above and independent of this, he thirsts for its continuance, and strives to banish the thought that he will at last have to part from those earthly luxuries and delights to which he has become enslaved, and which he regards as being inseparable from himself.

Persistence is the antithesis of immortality; and to be absorbed in it is spiritual death. Its very nature is change, impermanence. It is a continual living and dying.

The death of the body can never bestow upon a man immortality. Spirits are not different from men, and live their little feverish life of broken consciousness, and are still immersed in change and mortality. The mortal man, he who thirsts for the persistence of his pleasure-loving personality is still mortal after death, and only lives another life with a beginning and an end without memory of the past, or knowledge of the future.

The immortal man is he who has detached himself from the things of time by having ascended into that state of consciousness which is fixed and unvariable, and is not affected by passing events and sensations. Human life consists of an ever moving procession of events, and in this procession the mortal man is immersed, and he is carried along with it; and being so carried along, he has no knowledge of what is behind and before him. The immortal man is he who has stepped out of this procession, and he stands by unmoved and watches it; and from his fixed place he sees both the before, the behind and the middle of the moving thing called life. No longer identifying himself with the sensations and fluctuations of the personality, or with the outward changes which make up the life in time, he has become the passionless spectator of his own destiny and of the destinies of the men and nations.

The mortal man, also, is one who is caught in a dream, and he neither knows that he was formerly awake, nor that he will wake again; he is a dreamer without knowledge, nothing more. The immortal man is as one who has awakened out of his dream, and he knows that his dream was not an enduring reality, but a passing illusion. He is a man with knowledge, the knowledge of both states- that of persistence, and that of immortality,— and is in full possession of himself.

The mortal man lives in the time or world state of consciousness which begins and ends; the immortal man lives in the cosmic or heaven state of consciousness, in which there is neither beginning nor end, but an eternal now. Such a man remains poised and steadfast under all changes, and the death of his body will not in any way interrupt the eternal consciousness in which he abides. Of such a one it is said, "He shall not taste of death", because he has stepped out of the stream of mortality, and established himself in the abode of Truth. Bodies, personalities, nations, and worlds pass away, but Truth remains, and its glory is undimmed by time. The immortal man, then, is he who has conquered himself; who no longer identifies himself with the self-seeking forces of the personality, but who has trained himself to direct those forces with the hand of a master, and so has brought them into harmony with the causal energy and source of all things.

The fret and fever of life has ceased, doubt and fear are cast out, and death is not for him who has realized the fadeless splendor of that life of Truth by adjusting heart and mind to the eternal and unchangeable verities.

The Overcoming of Self

Many people have very confused and erroneous ideas concerning the terms "the overcoming of self", "the eradication of desire", and "the annihilation of the personality." Some (particularly the intellectual who are prone to theories) regard it as a metaphysical theory altogether apart from life and conduct; while others conclude that it is the crushing out of all life, energy and action, and the attempt to idealize stagnation and death. These errors and confusions, arising as they do in the minds of individuals, can only be removed by the individuals themselves; but perhaps it may make their removal a little less difficult (for those who are seeking Truth) by presenting the matter in another way.

The doctrine of the overcoming or annihilation of self is simplicity itself; indeed, so simple, practical, and close at hand is it that a child of five, whose mind has not yet become clouded with theories, theological schemes and speculative philosophies, would be far more likely to comprehend it than many older people who have lost their hold upon simple and beautiful truths by the adoption of complicated theories.

The annihilation of self consists in weeding out and destroying all those elements in the soul which lead to division, strife, suffering, disease and sorrow. It does not mean the destruction of any good and beautiful and peace-producing quality. For instance, when a man is tempted to irritability or anger, and by a great effort overcomes the selfish tendency, casts it from him, and acts from the spirit of patience and love, in that moment of self-conquest he practices the annihilation of self. Every noble man practices it in part, though he may deny it in his words, and he who carries out this practice to its completion, eradicating every selfish tendency until only the divinely beautiful qualities remain, he is said to have annihilated the personality (all the personal elements) and to have arrived at Truth.

The self which is to be annihilated is composed of the following ten worthless and sorrow-producing elements: lust, hatred, avarice, self-indulgence, self-seeking, vanity, pride, doubt, dark belief, delusion.

It is the total abandonment, the complete annihilation of these ten elements, for they comprise the body of desire. On the other hand it teaches the cultivation, practice, and preservation of the following ten divine qualities: purity, patience, humility, self-sacrifice, self-reliance, fearlessness, knowledge, wisdom, compassion, love.

These comprise the Body of Truth, and to live entirely in them is to be a doer and knower of the Truth, is to be an embodiment of Truth.

The combination of the ten elements is called Self or the Personality; the combination of the ten qualities produces what is called Truth; the Impersonal; the abiding, real and immortal Man.

It will thus be seen that it is not the destruction of any noble, true, and enduring quality that is taught, but only the destruction of those things that are ignoble, false and evanescent. Neither is this overcoming of self the deprivation of gladness, happiness and joy, but rather is it the constant possession of these things by living in the joy-begetting qualities. It is the abandonment of the lust for enjoyment, but not of enjoyment itself; the destruction of the thirst for pleasure, but not of pleasure itself; the annihilation of the selfish longing for love, and power, and possessions themselves. It is the preservation of all those things which draw and bind men together in unity and concord, and, far from idealizing stagnation and death, urges men to the practice of those qualities which lead to the highest, noblest, most effective, and enduring action. He whose actions proceed from some or all of the ten elements wastes his energies upon negations, and does not preserve his soul; but he whose actions proceed from some or all of the ten qualities, he truly and wisely acts and so preserves his soul.

He who lives largely in the ten earthly elements, and who is blind and deaf to the spiritual verities, will find no attraction in the doctrine of self-surrender, for it will appear to him as the complete extinction of his being; but he who is endeavoring to live in the ten heavenly qualities will see the glory and beauty of the doctrine, and will know it as the foundation of Life Eternal. He will also see that when men apprehend and practice it, industry, commerce, government, and every worldly activity will be purified; and action, purpose and intelligence, instead of being destroyed, will be intensified and enlarged, but freed from strife and pain.

The Uses of Temptation

The soul, in its journey towards perfection, passes through three distinct stages. The first is the animal stage, in which the man is content to live, in the gratification of his senses, unawakened to the knowledge of sin, or of his divine inheritance, and altogether unconscious of the spiritual possibilities within himself.

The second is the dual stage, in which the mind is continually oscillating between its animal and divine tendencies having become awakened to the consciousness of both. It is during this stage that temptation plays its part in the progress of the soul. It is a stage of continual fighting, of falling and rising, of sinning and repenting, for the man, still loving, and reluctant to leave, the gratifications in which he has so long lived, yet also aspires to the purity and excellence of the spiritual state, and he is continually mortified by an undecided choice.

Urged on by the divine life within him, this stage becomes at last one of deep anguish and suffering, and then the soul is ushered into the third stage, that of knowledge , in which the man rises above both sin and temptation, and enters into peace.

Temptation, like contentment in sin, is not a lasting condition, as the majority of people suppose; it is a passing phase, an experience through which the soul must pass; but as to whether a man will pass through that condition in this present life, and realize holiness and heavenly rest here and now, will depend entirely upon the strength of his intellectual and spiritual exertions, and upon the intensity and ardor with which he searches for Truth.

Temptation, with all its attendant torments can be overcome here and now, but it can only be overcome by knowledge. It is a condition of darkness or of semi-darkness. The fully enlightened soul is proof against all temptation. When a man fully understands the source, nature, and meaning of temptation, in that hour he will conquer it, and will rest from his long travail; but whilst he remains in ignorance, attention to religious observances, and much praying and reading of Scripture will fail to bring him peace.

If a man goes out to conquer an enemy, knowing nothing of his enemy's strength, tactics, or place of ambush, he will not only ignominiously fail, but will speedily fall into the hands of the enemy. He who would overcome his enemy the tempter, must discover his stronghold and place of concealment, and must also find out the unguarded gates in his own fortress where his enemy effects so easy an entrance. This necessitates continual meditation, ceaseless watchfulness, and constant and rigid introspection which lays bare, before the spiritual eyes of the tempted one, the vain and selfish motives of his soul. This is the holy warfare of the saints; it is the fight upon which every soul enters when it awakens out of its long sleep of animal indulgence.

Men fail to conquer, and the fight is indefinitely prolonged, because they labor, almost universally, under two delusions: first, that all temptations come from without; and second, that they are tempted because of their goodness. Whilst a man is held in bondage by these two delusions, he will make no progress; when he has shaken them off, he will pass on rapidly from victory to victory, and will taste of spiritual joy and rest.

Two searching truths must take the place of these two delusions, and those truths are: first, that all temptation comes from within; and second, that a man is tempted because of the evil that is within him. The idea that God, a devil, evil spirits, or outward objects are the source of temptation must be dispelled.

The source and cause of all temptation is in the inward desire; that being purified or eliminated, outward objects and extraneous powers are utterly powerless to move the soul to sin or to temptation. The outward object is merely the occasion of the temptation, never the cause; this is in the desire of the one tempted. If the cause existed in the object, all men would be tempted alike, temptation could never be overcome, and men would be hopelessly doomed to endless torment; but seated, as it is, in his own desires, he has the remedy in his own hands, and can become victorious over all temptation by purifying those desires. A man is tempted because there are within him certain desires or states of mind which he has come to regard as unholy. These desires may lie asleep for a long time, and the man may think that he has got rid of them, when suddenly, on the presentation of an outward object, the sleeping desire wakes up and thirsts of immediate gratification; and this is the state of temptation.

The good in a man is never tempted. Goodness destroys temptation. It is the evil in a man that is aroused and tempted. The measure of a man's temptations is the exact register of his own ungodliness. As a man purifies his heart, temptation ceases, for when a certain unlawful desire has been taken out of the heart, the object which formerly appealed to it can no longer do so, but becomes dead and powerless, for there is nothing left in the heart that can respond to it. The honest man cannot be tempted to steal, let the occasion be ever so opportune; the man of purified appetites cannot be tempted to gluttony and drunkenness, though the viands and wines be the most luscious; he of an enlightened understanding, whose mind is calm in the strength of inward virtue, can never be tempted to anger, irritability or revenge, and the wiles and charms of the wanton fall upon the purified heart as empty meaningless shadows.

Temptation shows a man just where he is sinful and ignorant, and is a means of urging him on to higher altitudes of knowledge and purity. Without temptation the soul cannot grow and become strong, there could be no wisdom, no real virtue; and though there would be lethargy and death, there could be no peace and no fullness of life. When temptation is understood and conquered, perfection is assured, and such perfection may become any man's who is willing to cast every selfish and impure desire by which he is possessed, into the sacrificial fire of knowledge. Let men, therefore, search diligently for Truth, realizing that whilst they are subject to temptation, they have not comprehended Truth, and have much to learn.

Ye who are tempted know, then, that ye are tempted of yourselves. "For every man is tempted when he is drawn away of his own lusts," says the Apostle James. You are tempted because you are clinging to the animal within you and are unwilling to let go; because you are living in the false mortal self which is ever devoid of all true knowledge, knowing nothing, seeking nothing, but its own immediate gratification, ignorant of every Truth, and of every divine Principle. Clinging to that self, you continually suffer the pains of three separate torments; the torment of desire, the torment of repletion, and the torment of remorse.

> "So flameth Trishna, lust and thirst of things.
> Eager, ye cleave to shadows, dote on dreams;
> A false self in the midst ye plant, and make
> A World around which seems;
> Blind to the height beyond; deaf to the sound
> Of sweet airs breathed from far past Indra's sky;
> Dumb to the summons of the true life kept
> For him who false puts by,
> So grow the strifes and lusts which make earth's war,
> So grieve poor cheated hearts and flow salt tears;
> So wax the passions, envies, angers, hates;
> So years chase blood-stained years
> With wild red feet."

In that false self lies the germ of every suffering, the blight of every hope, the substance of every grief. When you are ready to give it up; when you are willing to have laid bare before you all its selfishness, impurity, and ignorance, and to confess its darkness to the uttermost, then will you enter upon the life of self-knowledge and self-mastery; you will become conscious of the god within you, of that divine nature which, seeking no gratification, abides in a region of perpetual joy and peace where suffering cannot come and where temptation can find no foothold. Establishing yourself, day by day, more and more firmly in that inward Divinity, the time will at last come when you will be able to say with Him whom millions worship, few understand and fewer still follow, — "The Prince of this world cometh and hath nothing in me."

The Man of Integrity

There are times in the life of every man who takes his stand on high moral principles when his faith in, and knowledge of, those principles is tested to the uttermost, and the way in which he comes out of the fiery trial decides as to whether he has sufficient strength to live as a man of Truth, and join the company of the free, or shall still remain a slave and a hireling to the cruel taskmaster, Self.

Such times of trial generally assume the form of a temptation to do a wrong thing and continue in comfort and prosperity, or to stand by what is right and accept poverty and failure; and so powerful is the trial that, to the tempted one, it plainly appears on the face of things as though, if he chooses the wrong, his material success will be assured for the remainder of his life, but if he does what is right, he will be ruined for ever.

Frequently the man at once quails and gives way before this appalling prospect which the Path of Righteousness seems to hold out for him, but should he prove sufficiently strong to withstand this onslaught of temptation, then the inward seducer the spirit of self, assumes the grab of an Angel of Light, and whispers, "Think of your wife and children; think of those who are dependent upon you; will you bring them down to disgrace and starvation?"

Strong indeed and pure must be the man who can come triumphant out of such a trial, but he who does so, enters at once a higher realm of life, where his spiritual eyes are opened to see beautiful things; and then poverty and ruin which seemed inevitable do not come, but a more abiding success comes, and a peaceful heart and a quiet conscience. But he who fails does not obtain the promised prosperity, and his heart is restless and his conscience troubled.

The right-doer cannot ultimately fail, the wrong-doer cannot ultimately succeed, for "Such is the Law which moves to Righteousness/ Which none at last can turn aside or stay," and it is because justice is at the heart of things— because the Great Law is good— that the man of integrity is superior to fear, and failure, and poverty, and shame, and disgrace.

As the poet further says of this Law:"The heart of its Love, the end of it/Is peace and consummation sweet—obey."

The man who fearing the loss of present pleasures or material comforts, denies the Truth within him, can be injured, and robbed, and degraded, and trampled upon, because he has first injured, robbed and degraded, and trampled upon his own nobler self; but the man of steadfast virtue, of unblemished integrity, cannot be subject to such conditions, because he has denied the craven self within him and has taken refuge in Truth. It is not the scourge and the chains which make a man a slave, but the fact that he is a slave.

Slander, Accusation, and malice cannot affect the righteous man, nor call from him any bitter response, nor does he need to go about to defend himself and prove his innocence. His innocence and integrity alone are a sufficient answer to all that hatred may attempt against him. Nor can he ever be subdued by the forces of darkness, having subdued all those forces within himself; but he turns all evil things to good account — out of darkness he brings light, out of hatred love, out of dishonor honor; and slanders, envies, and misrepresentations only serve to make more bright the jewel of Truth within him, and to glorify his high and holy destiny.

Let the man of integrity rejoice and be glad when he is severely tried; let him be thankful that he has been given an opportunity of proving his loyalty to the noble principles which he has espoused; and let him think: "Now is the hour of holy opportunity! Now is the day of triumph for Truth! Though I lose the whole world I will note desert the right!" So thinking, he will return good for evil, and will think compassionately of the wrong-doer.

The slanderer, the backbiter, and the wrong-doer may seem to succeed for a time, but the Law of Justice prevails; the man of integrity may seem to fail for a time, but he is invincible, and in none of the worlds, visible or invisible, can there be forged a weapon that shall prevail against him.

Discrimination

There is one quality which is pre-eminently necessary to spiritual development, the quality of discrimination.

A man's spiritual progress will be painfully slow and uncertain until there opens with him the eye of discrimination, for without this testing, proving, searching quality, he will but grope in the dark, will be unable to distinguish the real from the unreal, the shadow from the substance, and will so confuse the false with the true as to mistake the inward promptings of his animal nature for those of the spirit of Truth.

A blind man left in a strange place may go grope his way in darkness, but not without much confusion and many painful falls and bruising. Without discrimination a man is mentally blind, and his life is a painful groping in darkness, a confusion in which vice and virtue are indistinguishable one from the other, where facts are confounded with truths; opinions with principles, and where ideas, events, men, and things appear to be out of all relation to each other.

A man's mind and life should be free from confusion. He should be prepared to meet every mental, material and spiritual difficulty, and should not be inextricably caught (as many are) in the meshes of doubt, indecision and uncertainty when troubles and so-called misfortunes come along. He should be fortified against every emergency that can come against him; but such mental preparedness and strength cannot be attained in any degree without discrimination, and discrimination can only be developed by bringing into play and constantly exercising the analytical faculty.

Mind, like muscle, is developed by use, and the assiduous exercise of the mind in any given direction will develop, in that direction, mental capacity and power. The merely critical faculty is developed and strengthened by continuously comparing and analyzing the ideas and opinions of others. But discrimination is something more and greater than criticism; it is a spiritual quality from which the cruelty and egotism which so frequently accompany criticism are eliminated, and by virtue of which a man sees things as they are, and not as he would like them to be.

Discrimination, being a spiritual quality, can only be developed by spiritual methods, namely, by questioning, examining, and analyzing one's own ideas, opinions, and conduct. The critical, fault finding faculty must be withdrawn from its merciless application to the opinions and conduct of others, and must be applied, with undiminished severity, to oneself. A man must be prepared to question his every opinion, his every thought, and his every line of conduct, and rigorously and logically test them; only in this way can the discrimination which destroys confusion will be developed.

Before a man can enter upon such mental exercise, he must make himself of a teachable spirit. This does not mean that he must allow himself to be led by others; it means that he must be prepared to yield up any cherished thoughts to which he clings, if it will not bear the penetrating light of reason, if it shrivels up before the pure flames of searching aspirations. The man who says, "I am right!" and who refuses to question his position in order to discover whether he is right, will continue to follow the line of his passions and prejudices, and will not acquire discrimination. The man who humbly asks, "Am I right?" and then proceeds to test and prove his position by earnest thought and the love of Truth, will always be able to discover the true and to distinguish it from the false, and he will acquire the priceless possession of discrimination.

The man who is afraid to think searchingly upon his opinions, and to reason critically upon his position, will have to develop moral courage before he can acquire discrimination.

A man must be true to himself, fearless with himself, before he can perceive the Pure Principles of Truth, before he can receive the all-revealing Light of Truth.

The more Truth is inquired of, the brighter it shines; it cannot suffer under examination and analysis.

The more error is questioned, the darker it grows; it cannot survive the entrance of pure and searching thought.

To "prove all things" is to find the good and throw the evil.

He who reasons and meditates learns to discriminate; he who discriminates discovers the eternally True.

Confusion, suffering and spiritual darkness follow the thoughtless.

Harmony, blessedness and the Light of Truth attend upon the thoughtful.

Passion and prejudice are blind, and cannot discriminate: they are still crucifying the Christ and releasing Barabbas.

Belief, The Basis of Action

Belief is an important word in the teachings of the wise, and it figures prominently in all religions. According to Jesus, a certain kind of belief is necessary to salvation or regeneration, and Buddha definitely taught that right belief is the first and most essential step in the Way of Truth, as without right belief there cannot be right conduct, and he who has not learned how to rightly govern and conduct himself, has not yet comprehended the simplest rudiments of Truth.

Belief as laid down by the Great Teachers, is not belief in any particular school, philosophy, or religion, but consists of an altitude of mind determining the whole course of one's life. Belief and conduct are, therefore inseparable, for the one determines the other.

Belief is the basis of all action, and, this being so, the belief which dominates the hearts or mind is shown in the life. Every man acts, thinks, lives in exact accordance with the belief which is rooted in his innermost being, and such is the mathematical nature of the laws which govern mind that it is absolutely impossible for anyone to believe in two opposing conditions at the same time. For instance, it is impossible to believe in justice and injustice, hatred and love, peace and strife, self and truth. Every man believes in one or the other of these opposites, never in both, and the daily conduct of every man indicates the nature of his belief. The man who believes in justice, who regards it as an eternal and indestructible Principle, never boils over with righteous indignation, does not grow cynical and pessimistic over the inequalities of life, and remains calm and untroubled through all trials and difficulties. It is impossible for him to act otherwise, for he believes that justice reigns, and that, therefore, all that is called injustice is fleeting and illusory.

The man who is continually getting enraged over the injustice of his fellow men, who talks about himself being badly treated, or who mourns over the lack of justice in the world around him, shows by his conduct, his attitude of mind, that he believes in injustice. However he may protest to the contrary, in his inmost heart he believes that confusion and chaos are dominant in the universe, the result being that he dwells in misery and unrest, and his conduct is faulty.

Again, he who believes in love, in its stability and power, practices it under all circumstances, never deviates from it, and bestows it alike upon enemies as upon friends. He who slanders and condemns, who speaks disparagingly of others, or regards them with contempt, believes not in love, but hatred; all his actions prove it, even though with tongue or pen he may eulogize love.

The believer in peace is known by his peaceful conduct. It is impossible for him to engage in strife. If attacked he does not retaliate, for he has seen the majesty of the angel of peace, and he can no longer pay homage to the demon of strife. The stirrer-up of strife, the lover of argument, he who rushes into self-defense upon any or every provocation, believes in strife, and will have naught to do with peace.

Further, he who believes in Truth renounces himself— that is, he refuses to center his life in those passions, desires, and characteristics which crave only their own gratification, and by thus renouncing he becomes steadfastly fixed in Truth, and lives a wise, beautiful, and blameless life. The believer in self is known by his daily indulgences, gratifications, and vanities, and by the disappointments, sorrows, and mortifications which he continually suffers.

The believer in Truth does not suffer, for he has given up that self which is the cause of such suffering.

It will be seen by the foregoing that every man believes either in permanent and eternal Principles directing human life towards law and harmony, or in the negation of those Principles, with the resultant chaos in human affairs and in his own life.

Belief in the divine Principles of Justice, Compassion, Love, constitutes the right belief laid down by Buddha as being the basis of right conduct, and also the belief unto salvation as emphasized in the Christian Scriptures, for he who so believes cannot do otherwise than build his whole life upon these Principles, and so purifies his heart, and perfects his life.

Belief in the negation of this divine principle constitutes what is called in all religious unbelief and this unbelief is manifested as a sinful, troubled, and imperfect life.

Where there is Right Belief there is a blameless and perfect life; where there is false belief there is sin, there is sorrow, the mind and life are improperly governed, and there is affliction and unrest. "By their fruits ye shall know them."

There is much talk about, "belief in Jesus," but what does belief in Jesus mean? It means belief in his words, in the Principles he enunciated— and lived, in his commandments and in his exemplary life of perfection. He who declares belief in Jesus, and yet is all the time living in his lusts and indulgences, or in the spirit of hatred and condemnation, is self deceived. He believes not in Jesus. He believes in his own animal self. As a faithful servant delights in carrying out the commands of his master, so he who believes in Jesus carries out his commandments, and so is saved from sin. The supreme test of belief in Jesus is this: Do I keep his commandments? And this test is applied by St. John himself in the following words: "He that saith. I know him

(Jesus), and keepeth not His Commandments, is a liar, and the truth is not in him. But whoso keepeth his word, in him verily is the word of God perfected."

It will be found after a rigid and impartial analysis, that belief lies at the root of all human conduct. Every thought, every act, every habit, is the direct outcome of a certain fixed belief, and one's conduct alters only as one's belief are modified. What we cling to, in that we believe; what we practice, in that we believe. When our belief in a thing ceases, we can no longer cling to or practice it; it falls away from us as a garment out-worn. Men cling to their lusts, and lies, and vanities, because they believe in them, believe there is gain and happiness in them. When they transfer their belief to the divine qualities of purity and humility, those sins trouble them no more.

Men are saved from error by belief in the supremacy of Truth. They are saved from sin by belief in Holiness or Perfection. They are saved from evil by belief in Good, for every belief is manifested in the life. It is not necessary to inquire as to a man's theological belief, for that is of little or no account, for what can it avail a man to believe that Jesus died for him, or that Jesus is God, or that he is "justified by faith," if he continues to live in his lower, sinful nature? All that is necessary to ask is this: "How does a man live?" "How does he conduct himself under trying circumstances?" The answer to these questions will show whether a man believes in the power of evil or in the power of Good.

He who believes in the power of Good, lives a good, spiritual, or godly life, for Goodness is God, yea, verily is God Himself, and he will soon leave behind him all sins and sorrows who believes, with steadfast and unwavering faith, in the Supreme Good.

The Belief That Saves

It has been said that a man's whole life and character is the outcome of his belief, and also that his belief has nothing whatever to do with his life. Both statements are true. The confusion and contradiction of these two statements are only apparent, and are quickly dispelled when it is remembered that there are two entirely distinct kinds of beliefs, namely, Head-belief and Heart-belief.

Head, or intellectual belief, is not fundamental and causative, but it is superficial and consequent, and that it has no power in the molding of a man's character, the most superficial observer may easily see. Take, for instance, half a dozen men from any creed. They not only hold the same theological belief, but confess the same articles of faith in every particular, and yet their characters are vastly different. One will be just as noble as another is ignoble; one will be mild and gentle, another coarse and irascible; one will be honest, another dishonest; one will indulge certain habits which another will rigidly abjure, and so on, plainly indicating that theological belief is not an influential factor in a man's life.

A man's theological belief is merely his intellectual opinion or view of the universe. God, The Bible, etc., and behind and underneath this head-belief there lies, deeply rooted in his innermost being, the hidden, silent, secret belief of his heart, and it is this belief which molds and makes his whole life. It is this which makes those six men who, whilst holding the same theology, are yet so vastly at variance in their deeds— they differ in the vital belief of the heart.

What, then, is this heart-belief?

It is that which a man loves and clings to and fosters in his soul; for he thus loves and clings to and fosters in his heart, because he believes in them, and believing in them and loving them, he practices them; thus is his life the effect of his belief, but it has no relation to the particular creed which comprises his intellectual belief. One man clings to impure and immoral things because he believes in them; another does not cling to them because he has ceased to believe in them. A man cannot cling to anything unless he believes in it; belief always precedes action, therefore a man's deeds and life are the fruits of his belief.

The Priest and the Levite who passed by the injured and helpless man, held, no doubt, very strongly to the theological doctrines of their fathers— that was their intellectual belief,— but in their hearts they did not believe in mercy, and so lived and acted accordingly. The good Samaritan may or may not have had any theological beliefs nor was it necessary that he should have; but in his heart he believed in mercy, and acted accordingly.

Strictly speaking, there are only two beliefs which vitally affect the life, and they are, belief in good and belief in evil.

He who believes in all those things that are good, will love them, and live in them; he who believes in those things that are impure and selfish, will love them, and cling to them. The tree is known by its fruits.

A man's beliefs about God, Jesus, and the Bible are one thing; his life, as bound up in his actions, is another; therefore a man's theological belief is of no consequence; but the thoughts which he harbors, his attitude of mind towards others, and his actions, these, and these only, determine and demonstrate whether the belief of a man's heart is fixed in the false or true.

Thought And Action

As the fruit to the tree and the water to the spring, so is action to thought. It does not come into manifestation suddenly and without a cause. It is the result of a long and silent growth; the end of a hidden process which has long been gathering force. The fruit of the tree and the water gushing from the rock are both the effect of a combination of natural processes in air and earth which have long worked together in secret to produce the phenomenon; and the beautiful acts of enlightenment and the dark deeds of sin are both the ripened effects of trains of thought which have long been harbored in the mind.

The sudden falling, when greatly tempted, into some grievous sin by one who was believed, and who probably believed himself, to stand firm, is seen neither to be a sudden nor a causeless thing when the hidden process of thought which led up to it are revealed. The falling was merely the end, the outworking, the finished result of what commenced in the mind probably years before. The man had allowed a wrong thought to enter his mind; and a second and a third time he had welcomed it, and allowed it to nestle in his heart. Gradually he became accustomed to it, and cherished, and fondled, and tended it; and so it grew, until at last it attained such strength and force that it attracted to itself the opportunity which enabled it to burst forth and ripen into act. As falls the stately building whose foundations have been gradually undermined by the action of water, so at last falls the strong man who allows corrupt thoughts to creep into his mind and secretly undermine his character.

When it is seen that all sin and temptation are the natural outcome of the thoughts of the individual, the way to overcome sin and temptation becomes plain, and its achievement a near possibility, and, sooner or later, a certain reality; for if a man will admit, cherish, and brood upon thoughts that are pure and good, those thoughts, just as surely as the impure, will grow and gather force, and will at last attract to themselves the opportunities which will enable them to ripen into act.

"There is nothing hidden that shall not be revealed," and every thought that is harbored in the mind must, by virtue of the impelling force which is inherent in the universe, at last blossom into act good or bad according to its nature. The divine Teacher and the sensualist are both the product of their own thoughts, and have become what they are as the result of the seeds of thought which they have implanted, are allowed to fall, into the garden of the heart, and have afterwards watered, tended, and cultivated.

Let no man think he can, overcome sin and temptation by wrestling with opportunity; he can only overcome them by purifying his thoughts; and if he will, day by day, in the silence of his soul, and in the performance of his duties, strenuously overcome all erroneous inclination, and put in its place thoughts that are true and that will endure the light, opportunity to do evil will give place to opportunity for accomplishing good, for a man can only attract that to him which is in harmony with his nature, and no temptation can gravitate to a man unless there is that in his heart which is capable of responding to it.

Guard well your thoughts, reader, for what you really are in your secret thoughts today, be it good or evil, you will, sooner or later, become in actual deed. He who unwearyingly guards the portals of his mind against the intrusion of sinful thoughts, and occupies himself with loving thoughts, with pure, strong, and beautiful thoughts, will, when the season of their ripening comes, bring forth the fruits of gentle and holy deeds, and no temptation that can come against him shall find him unarmed or unprepared.

Your Mental Attitude

As a being of thought, your dominant mental attitude will determine your condition in life. It will also be the gauge of your knowledge and the measures of your attainment. The so-called limitations of your nature are the boundary lines of your thoughts; they are self-erected fences, and can be drawn to a narrower circle, extended to a wider, or be allowed to remain.

You are the thinker of your thoughts and as such you are the maker of yourself and condition. Thought is causal and creative, and appears in your character and life in the form of results. There are no accidents in your life. Both its harmonies and antagonisms are the responsive echoes of your thoughts. A man thinks, and his life appears.

If your dominant mental attitude is peaceable and lovable, bliss and blessedness will follow you; if it be resistant and hateful, trouble and distress will cloud your pathway. Out of ill-will will come grief and disaster; out of good-will, healing and reparation.

You imagine your circumstances as being separate from yourself, but they are intimately related to your thought world. Nothing appears without an adequate cause. Everything that happens is just. Nothing is fated, everything is formed.

As you think, you travel; as you love, you attract. You are today where your thoughts have brought you; you will be tomorrow where your thoughts take you. You cannot escape the result of your thoughts, but you can endure and learn, can accept and be glad.

You will always come to the place where your love (your most abiding and intense thought) can receive its measure of gratification. If your love be base, you will come to a base place; if it be beautiful, you will come to a beautiful place.

You can alter your thoughts, and so alter your condition. Strive to perceive the vastness and grandeur of your responsibility. You are powerful, not powerless. You are as powerful to obey as you are to disobey; as strong to be pure as to be impure; as ready for wisdom as for ignorance. You can learn what you will, can remain as ignorant as you choose. If you love knowledge you will obtain it; if you love wisdom you will secure it; if you love purity you will realize it. All things await your acceptance, and you choose by the thoughts which you entertain.

A man remains ignorant because he loves ignorance, and chooses ignorant thoughts; a man becomes wise because he loves wisdom and chooses wise thoughts. No man is hindered by another; he is only hindered by himself. No man suffers because of another; he suffers only because of himself. By the noble Gateway of Pure Thought you can enter the highest Heaven; by the ignoble doorway of impure thought you can descend into the lowest hell.

Your mental attitude towards others will faithfully react upon yourself, and will manifest itself in every relation of your life. Every impure and selfish thought that you send out comes back to you in your circumstances in some form of suffering; every pure and unselfish thought returns to you in some form of blessedness. Your circumstances are effects of which the cause is inward and invisible. As the father-mother of your thoughts you are the maker of your state and condition. When you know yourself, you will perceive, that every event in your life is weighed in the faultless balance of equity. When you understand the law within your mind you will cease to regard yourself as the impotent and blind tool of circumstances, and will become the strong and seeing master.

Sowing And Reaping

Go into the fields and country lanes in the spring-time, and you will see farmers and gardeners busy sowing seeds in the newly prepared soil. If you were to ask any one of those gardeners or farmers what kind of produce he expected from the seed he was sowing, he would doubtless regard you as foolish, and would tell you that he does not "expect" at all, that it is a matter of common knowledge that his produce will be of the kind which he is sowing, and that he is sowing wheat, or barley, or turnips, as the case may be, in order to reproduce that particular kind.

Every fact and process in Nature contains a moral lesson for the wise man. There is no law in the world of Nature around us which is not to be found operating with the same mathematical certainty in the mind of man and in human life. All the parables of Jesus are illustrative of this truth, and are drawn from the simple facts of Nature. There is a process of seed-sowing in the mind and life a spiritual sowing which leads to a harvest according to the kind of seed sown. Thoughts, words, and acts are seeds sown, and, by the inviolable law of things, they produce after their kind.

The man who thinks hateful thoughts brings hatred upon himself. The man who thinks loving thoughts is loved. The man whose thoughts, words and acts are sincere, is surrounded by sincere friends; the insincere man is surrounded by insincere friends. The man who sows wrong thoughts and deeds, and prays that God will bless him, is in the position of a farmer who, having sown tares, asks God to bring forth for him a harvest of wheat.

> "That which ye sow, ye reap; see yonder fields
> The Sesamum was Sesamum, the corn
> Was corn; the silence and the darkness knew;
> So is a man's fate born."
> "He cometh reaper of the things he sowed."

He who would be blest, let him scatter blessings. He who would be happy, let him consider the happiness of others.

Then there is another side to this seed sowing. The farmer must scatter all his seed upon the land, and then leave it to the elements. Were he to covetously hoard his seed, he would lose both it and his produce, for his seed would perish. It perishes when he sows it, but in perishing it brings forth a great abundance. So in life, we get by giving;

we grow rich by scattering. The man who says he is in possession of knowledge which he cannot give out because the world is incapable of receiving it, either does not possess such knowledge, or, if he does, will soon be deprived of it — if he is not already so deprived. To hoard is to lose; to exclusively retain is to be dispossessed.

Even the man who would increase his material wealth must be willing to part with (invest) what little capital he has, and then wait for the increase. So long as he retains his hold on his precious money, he will not only remain poor, but will be growing poorer everyday. He will, after all, lose the thing he loves, and will lose it without increase. But if he wisely lets it go; if, like the farmer, he scatters his seeds of gold, then he can faithfully wait for, and reasonably expect, the increase.

Men are asking God to give them peace and purity, and righteousness and blessedness, but are not obtaining these things; and why not? Because they are not practicing them, not sowing them. I once heard a preacher pray very earnestly for forgiveness, and shortly afterwards, in the course of his sermon, he called upon his congregation to "show no mercy to the enemies of the church." Such self-delusion is pitiful, and men have yet to learn that the way to obtain peace and blessedness is to scatter peaceful and blessed thoughts, words, and deeds.

Men believe that they can sow the seeds of strife, impurity, and unbrotherliness, and then gather in a rich harvest of peace, purity and concord by merely asking for it. What more pathetic sight than to see an irritable and quarrelsome man praying for peace. Men reap that which they sow, and any man can reap all blessedness now and at once, if he will put aside selfishness, and sow broadcast the seeds of kindness, gentleness, and love.

If a man is troubled, perplexed, sorrowful, or unhappy, let him ask: "What mental seeds have I been sowing?" "What seeds am I sowing?" "What have I done for others?" "What is my attitude towards others?" "What seeds of trouble and sorrow and unhappiness have I sown that I should thus reap these bitter weeds?"

Let him seek within and find, and having found, let him abandon all the seeds of self, and sow, henceforth, only the seeds of Truth.

Let him learn of the farmer the simple truths of wisdom.

The Reign Of Law

The little party gods have had their day. The arbitrary gods, creatures of human caprice and ignorance, are falling into disrepute. Men have quarreled over and defended them until they have grown weary of the strife, and now, everywhere, they are relinquishing and breaking up these helpless idols of their long worship.

The god of revenge, hatred and jealousy, who gloats over the downfall of his enemies; the partial god who gratifies all our narrow and selfish desires; the god who saves only the creatures of his particular special creed; the god of exclusiveness and favoritism; such were the gods (miscalled by us God) of our soul's infancy, gods base and foolish as ourselves, the fabrications of our selfish self. And we relinquished our petty gods with bitter tears and misgivings, and broke our idols with bleeding hands. But in so doing we did not lose sight of God; nay we drew nearer to the great, silent Heart of Love. Destroying the idols of self, we began to comprehend somewhat of the Power which cannot be destroyed, and entered into a wider knowledge of the God of Love, of Peace, of Joy; the God in whom revenge and partiality cannot exist; the God of Light, from whose presence the darkness of fear and doubt and selfishness cannot choose but flee.

We have reached one of those epochs in the world's progress which witnesses the passing of the false gods; the gods of human selfishness and human illusion. The new-old revelation of one universal impersonal Truth has again dawned upon the world, and its searching light has carried consternation to the perishable gods who take shelter under the shadow of self.

Men have lost faith in a god who can be cajoled, who rules arbitrarily and capriciously, subverting the whole order of things to gratify the wishes of his worshipers, and are turning, with a new light in their eyes and a new joy in their hearts, to the God of Law.

And to Him they turn, not for personal happiness and gratification, but for knowledge, for understanding, for wisdom, for liberation from the bondage of self. And thus turning, they do not seek in vain, nor are they sent away empty and discomfited. They find within themselves the reign of Law, that every thought, every impulse, every act and word brings about a result in exact accordance with its own nature; that thoughts of love bring about beautiful and blissful conditions, that hateful thoughts bring about distorted and painful conditions, that thoughts and acts good and evil are weighed in the faultless balance of the Supreme Law, and receive their equal measure of blessedness on the one hand, and misery on the other. And thus finding they enter a new Path, the Path of Obedience to the Law. Entering that Path they no longer accuse, no longer doubt, no longer fret and despond, for they know that God is right, the universal laws are right, the cosmos is right, and that they themselves are wrong, if wrong there is, and that their salvation depends upon themselves, upon their own efforts, upon their personal acceptance of that which is good and deliberate rejection of that which is evil. No longer merely hearers, they become doers of the Word, and they acquire knowledge, they receive understanding, they grow in wisdom, and they enter into the glorious life of liberation from the bondage of self.

"The Law of the Lord is perfect, enlightening the eyes." Imperfection lies in man's ignorance, in man's blind folly. Perfection, which is knowledge of the Perfect Law, is ready for all who earnestly seek it; it belongs to the order of things; it is yours and mine now if we will only put self-seeking on one side, and adopt the life of self-obliteration.

The knowledge of Truth, with its unspeakable joy, its calmness and quiet strength, is not for those who persist in clinging to their "rights," defending their "interests," and fighting for their "opinions"; whose works are imbued with the personal "I," and who build upon the shifting sands of selfishness and egotism. It is for those who renounce these causes of strife, these sources of pain and sorrow; and they are, indeed, Children of Truth, disciples of the Master, worshipers of the most High.

The Children of Truth are in the world today; they are thinking, acting, writing, speaking; yea, even prophets are amongst us, and their influence is pervading the whole earth. An undercurrent of holy joy is gathering force in the world, so that men and women are moved with new aspirations and hopes, and even those who neither see nor hear, feel within themselves strange yearnings after a better and fuller life.

The Law reigns, and it reigns in men's hearts and lives; and they have come to understand the reign of Law who have sought out the Tabernacle of the true God by the fair pathway of unselfishness.

God does not alter for man, for this would mean that the perfect must become imperfect; man must alter for God, and this implies that the imperfect must become perfect. The Law cannot be broken for man, otherwise confusion would ensue; man must obey the Law; this is in accordance with harmony, order, justice.

There is no more painful bondage than to be at the mercy of one's inclinations; no greater liberty than utmost obedience to the Law of Being. And the Law is that the heart shall be purified, the mind regenerated, and the whole being brought in subjection to Love till self is dead and Love is all in all, for the reign of Law is the reign of Love. And Love waits for all , rejecting none. Love may be claimed and entered into now, for it is the heritage of all.

Ah, beautiful Truth! To know that now man may accept his divine heritage, and enter the Kingdom of Heaven!

Oh, pitiful error! To know that man rejects it because of love of self!

Obedience to the Law means the destruction of sin and self, and the realization of unclouded joy and undying peace.

Clinging to one's selfish inclinations means the drawing about one's soul clouds of pain and sorrow which darken the light of Truth; the shutting out of oneself from all real blessedness; for "whatsoever a man sows that shall he also reap."

Verily the Law reigneth, and reigneth for ever, and Justice and Love are its eternal ministers.

The Supreme Justice

The material universe is maintained and preserved by the equilibrium of its forces.

The moral universe is sustained and protected by the perfect balance of its equivalents.

As in the physical world Nature abhors a vacuum, so in the spiritual world disharmony is annulled.

Underlying the disturbances and destructions of Nature, and behind the mutability of its forms, there abides the eternal and perfect mathematical symmetry; and at the heart of life, behind all its pain, uncertainty, and unrest, there abide the eternal harmony, the unbroken peace, and inviolable Justice.

Is there, then, no injustice in the universe? There is injustice, and there is not. It depends upon the kind of life and the state of consciousness from which a man looks out upon the world and judges. The man who lives in his passions sees injustice everywhere; the man who has overcome his passions, sees the operations of Justice in every department of human life. Injustice is the confused, feverish dream of passion, real enough to those who are dreaming it; Justice is the permanent reality in life, gloriously visible to those who have wakened out of the painful nightmare of self.

The Divine Order cannot be perceived until passion and self are transcended; the Faultless Justice cannot be apprehended until all sense of injury and wrong is consumed in the pure flames of all-embracing Love.

The man who thinks, "I have been slighted, I have been injured, I have been insulted, I have been treated unjustly," cannot know what Justice is; blinded by self, he cannot perceive the pure Principles of Truth, and brooding upon his wrongs, he lives in continual misery.

In the region of passion there is a ceaseless conflict of forces causing suffering to all who are involved in them. There is action and reaction, deed and consequence, cause and effect; and within and above all is the Divine Justice regulating the play of forces with the utmost mathematical accuracy, balancing cause and effect with the finest precision. But this Justice is not perceived — cannot be perceived — by those who are engaged in the conflict; before this can be done, the fierce warfare of passion must be left behind.

The world of passion is the abode of schisms, quarrellings, wars, lawsuits, accusations, condemnations, impurities, weaknesses, follies, hatreds, revenges, and resentments. How can a man perceive Justice or understand Truth who is even partly involved in the fierce play of its blinding elements? As well expect a man caught in the flames of a burning building to sit down and reason out the cause of the fire.

In this realm of passion, men see injustice in the actions of others because, seeing only immediate appearances, they regard every act as standing by itself, undetached from cause and consequence. Having no knowledge of cause and effect in the moral sphere, men do not see the exacting and balancing process which is momentarily proceeding, nor do they ever regard their own actions as unjust, but only the actions of others. A boy beats a defenseless animal, then a man beats the defenseless boy for his cruelty, then a stronger man attacks the man for his cruelty to the boy. Each believes the other to be unjust and cruel, and himself to be just and humane; and doubtless most of all would the boy justify his conduct toward the animal as altogether necessary. Thus does ignorance keep alive hatred and strife; thus do men blindly inflict suffering upon themselves, living in passion and resentment, and not finding the true way in life. Hatred is met with hatred, passion with passion, strife with strife. The man who kills is himself killed; the thief who lives by depriving others is himself deprived; the beast that preys on others is hunted and killed; the accuser is accused, the condemner is condemned, the denouncer is persecuted.

> "By this the slayer's knife doth stab himself,
> The unjust judge has lost his own defender,
> The false tongue dooms its lie, the creeping thief
> And spoiler rob to render.
> Such is the Law."

Passion, also has its active and passive sides. Fool and fraud, oppressor and slave, aggressor and retaliator, the charlatan and the superstitious, complement each other, and come together by the operation of the Law of Justice. Men unconsciously cooperate in the mutual production of affliction; "the blind lead the blind, and both fall together into the ditch." Pain, grief, sorrow, and misery are the fruits of which passion is the flower.

Where the passion-bound soul sees only injustice, the good man, he who has conquered passion, sees cause and effect, sees the Supreme Justice. It is impossible for such a man to regard himself as treated unjustly, because he has ceased to see injustice. He knows that no one can injure or cheat him, having ceased to injure or cheat himself. However passionately or ignorantly men may act towards him, it cannot possibly cause him any pain, for he knows that whatever comes to him (it may be abuse and persecution) can only come as the effect of what he himself has formerly sent out. He therefore regards all things as good, rejoices in all things, loves his enemies and blesses them that curse him, regarding them as the blind but beneficent instruments by which he is enabled to pay his moral debts to the Great Law.

The good man, having put away all resentment, retaliation, self-seeking, and egotism, has arrived at a state of equilibrium, and has thereby become identified with the Eternal and Universal Equilibrium. Having lifted himself above the blind forces of passion, he understands those forces, contemplates them with a calm penetrating insight, like the solitary dweller upon a mountain who looks down upon the conflict of the storms beneath his feet. For him, injustice has ceased, and he sees ignorance and suffering on the one hand and enlightenment and bliss on the other. He sees that not only do the fool and the slave need his sympathy, but that the fraud and the oppressor are equally in need of it, and so his compassion is extended towards all.

The Supreme Justice and the Supreme Love are one. Cause and effect cannot be avoided; consequences cannot be escaped.

While a man is given to hatred, resentment, anger and condemnation, he is subject to injustice as the dreamer to his dream, and cannot do otherwise than see injustice; but he who has overcome those fiery and binding elements, knows that unerring Justice presides over all, that in reality there is no such thing as injustice in the whole of the universe.

The Use Of Reason

We have heard it said that reason is a blind guide, and that it draws men away from Truth rather than leads them to it. If this were true, it were better to remain, or to become, unreasonable, and to persuade others so to do. We have found, however, that the diligent cultivation of the divine faculty of reason brings about calmness and mental poise, and enables one to meet cheerfully the problems and difficulties of life.

It is true there is a higher light than reason; even that of the Spirit of Truth itself, but without the aid of reason, Truth cannot be apprehended. They who refuse to trim the lamp of reason will never, whilst they so refuse, perceive the light of Truth, for the light of reason is a reflection of that Light.

Reason is a purely abstract quality, and comes midway between the animal and divine consciousness in man, and leads, if rightly employed, from the darkness of one to the Light of the other. It is true that reason may be enlisted in the service of the lower, self-seeking nature, but this is only a result of its partial and imperfect exercise. A fuller development of reason leads away from the selfish nature, and ultimately allies the soul with the highest, the divine.

That spiritual Perceival who, searching for the Holy Grail of the Perfect Life, is again and again "left alone, and wearying in a land of sand and thorns,"

is not so stranded because he has followed reason, but because he is still clinging to, and is reluctant to leave, some remnants of his lower nature. He who will use the light of reason as a torch to search for Truth will not be left at last in comfortless darkness.

"Come, now, and let us reason together, saith the Lord; though your sins be as scarlet, they shall be as white as snow."

Many men and women pass through untold sufferings, and at last die in their sins, because they refuse to reason; because they cling to those dark delusions which even a faint glimmer of the light of reason would dispel; and all must use their reason freely, fully, and faithfully, who would exchange the scarlet robe of sin and suffering for the white garment of blamelessness and peace.

It is because we have proved and know these truths that we exhort men to "tread the middle road, whose course bright reason traces, and soft quiet smooths,"

for reason leads away from passion and selfishness into the quiet ways of sweet persuasion and gentle forgiveness, and he will never be led astray, nor will he follow blind guides, who faithfully adheres to the Apostolic injunction, "Prove all things, and hold fast that which is good." They, therefore, who despise the light of reason, despise the Light of Truth.

Large numbers of people are possessed of the strange delusion that reason is somehow intimately connected with the denial of the existence of God. This is probably due to the fact that those who try to prove that there is no God usually profess to take their stand upon reason, while those who try to prove the reverse generally profess to take their stand on faith. Such argumentative combatants, however, are frequently governed more by prejudice than either reason or faith, their object being not to find Truth, but to defend and confirm a preconceived opinion.

Reason is concerned, not with ephemeral opinions, but with the established truth of things, and he who is possessed of the faculty of reason in its purity and excellence can never be enslaved by prejudice, and will put from him all preconceived opinions as worthless. He will neither attempt to prove nor disprove, but after balancing extremes and bringing together all apparent contradictions, he will carefully and dispassionately weigh and consider them, and so arrive at Truth.

Reason is, in reality, associated with all that is pure and gentle, moderate and just. It is said of a violent man that he is "unreasonable," of a kind and considerate man that he is "reasonable," and of an insane man that he has "lost his reason." Thus it is seen that the word is used, even to a great extent unconsciously, though none the less truly, in a very comprehensive sense, and though reason is not actually love and thoughtfulness and gentleness and sanity, it leads to and is intimately connected with these divine qualities, and cannot, except for purposes of analysis, be dissociated from them.

Reason represents all that is high and noble in man. It distinguishes him from the brute which blindly follows its animal inclinations, and just in the degree that man disobeys the voice of reason and follows his inclinations does he become brutish. As Milton says:

"Reason in man obscured, or not obeyed,
Immediately inordinate desires
And upstart passions catch the government
From reason, and to servitude reduce
Man till then free."

The following definition of "reason" from Nuttall's Dictionary will give some idea of the comprehensiveness of the word: The cause, ground, principle, or motive of anything said or done; efficient cause; final cause; the faculty of intelligence in man; especially the faculty by which we arrive at necessary truth. It will thus be seen that "reason" is a term, the breadth of which is almost sufficient to embrace even Truth itself, and Archbishop Trench tells us in his celebrated work On the

Study of Words that the terms Reason and Word "are indeed so essentially one and the same that the Greek language has one word for them both," so that the Word of God is the Reason of God; and one of the renderings of Lao-tze's "Tao" is Reason, so that in the Chinese translation of our New Testament, St. John's Gospel runs; "In the beginning was the Tao."

To the undeveloped and uncharitable mind all words have narrow applications, but as a man enlarges his sympathies and broadens his intelligence, words become filled with rich meanings and assume comprehensive proportions. Let us therefore cease from foolish quarrellings about words, and, like reasonable beings, search for principles and practice those things which make for unity and peace.

Self-Discipline

A man does not live until he begins to discipline himself; he merely exists. Like an animal he gratifies his desires and pursues his inclinations just where they may lead him. He is happy as a beast is happy, because he is not conscious of what he is depriving himself; he suffers as the beast suffers, because he does not know the way out of suffering. He does not intelligently reflect upon life, and lives in a series of sensations, longings, and confused memories which are unrelated to any central idea or principle. A man whose inner life is so ungoverned and chaotic must necessarily manifest this confusion in the visible conditions of his outer life in the world; and though for a time, running with the stream of his desires, he may draw to himself a more or less large share of the outer necessities and comforts of life, he never achieves any real success nor accomplishes any real good, and sooner or later worldly failure and disaster are inevitable, as the direct result of the inward failure to properly adjust and regulate those mental forces which make the outer life.

Before a man accomplish anything of an enduring nature in the world he must first of all acquire some measure of success in the management of his own mind. This is as mathematical a truism as that two and two are four, for, "out of the heart are the issues of life." If a man cannot govern the forces within himself, he cannot hold a firm hand upon the outer activities which form his visible life. On the other hand, as a man succeeds, in governing himself he rises to higher and higher levels of power and usefulness and success in the world.

The only difference between the life of the beast and that of the undisciplined man is that the man has a wider variety of desires, and experiences a greater intensity of suffering. It may be said of such a man that he is dead, being truly dead to self-control, chastity, fortitude, and all the nobler qualities which constitute life. In the consciousness of such a man the crucified Christ lies entombed, awaiting that resurrection which shall revivify the mortal sufferer, and wake him up to a knowledge of that realities of his existence.

With the practice of self-discipline a man begins to live, for he then commences to rise above the inward confusion and to adjust his conduct to a steadfast center within himself. He ceases to follow where inclination leads him, reins in the steed of his desires, and lives in accordance with the dictates of reason and wisdom. Hitherto his life has been without purpose or meaning, but now he begins to consciously could his own destiny; he is "clothed and in his right mind."

In the process of self-discipline there are three stages namely; Control, Purification, Relinquishment.

A man begins to discipline himself by controlling those passions which have hitherto controlled him; he resists temptation and guards himself against all those tendencies to selfish gratifications which are so easy and natural, and which have formerly dominated him. He brings his appetite into subjection, and begins to eat as a reasonable and responsible being, practicing moderation and thoughtfulness in the selection of his food, with the object of making his body a pure instrument through which he may live and act as becomes a man, and no longer degrading that body by pandering to gustatory pleasure. He puts a check upon his tongue, his temper, and, in fact, his every animal desire and tendency, and this he does by referring all his acts to a fixed center within himself. It is a process of living from within outward, instead of, as formerly, from without inward. He conceives of an ideal, and, enshrining that ideal in the sacred recesses of his heart, he regulates his conduct in accordance with its exaction and demands.

There is a philosophical hypothesis that at the heart of every atom and every aggregation of atoms in the universe there is a motionless center which is the sustaining source of all the universal activities. Be this as it may, there is certainly in the heart of every man and woman a selfless center without which the outer man could not be, and the ignoring of which leads to suffering and confusion. This selfless center which takes the form, in the mind, of an ideal of unselfishness and spotless purity, the attainment of which is desirable, is man's eternal refuge from the storms of passion and all the conflicting elements of his lower nature. It is the Rock of Ages, the Christ within, the divine and immortal in all men.

As a man practices self-control he approximates more and more to this inward reality, and is less and less swayed by passion and grief, pleasure and pain, and lives a steadfast and virtuous life, manifesting manly strength and fortitude. The restraining of the passions, however, is merely the initial stage in self-discipline, and is immediately followed by the process of Purification. By this a man so purifies himself as to take passion out of the heart and mind altogether; not merely restraining it when it rises within him, but preventing it from rising altogether. By merely restraining his passions a man can never arrive at peace, can never actualize his ideal; he must purify those passions.

It is in the purification of his lower nature that a man becomes strong and god-like, standing firmly upon the ideal center within, and rendering all temptations powerless and ineffectual. This purification is effected by thoughtful care, earnest meditation, and holy aspiration; and as success is achieved confusion of mind and life pass away, and calmness of mind and spiritualized conduct ensure.

True strength and power and usefulness are born of self-purification, for the lower animal forces are not lost, but are transmuted into intellectual and spiritual energy. The pure life (Pure in thought and deed) is a life of conservation of energy; the impure life (even should the impurity not extent beyond thought) is a life of dissipation of energy. The pure man is more capable, and therefore more fit to succeed in his plans and to accomplish his purposes than the impure. Where the impure man fails, the pure man will step in and be victorious, because he directs his energies with a calmer mind and a greater definiteness and strength of purpose.

With the growth in purity; all the elements which constitute a strong and virtuous manhood are developed in an increasing degree of power, and as a man brings his lower nature into subjection, and makes his passions do his bidding, just so much will he could the outer circumstances of his life, and influence others for good.

The third stage of self-discipline, that of Relinquishment, is a process of letting the lower desires and all impure and unworthy thoughts drop out of the mind, and also refusing to give them any admittance, leaving them to perish. As a man grows purer, he perceives that all evil is powerless, unless it receives his encouragement, and so he ignores it, and lets it pass out of his life. It is by pursuing this aspect of self-discipline that a man enters into and realizes the divine life, and manifests those qualities which are distinctly divine, such as wisdom, patience, non-resistance, compassion, and love. It is here, also, where a man becomes consciously immortal, rising above all the fluctuations and uncertainties of life, and living in and intelligent and unchangeable peace.

By self-discipline a man attains to every degree of virtue and holiness, and finally becomes a purified son of God, realizing his oneness with the central heart of all things.

Without self-discipline a man drifts lower and lower, approximating more and more nearly to the beast, until at last he grovels, a lost creature, in the mire of his own befoulment. By self-discipline a man rises higher and higher, approximating more and more nearly to the divine, until at last he stands erect in his divine dignity, a saved soul, glorified by the radiance of his purity. Let a man discipline himself, and he will live; let a man cease to discipline himself, and he will perish. As a tree grows in beauty, health, and fruitfulness by being carefully pruned and tended, so a man grows in grace and beauty of life by cutting away all the branches of evil from his mind, and as he tends and develops the good by constant and unfailing effort.

As a man by practice acquires proficiency in his craft, so the earnest man acquires proficiency in goodness and wisdom. Men shrink from self-discipline because in its early stages it is painful and repellent, and the yielding to desire is, at first, sweet and inviting; but the end of desire is darkness and unrest, whereas the fruits of discipline are immortality and peace.

Resolution

Resolution is the directing and impelling force in individual progress. Without it no substantial work can be accomplished. Not until a man brings resolution to bear upon his life does he consciously and rapidly develop, for a life without resolution is a life without aims, and a life without aims is a drifting and unstable thing.

Resolution may of course be linked to downward tendencies, but it is more usually the companion of noble aims and lofty ideals, and I am dealing with it in this its highest use and application.

When a man makes a resolution, it means that he is dissatisfied with his condition, and is commencing to take himself in hand with a view to producing a better piece of workmanship out of the mental materials of which his character and life are composed, and in so far as he is true to his resolution he will succeed in accomplishing his purpose.

The vows of the saintly once are holy resolutions directed toward some victory over self, and the beautiful achievements of holy men and the glorious conquests of the Divine Teachers were rendered possible and actual by the pursuit of unswerving resolution.

To arrive at the fixed determination to walk a higher path than heretofore, although it reveals the great difficulties which have to be surmounted, it yet makes possible the treading of that path, and illuminates its dark places with the golden halo of success.

The true resolution is the crisis of long thought, protracted struggle, or fervent but unsatisfied aspiration. It is no light thing, no whimsical impulse or vague desire, but a solemn and irrevocable determination not to rest nor cease from effort until the high purpose which is held in view is fully accomplished.

Half-hearted and premature resolution is no resolution at all, and is shattered at the first difficulty.

A man should be slow to form a resolution. He should searchingly examine his position and take into consideration every circumstance and difficulty connected with his decision, and should be fully prepared to meet them. He should be sure that he completely understands the nature of his resolution, that his mind is finally made up, and that he is without fear and doubt in the matter. With the mind thus prepared, the resolution that is formed will not be departed from, and by the aid of it a man will, in due time, accomplish his strong purpose.

Hasty resolutions are futile.

The mind must be fortified to endure.

Immediately the resolution to walk a higher path is made, temptation and trial begin. Men have found that no sooner have they decided to lead a truer and nobler life than they have been overwhelmed with such a torrent of new temptations and difficulties as make their position almost unendurable, and many men, because of this, relinquish their resolution.

But these temptations and trials are a necessary part of the work of regeneration upon which the man has decided and must be hailed as friends and met with courage if the resolution is to do its work. For what is the real nature of a resolution? Is it not the sudden checking of a particular stream of conduct, and the Endeavor to open up an entirely new channel? Think of an engineer who decides to turn the course of a powerfully running stream or river in another direction. He must first cut his new channel, and must take every precaution to avoid failure in the carrying out of his undertaking. But when he comes to the all-important task of directing the stream into its new channel, then the flowing force, which for ages has steadily pursued its accustomed course, becomes refractory, and all the patience and care and skill of the engineer will be required for the successful completion of the work. It is even so with the man who determines to turn his course of conduct in another and higher direction. Having prepared his mind, which is the cutting of a new channel, he then proceeds to the work of redirecting his mental forces — which have hitherto flowed on uninterruptedly — into the new course. Immediately this is attempted, the arrested energy begins to assert itself in the form of powerful temptations and trials hitherto unknown and unencountered. And this is exactly as it should be; it is the law; and the same law that is in the water is in the mind. No man can improve upon the established law of things, but he can learn to understand the law instead of complaining, and wishing things were different. The man who understands all that is involved in the regeneration of his mind will "glory in tribulations," knowing that only by passing through them can he gain strength, obtain purity of heart, and arrive at peace. And as the engineer at last (perhaps after many mistakes and failures) succeeds in getting the stream to flow on peacefully in the broader and better channel, and the turbulence of the water is spent, and all dams can be removed, so the man of resolution at last succeeds in directing his thoughts and acts into the better and nobler way to which he aspires, and temptations and trials give place to steadfast strength and settled peace.

He whose life is not in harmony with his conscience and who is anxious to remedy his mind and conduct in a particular direction, let him first mature his purpose by earnest thought and self-examination, and having arrived at a final conclusion, let him frame his resolution, and having done so let him not swerve from it, let him remain true to his decision under all circumstances, and he cannot fail to achieve his good purpose; for the Great Law ever shields and protects him who, no matter how deep his sins, or how great and many his failures and mistakes, has, deep in his heart, resolved upon the finding of a better way, and every obstacle must at last give way before a matured and unshaken resolution.

The Glorious Conquest

Truth can only be apprehended by the conquest of self.
Blessedness can only be arrived at by overcoming the lower nature.
The way of Truth is barred by a man's self.

The only enemies that can actually hinder him are his own passions and delusions.

Until a man realizes this, and commences to cleanse his heart, he has not found the Path which leads to knowledge and peace.

Until passion is transcended, Truth remains unknown. This is the Divine Law.

A man cannot keep his passions and have Truth as well.

Error is not slain until selfishness is dead.

The overcoming of self is no mystical theory, but a very real and practical thing.

It is a process which must be pursued daily and hourly, with unswerving faith and undaunted resolution if any measure of success is to be achieved.

The process is one of orderly growth, having its sequential stages, like the growth of a tree; and as fruit can only be produced by carefully and patiently training the tree even so the pure and satisfying fruits of holiness can only be obtained by faithfully and patiently training the mind in the growth of right thought and conduct.

There are five steps in the overcoming of passion (which includes all bad habits and particular forms of wrong-doing) which I will call: repression, endurance, elimination, understanding, victory

When men fail to overcome their sins, it is because they try to begin at the wrong end. They want to have the stage of Victory without passing through the previous four stages. They are in the position of a gardener who wants to produce good fruit without training and attending to his trees.

Repression consists in checking and controlling the wrong act (such as an outburst of temper, a hasty or unkind word, a selfish indulgence etc.), and not allowing it to take actual form. This is equivalent to the gardener nipping off the useless buds and branches from his tree. It is a necessary process, but a painful one. The tree bleeds while undergoing the process, and the gardener knows that it must not be taxed too severely. The heart also bleeds when it refuses to return passion for passion, when it ceases to defend and justify itself. It is the process of "mortifying the members" of which St. Paul speaks.

But this repression is only the beginning of self-conquest. When it is made an end in itself, and there is no object of finally purifying the heart, that is a stage of hypocrisy; a hiding of one's true nature, and striving to appear better in the eyes of others than one really is. In that case it is an evil, but when adopted as the first stage toward complete purification, it is good. Its practice leads to the second stage of Endurance, or forbearance, in which one silently endures the pain which arises in the mind when it is brought in contact with certain actions and attitudes of other minds toward one. As success is attained in this stage, the striver comes to see that all his pain actually arises in his own weaknesses, and not in the wrong attitudes of others toward him, these latter being merely the means by which his sins are brought to the surface and revealed to him. He thus gradually exonerates all others from blame in his falls and lapses of conduct, and accuses only himself, and so learns to love those who thus unconsciously reveal to him his sins and shortcomings.

Having passed through these two stages of self-crucifixion, the disciple enters the third, that of Elimination, in which the wrong thought which lay behind the wrong act is cast from the mind immediately it appears. At this stage, conscious strength and holy joy begin to take the place of pain, and the mind having become comparatively calm, the striver is enabled to gain a deeper insight into the complexities of his mind, and thus to understand the inception, growth, and outworking of sin. This is the stage of Understanding.

Perfection in understanding leads to the final conquest of self, a conquest so complete that the sin can no more rise in the mind even as a thought or impression; for when the knowledge of sin is complete; when it is known in its totality, from its inception as a seed in the mind to its ripened outgrowth as act and consequence, then it can no more be allowed a place in life, but it is abandoned for ever. Then the mind is at peace. The wrong acts of others no longer arouse wrong and pain in the mind of the disciple. He is glad and calm and wise. He is filled with Love, and blessedness abides with him. And this is Victory!

Contentment In Activity

The confounding of a positive spiritual virtue or principle with a negative animal vice is common amongst writers even of what is called the "Advance Thought School," and much valuable energy is frequently expended in criticizing and condemning, where a little calm reasoning would have revealed a greater light, and led to the exercise of a broader charity.

The other day I came across a vigorous attack upon the teaching of "Love," wherein the writer condemned such teaching as weakly, foolish, and hypocritical. Needless to say, that which he was condemning as "Love," was merely weak sentimentality and hypocrisy.

Another writer in condemning "meekness" does not know that what he calls meekness is only cowardice, while another who attacks "chastity" as "a snare," is really confusing painful and hypocritical restraint with the virtue of chastity. And just lately I received a long letter from a correspondent who took great pains to show me that "contentment" is a vice, and is the source of innumerable evils.

That which my correspondent called "contentment" is, of course animal indifference. The spirit of indifference is incompatible with progress, whereas the spirit of contentment may, and does, attend the highest form of activity, the truest advancement and development. Indolence is the twin sister of indifference, but cheerful and ready action is the friend of contentment.

Contentment is a virtue which becomes lofty and spiritual in its later developments, as the mind is trained to perceive and the heart to receive the guidance, in all things, of a merciful law.

To be contented does not mean to forego effort; it means to free effort from anxiety; it does not mean to be satisfied with sin and ignorance and folly, but to rest happily in duty done, work accomplished.

A man may be said to be content to lead a groveling life, to remain in sin and in debt, but such a man's true state is one of indifference to his duty, his obligations, and the just claims of his fellow-men. He cannot truly be said to possess the virtue of contentment; he does not experience the pure and abiding joy which is the accompaniment of active contentment; so far as his true nature is concerned he is a sleeping soul, and sooner or later will be awakened by intense suffering, having passed through which he will find that true contentment which is the outcome of honest effort and true living.

There are three things with which a man should be content: With whatever happens. With his friendships and possessions. With his pure thoughts.

Contented with whatever happens, he will escape grief; with his friends and possessions, he will avoid anxiety and wretchedness; and with his pure thoughts, he will never go back to suffer and grovel in impurities.

There are three things with which a man should not be content: With his opinions. With his character. With his spiritual condition.

Not content with his opinions, he will continually increase in intelligence; not content with his character, he will ceaselessly grow in strength and virtue; and not content with his spiritual condition, he will, everyday, enter into a larger wisdom and fuller blessedness. In a word, a man should be contented, but not indifferent to his development as a responsible and spiritual being.

The truly contented man works energetically and faithfully, and accepts all results with an untroubled spirit, trusting, at first, that all is well, but afterwards, with the growth of enlightenment, knowing that results exactly correspond with efforts. Whatsoever material possessions come to him, come not by greed and anxiety and strife, but by right thought, wise action, and pure exertion.

The Temple Of Brotherhood

Universal Brotherhood is the supreme Ideal of Humanity, and towards that Ideal the world is slowly but surely moving.

Today, as never before, numbers of earnest men and women are striving to make this Ideal tangible and real; Fraternities are springing up on every hand, and Press and Pulpit, the world over, are preaching the Brotherhood of Man.

The unselfish elements in all such efforts cannot fail to have their effect upon the race, and are with certainty urging it towards the goal of its noblest aspirations; but the ideal state has not yet manifested through any outward organization, and societies formed for the purpose of propagating Brotherhood are continually being shattered to pieces by internal dissension.

The Brotherhood for which Humanity sighs is withheld from actuality by Humanity itself; nay, more, it is frustrated even by men who work zealously for it is a desirable possibility; and this because the purely spiritual nature of Brotherhood is not perceived, and the principles involved, as well as the individual course of conduct necessary to perfect unity, are not comprehended.

Brotherhood as a human organization cannot exist so long as any degree of self-seeking reigns in the hearts of men and women who band themselves together for any purpose, as such self-seeking must eventually rend the Seamless Coat of loving unity. But although organized Brotherhood has so far largely failed, any man may realize Brotherhood in its perfection, and know it in all its beauty and completion, if he will make himself of a wise, pure, and loving spirit, removing from his mind every element of strife, and learning to practice those divine qualities without which Brotherhood is but a mere theory, opinion, or illusive dream.

For Brotherhood is at first spiritual, and its outer manifestation in the world must follow as a natural sequence.

As a spiritual reality it must be discovered by each man for himself, and in the only place where spiritual realities can be found — within himself, and it rests with each whether he shall choose or refuse it.

There are four chief tendencies in the human mind which are destructive of Brotherhood, and which bar the way to its comprehension, namely: pride, self-love, hatred, condemnation .

Where these are there can be no Brotherhood; in whatsoever heart these hold sway, discord rules, and Brotherhood is not realized, for these tendencies are, in their very nature, dark and selfish always make for disruption and destruction. From these four things proceeds that serpent brood of false actions and conditions which poison the heart of man, and fill the world with suffering and sorrow.

Out of the spirit of pride proceed envy, resentment, and opinionativeness. Pride envies the position, influence, or goodness of others; it thinks, "I am more deserving than this man or this woman"; it also continually finds occasion for resenting the actions of others, and says, "I have been snubbed," "I have been insulted," and thinking altogether of his own excellence, it sees no excellence in others.

From the spirit of self-love proceed egotism, lust for power, and disparagement and contempt. Self-love worships the personality in which it moves; it is lost in the adoration and glorification of that "I", that "self" which has no real existence, but is a dark dream and a delusion. It desires pre-eminence over others, and thinks, "I am great," "I am more important than others"; it also disparages others, and bestows upon them contempt, seeing no beauty in them, being lost in the contemplation of its own beauty.

From the spirit of hatred proceed slander, cruelty, reviling, and anger. It strives to overcome evil by adding evil to it. It says, "This man has spoken of me ill, I will speak still more ill of him and thus teach him a lesson." It mistakes cruelty for kindness, and causes its possessor to revile a reproving friend. It feeds the flames of anger with bitter and rebellious thoughts.

From the spirit of condemnation proceed accusation, false pity, and false judgment. It feeds itself on the contemplation of evil, and cannot see the good. It has eyes for evil only, and finds it in almost every thing and every person. It sets up an arbitrary standard of right and wrong by which to judge others, and it thinks, "This man does not do as I would have him do, he is therefore evil, and I will denounce him." So blind is the spirit of condemnation that whilst rendering its possessor incapable of judging himself, it causes him to set himself up as the judge of all the earth.

From the four tendencies enumerated, no element of brotherliness can proceed. They are deadly mental poisons, and he who allows them to rankle in his mind, cannot apprehend the peaceful principles on which Brotherhood rests.

Then there are chiefly four divine qualities which are productive of Brotherhood; which are, as it were, the foundation stones on which it rests, namely: humility, self-surrender, love, compassion .

Wheresoever these are, there Brotherhood is active. In whatsoever heart these qualities are dominant, there Brotherhood is an established reality, for they are, in their very nature, unselfish and are filled with the revealing Light of Truth. There is no darkness in them, and where they are, so powerful is their light, that the dark tendencies cannot remain, but are dissolved and dissipated.

Out of these four qualities proceed all those angelic actions and conditions which make for unity and bring gladness to the heart of man and to the world.

From the spirit of Humility proceed meekness and peacefulness; from self-surrender come patience, wisdom, and true judgment; from Love spring kindness, joy, and harmony; and from Compassion proceed gentleness and forgiveness.

He who has brought himself into harmony with these four qualities is divinely enlightened; he sees whence the actions of men proceed and whither they tend, and therefore can no longer live in the exercise of the dark tendencies. He has realized Brotherhood in its completion as freedom from malice; from envy, from bitterness, from contention, from condemnation. All men are his brothers, those who live in the dark tendencies, as well as those who live in the enlightened qualities, for he knows that when they have perceived the glory and beauty of the Light of Truth, the dark tendencies will be dispelled from their minds. He has but one attitude of mind towards all, that of good-will.

Of the four dark tendencies are born ill-will and strife; of the four divine qualities are born good-will and peace.

Living in the four tendencies a man is a strife-producer. Living in the four qualities a man is a peace-maker.

Involved in the darkness of the selfish tendencies, men believe that they can fight for peace, kill to make alive, slay injury by injuring, restore love by hatred, unity by contention, kindness by cruelty, and establish brotherhood by erecting their own opinions (which they themselves will, in the course of time, abandon as worthless) as objects of universal adoration.

The wished-for Temple of Brotherhood will be erected in the world when its four foundation stones of Humility, Self-surrender, Love, and Compassion are firmly laid in the hearts of men, for Brotherhood consists, first of all, in the abandonment of self by the individual, and its after-effects is unity between man and man.

Theories and schemes for propagating Brotherhood are many, but Brotherhood itself is one and unchangeable and consists in the complete cessation from egotism and strife, and in practicing good-will and peace; for Brotherhood is a practice and not a theory. Self-surrender and Good-will are its guardian angels, and peace is its habitation.

Where two are determined to maintain an opposing opinion, the clinging to self and ill-will are there, and Brotherhood is absent.

Where two are prepared to sympathize with each other, to see no evil in each other, to serve and not to attack each other; the Love of Truth and Good-will are there, and Brotherhood is present.

All strifes, divisions, and wars inhere in the proud, unyielding self; all peace, unity, and concord inhere in the Principles which the yielding up of self reveals.

Brotherhood is only practiced and known by him whose heart is at peace with all the world.

Pleasant Pastures Of Peace

He who aspires to the bettering of himself and humanity should ceaselessly strive to arrive at the exercise of that blessed attitude of mind by which he is enabled to put himself, mentally and sympathetically in the place of others, and so, instead of harshly and falsely judging them, and thereby making himself unhappy without adding to the happiness of those others, he will enter into their experience, will understand their particular frame of mind, and will feel for them and sympathize with them.

One of the great obstacles to the attainment of such an attitude of mind is, prejudice, and until this is removed it is impossible to act toward others as we would wish others to act toward us.

Prejudice is destructive of kindness, sympathy, love and true judgment, and the strength of a man's prejudice will be the measure of his harshness and unkindness toward others, for prejudice and cruelty are inseparable.

There is no rationality in prejudice, and, immediately it is aroused in a man he ceases to act as a reasonable being, and gives way to rashness, anger, and injurious excitement. He does not consider his words nor regard the feelings and liberties of those against whom his prejudices are directed. He has, for the time being, forfeited his manhood, and has descended to the level of an irrational creature.

While a man is determined to cling to his preconceived opinions, mistaking them for Truth, and refuses to consider dispassionately the position of others, he cannot escape hatred nor arrive at blessedness.

The man who strives after gentleness, who aspires to act unselfishly toward others, will put away all his passionate prejudice and petty opinions, and will gradually acquire the power of thinking and feeling for others, of understanding their particular state of ignorance or knowledge, and thereby entering fully into their hearts and lives, sympathizing with them and seeing them as they are.

Such a man will not oppose himself to the prejudices of others by introducing his own, but will seek to allay prejudice by introducing sympathy and love, striving to bring out all that is good in men, encouraging the good by appealing to it, and discouraging the evil by ignoring it. He will realize the good in the unselfish efforts of others, though their outward methods may be very different from his own, and will so rid his heart of hatred, and will fit it with love and blessedness.

When a man is prone to harshly judge and condemn others, he should inquire how far he falls short himself; he should also reconsider those periods of suffering when he himself was misjudged and misunderstood, and, gathering wisdom and love from his own bitter experience, should studiously and self-sacrificingly refrain from piercing with anguish hearts that are as yet too weak to ignore, too immature and uninstructed to understand.

Sympathy is not required towards those who are purer and more enlightened than one's self, as the purer one lives above the necessity for it. In such a case reverence should be exercised, with a striving to lift one's self up to the purer level, and so enter into possession of the larger life. Nor can a man fully understand one who is wiser than himself, and before condemning, he should earnestly ask himself whether he is, after all, better than the man whom he has singled out as the object of his bitterness. If he is, let him bestow sympathy. If he is not, let him exercise reverence.

For thousands of years the sages have taught, both by precept and example, that evil is only overcome by good, yet still that lesson for the majority, remains unlearned. It is a lesson profound in its simplicity, and difficult to learn because men are blinded by the illusions of self. Men are still engaged in resenting, condemning, and fighting the evil in their own fellow-men, thereby increasing the delusion in their own hearts, and adding to the world's sum of misery and suffering. When they find out that their own resentment must be eradicated, and love put in its place, evil will perish for lack of sustenance.

Byways to Blessedness

Foreword

Along the highways of Burma there is placed, at regular distances away from the dust of the road, and under the cool shade of a group of trees, a small wooden building called a "rest-house", where the weary traveler may rest a while, and allay his thirst and assuage his hunger and fatigue by partaking of the food and water which the kindly inhabitants place there as a religious duty.

Along the great highway of life there are such resting places; away from the heat of passion and the dust of disappointment, under the cool and refreshing shade of lowly Wisdom, are the humble, unimposing "rest-houses" of peace, and the little, almost unnoticed, byways of blessedness, where alone the weary and footsore can find strength and healing.

Nor can these byways be ignored without suffering. Along the great road of life, hurrying, and eager to reach some illusive goal, presses the multitude, despising the apparently insignificant "rest-houses" of true thought, not heeding the narrow little byways of blessed action, which they regard as unimportant; and hour by hour men are fainting and falling, and numbers that cannot be counted perish of heart-hunger, heart-thirst, and heart-fatigue.

But he who will step aside from the passionate press, and will deign to notice and to enter the byways which are here presented, his dusty feet shall press the incomparable flowers of blessedness, his eyes be gladdened with their beauty, and his mind refreshed with their sweet perfume. Rested and sustained, he will escape the fever and the delirium of life, and, strong and happy, he will not fall fainting in the dust, nor perish by the way, but will successfully accomplish his journey.

Right Beginnings

"All common things, each day's events,
That with the hour begin and end;
Our pleasures and our discontents
Are rounds by which we may ascend."
"We have not wings, we cannot soar;
But we have feet to scale and climb." — Longfellow.

"For common life, its wants
And ways, would I set forth in beauteous hues." — Browning.

Life is full of beginnings. They are presented every day and every hour to every person. Most beginnings are small, and appear trivial and insignificant, but in reality they are the most important things in life.

See how in the material world everything proceeds from small beginnings. The mightiest river is at first a rivulet over which the grasshopper could leap; the great flood commences with a few drops of rain; the sturdy oak, which has endured the storms of a thousand winters, was once an acorn; and the smouldering match, carelessly dropped, may be the means of devastating a whole town by fire.

Consider, also, how in the spiritual world the greatest things proceed from smallest beginnings. A light fancy may be the inception of a wonderful invention or an immortal work of art; a spoken sentence may turn the tide of history; a pure thought entertained may lead to the exercise of a world-wide regenerative power; and a momentary animal impulse may lead to the darkest crime.

Have you yet discovered the vast importance of beginnings? Do you really know what is involved in a beginning? Do you know the number of beginnings you are continuously making, and realize their full import? If not, come with me for a short time, and thoughtfully explore this much ignored byway of blessedness, for blessed it is when wisely resorted to, and much strength and comfort it holds for the understanding mind.

A beginning is a cause, and as such it must be followed by an effect, or a train of effects, and the effect will always be of the same nature as the cause. The nature of an initial impulse will always determine the body of its results. A beginning also presupposes an ending, a consummation, achievement, or goal. A gate leads to a path, and the path leads to some particular destination; so a beginning leads to results, and results lead to a completion.

There are right beginnings and wrong beginnings, which are followed by effects of a like nature. You can, by careful thought, avoid wrong beginnings and make right beginnings, and so escape evil results and enjoy good results.

There are beginnings over which you have no control and authority — these are without, in the universe, in the world of nature around you, and in other people who have the same liberty as yourself.

Do not concern yourself with these beginnings, but direct your energies and attention to those beginnings over which you have complete control and authority, and which bring about the complicated web of results which compose your life. These beginnings are to be found in the realm of your own thoughts and actions; in your mental attitude under the variety of circumstances through which you pass; in your conduct day by day — in short, in your life as you make it, which is your world of good or ill.

In aiming at the life of Blessedness one of the simplest beginnings to be considered and rightly made is that which we all make everyday — namely, the beginning of each day's life.

How do you begin each day? At what hour do you rise? How do you commence your duties? In what frame of mind do you enter upon the sacred life of a new day? What answer can you give your heart to these important questions? You will find that much happiness or unhappiness follows upon the right or wrong beginning of the day, and that, when every day is wisely begun, happy and harmonious sequences will mark its course, and life in its totality will not fall far short of the ideal blessedness.

It is a right and strong beginning to the day to rise at an early hour. Even if your worldly duty does not demand it, it is wise to make of it a duty, and begin the day strongly by shaking off indolence. How are you to develop strength of will and mind and body if you begin every day by yielding to weakness? Self-indulgence is always followed by unhappiness. People who lie in bed till a late hour are never bright and cheerful and fresh, but are the prey of irritabilities, depressions, debilities, nervous disorders, abnormal fancies, and all unhappy moods. This is the heavy price which they have to pay for their daily indulgence. Yet, so blinding is the pandering to self that, like the drunkard who takes his daily dram in the belief that it is bracing up the nerves which it is all the time shattering, so the lie-a-bed is convinced that long hours of ease are necessary for him as a possible remedy for those very moods and weaknesses and disorders of which his indulgence is the cause. Men and women are totally unaware of the great losses which they entail by this common indulgence: loss of strength both of mind and body, loss of prosperity, loss of knowledge, and loss of happiness.

Begin the day, then, by rising early. If you have no object in doing so, never mind; get up, and go out for a gentle walk among the beauties of nature, and you will experience a buoyancy, a freshness, and a delight, not to say a peace of mind, which will amply reward you for your effort. One good effort is followed by another; and when a man begins the day by rising early, even though with no other purpose in view, he will find that the silent early hour is conducive to clearness of mind and calmness of thought, and that his early morning walk is enabling him to become a consecutive thinker, and so to see life and its problems, as well as himself and his affairs, in a clearer light; and so in time he will rise early with the express purpose of preparing and harmonizing his mind to meet any and every difficulty with wisdom and calm strength.

There is, indeed, a spiritual influence in the early morning hour, a divine silence and an inexpressible repose, and he who, purposeful and strong, throws off the mantle of ease and climbs the hills to greet the morning sun will thereby climb no inconsiderable distance up the hills of blessedness and truth.

The right beginning of the day will be followed by cheerfulness at the morning meal, permeating the house-hold with a sunny influence; and the tasks and duties of the day will be undertaken in a strong and confident spirit, and the whole day will be well lived.

Then there is a sense in which every day may be regarded as the beginning of a new life, in which one can think, act, and live newly, and in a wiser and better spirit.

"Every day is a fresh beginning;
Every morn is the world made new,
Ye who are weary of sorrow and sinning,
Here is a beautiful hope for you,
A hope for me and a hope for you."

Do not dwell upon the sins and mistakes of yesterday so exclusively as to have no energy and mind left for living rightly today, and do not think that the sins of yesterday can prevent you from living purely today. Begin today aright, and, aided by the accumulated experiences of all your past days, live it better than any of your previous days; but you cannot possibly live it better unless you begin it better. The character of the whole day depends upon the way it is begun.

Another beginning which is of great importance is the beginning of any particular and responsible undertaking. How does a man begin the building of a house? He first secures a plan of the proposed edifice and then proceeds to build according to the plan, scrupulously following it in every detail, beginning with the foundation. Should he neglect the beginning — namely, the obtaining of a mathematical plan — his labor would be wasted, and his building, should it reach completion without tumbling to pieces, would be insecure and worthless. The same law holds good in any important work: the right beginning and first essential is a definite mental plan on which to build. Nature will have no slipshod work, no slovenliness, and she annihilates confusion, or rather, confusion is in itself annihilation. Order, definiteness, purpose eternally and universally prevail, and he who in his operations ignores these mathematical elements at once deprives himself of substantiality, completeness, success.

> "Life without a plan,
> As useless as the moment it began,
> Serves merely as a soil for discontent
> To thrive in, an encumbrance ere half spent."

Let a man start in business without having in his mind a perfectly formed plan to systematically pursue and he will be incoherent in his efforts and will fail in his business operations. The laws which must be observed in the building of a house also operate in the building up of a business. A definite plan is followed by coherent effort; and coherent effort is followed by well-knit and orderly results — to wit, completeness, perfection, success, happiness.

But not only mechanical and commercial enterprise — all undertakings, of whatsoever nature, come under this law. The author's book, the artist's picture, the orator's speech, the reformer's work, the inventor's machine, the general's campaign, are all carefully planned in the mind before the attempt to actualize them is commenced; and in accordance with the unity, solidarity, and perfection of the original mental plan will be the actual and ultimate success of the undertaking.

Successful men, influential men, good men are those who, amongst other things, have learned the value and utilized the power which lies hidden in those obscure beginnings which the foolish man passes by as "insignificant."

But the most important beginning of all— that upon which afflication or blessedness inevitably depends, yet is most neglected and least understood— is the inception of thought in the hidden, but causal region of the mind. Your whole life is a series of effects having their cause in thought— in your own thought. All conduct is made and molded by thought; all deeds, good or bad, are thoughts made visible. A seed put into the ground is the beginning of a plant or tree; the seed germinates, the plant or tree comes forth into the light and evolves. A thought put into the mind is the beginning of a line of conduct: the thought first sends down its roots into the mind, and then pushes forth into the light in the forms of actions or conduct, which evolve into character and destiny.

Hateful, angry, envious, covetous, and impure thoughts are wrong beginnings, which lead to painful results. Loving, gentle, kind, unselfish and pure thoughts are right beginnings, which lead to blissful results. This is so simple, so plain, so absolutely true! and yet how neglected, how evaded, and how little understood!

The gardener who most carefully studies how, when, and where to put in his seeds obtains the best results and gains the greater horticultural knowledge. The best crops gladden the soul of him who makes the best beginning. The man who most patiently studies how to put into his mind the seeds of strong, wholesome, and charitable thoughts, will obtain the best results in life, and will gain greater knowledge of truth. The greatest blessedness comes to him, who infuses into his mind the purest and noblest thoughts.

None but right acts can follow right thoughts; none but a right life can follow right acts— and by living a right life all blessedness is achieved.

He who considers the nature and import of his thoughts, who strives daily to eliminate bad thoughts and supplant them with good, comes at last to see that thoughts are the beginnings of results which affect every fibre of his being, which potently influence every event and circumstance of his life. And when he thus sees, he thinks only right thoughts, chooses to make only those mental beginnings which lead to peace and blessedness.

Wrong thoughts are painful in their inception, painful in their growth, and painful in their fruitage. Right thoughts are blissful in their inception, blissful in their growth, and blissful in their fruitage.

Many are the right beginnings which a man must discover and adopt on his way to wisdom; but that which is first and last, most important and all embracing, which is the source and fountain of all abiding happiness, is the right beginning of the mental operations— this implies the steady development of self-control, will-power, steadfastness, strength, purity, gentleness, insight, and comprehension. It leads to the perfecting of life, for he who thinks perfectly has abolished all unhappiness, his every moment is peaceful, his years are rounded with bliss— he has attained to the complete and perfect blessedness.

Small Tasks And Duties

"Wrapped in our nearest duty is the key
Which shall unlock for us the Heavenly Gate:
Unveiled, the Heavenly Vision he shall see,
Who cometh not too early nor too late."
"Like the star
That shines afar,
Without haste
And without rest,
Let each man wheel with steady sway
Round the task that rules the day,
And do his best."— Goethe

As pain and bliss inevitably follow on wrong and right beginnings, so unhappiness and blessedness are inseparably bound up with small tasks and duties. Not that a duty has any power of itself to bestow happiness or the reverse— this is contained in the attitude of the mind which is assumed towards the duty— and everything depends upon the way in which it is approached and done.

Not only great happiness but great power arises from doing little things unselfishly, wisely, and perfectly, for life in its totality is made up of little things. Wisdom inheres in the common details of everyday existence, and when the parts are made perfect the Whole will be without blemish.

Everything in the universe is made up of little things, and the perfection of the great is based upon the perfection of the small. If any detail of the universe were imperfect the Whole would be imperfect. If any particle were omitted the aggregate would cease to be. Without a grain of dust there could be no world, and the world is perfect because the grain of dust is perfect. Neglect of the small is confusion of the great. The snowflake is as perfect as the star; the dew drop is as symmetrical as the planet; the microbe is not less mathematically proportioned than the man. By laying stone upon stone, plumbing and fitting each with perfect adjustment, the temple at last stands forth in all its architectural beauty. The small precedes the great. The small is not merely the apologetic attendant of the great, it is its master and informing genius.

Vain men are ambitious to be great, and look about to do some great thing, ignoring and despising the little tasks which call for immediate attention, and in the doing of which there is no vainglory, regarding such "trivialities" as beneath the notice of great men. The fool lacks knowledge because he lacks humility, and, inflated with the thought of self-importance, he aims at impossible things.

The great man has become such by the scrupulous and unselfish attention which he has given to small duties. He has become wise and powerful by sacrificing ambition and pride in the doing of those necessary things which evoke no applause and promise no reward. He never sought greatness; he sought faithfulness, unselfishness, integrity, truth; and in finding these in the common round of small tasks and duties he unconsciously ascended to the level of greatness.

The great man knows the vast value that inheres in moments, words, greetings, meals, apparel, correspondence, rest, work, detached efforts, fleeting obligations, in the thousand-and-one little things which press upon him for attention— briefly, in the common details of life. He sees everything as divinely apportioned, needing only the application of dispassionate thought and action on his part to render life blessed and perfect. He neglects nothing; does not hurry; seeks to escape nothing but error and folly; attends to every duty as it is presented to him, and does not postpone and regret. By giving himself unreservedly to his nearest duty, forgetting alike pleasure and pain, he attains to that combined childlike simplicity and unconscious power which is greatness.

The advice of Confucius to his disciples: "Eat at your own table as you would at the table of a king," emphasizes the immeasurable importance of little things, as also does that aphorism of another great teacher, Buddha: "If anything is to be done, let a man do it, let him attack it vigorously." To neglect small tasks, or to execute them in a perfunctory or slovenly manner, is a mark of weakness and folly.

The giving of one's entire and unselfish attention to every duty in its proper place evolves, by a natural growth, higher and ever higher combinations of duties, because it evolves power and develops talent, genius, goodness, character. A man ascends into greatness as naturally and unconsciously as the plant evolves a flower, and in the same manner, by fitting, with unabated energy and diligence, every effort and detail in its proper place, thus harmonizing his life and character without friction or waste of power.

Of the almost innumerable recipes for the development of "will-power" and "concentration" which are now scattered abroad, one looks almost in vain for any wholesome hint applicable to vital experience. "Breathings," "postures," "visualizings," "occult methods" are practices as delusive as they are artificial and remote from all that is real and essential in life; while the true path— the path of duty, of earnest and undivided application to one's daily task— along which alone will-power and concentration of thought can be wholesomely and normally developed, remains unknown, untrodden, unexplored even by the elect.

All unnatural forcing and straining in order to gain "power" should be abandoned. There is no way from childhood to manhood but by growth; nor is there any other way from folly to wisdom, from ignorance to knowledge, from weakness to strength. A man must learn how to grow little by little and day after day, by adding thought to thought, effort to effort, deed to deed.

It is true the fakir gains some sort of power by his long persistence in "postures" and "mortifications," but it is a power which is bought at a heavy price, and that price is an equal loss of strength in another direction. He is never a strong, useful character, but a mere fantastic specialist in some psychological trick. He is not a developed man, he is a maimed man.

True will-power consists in overcoming the irritabilities, follies, rash impulses and moral lapses which accompany the daily life of the individual, and which are apt to manifest themselves on every slight provocation; and in developing calmness, self-possession, and dispassionate action in the press and heat of worldly duties, and in the midst of the passionate and unbalanced throng. Anything short of this is not true power, and this can only be developed along the normal pathway of steady growth in executing ever more and more masterfully, unselfishly, and perfectly the daily round of legitimate tasks and pressing obligations.

The master is not he whose "psychological accomplishments," rounded by mystery and wonder, leave him in unguarded moments the prey of irritability, of regret, of peevishness, or other petty folly or vice, but he whose "mastery" is manifested in fortitude, non-resentment, steadfastness, calmness, and infinite patience. The true Master is master of himself; anything other than this is not mastery but delusion.

The man who sets his whole mind on the doing of each task as it is presented, who puts into it energy and intelligence, shutting all else out from his mind, and striving to do that one thing, no matter how small, completely and perfectly, detaching himself from all reward in his task— that man will every day be acquiring greater command over his mind, and will, by ever-ascending degrees, become at last a man of power— a Master.

Put yourself unreservedly into your present task, and so work, so act, so live that you shall leave each task a finished piece of labor— this is the true way to the acquisition of will-power, concentration of thought, and conservation of energy. Look not about for magical formulas, for strained and artificial methods. Every resource is already with you and within you. You have but to learn how wisely to apply yourself in that place which you now occupy. Until this is done those other and higher places which are waiting for you cannot be taken possession of, cannot be reached.

There is no way to strength and wisdom but by acting strongly and wisely in the present moment, and each present moment reveals its own task. The great man, the wise man does small things greatly regarding nothing as "trivial" that is necessary. The weak man, the foolish man, does small things carelessly, and meanly, hankering the while after, some greater work for which, in his neglect and inability in small matters, he is ceaselessly advertising his incapacity. The man who leasts governs himself is always more ambitious to govern others and assume important responsibilities. "Who so neglects a thing which he suspects he ought to do because it seems too small a thing is deceiving himself; it is not too little but too great for him that he doeth it not."

And just as the strong doing of small tasks leads to greater strength, so the doing of those tasks weakly leads to greater weakness. What a man is in his fractional duties that he is in the aggregate of his character. Weakness is as great a source of suffering as sin, and there can be no true blessedness until some measure of strength of character is evolved. The weak man becomes strong by attaching value to little things and doing them accordingly. The strong man becomes weak by falling into looseness and neglect concerning small things, thereby forfeiting his simple wisdom and squandering his energy. Herein we see the beneficent operation of that law of growth which is expressed in the little understood words: "To him that hath shall be given, and from him that hath not shall be taken away even that which he hath." Man instantly gains or loses by every thought he thinks, every word he says, every act he does, and every work to which he puts hand and heart. His character from moment to moment is a graduating quantity, to or from which some measure of good is added or subtracted during every moment, and the gain or loss is involved, even to absoluteness, in each thought, word, and deed as these follow each other in rapid sequence.

He who masters the small becomes the rightful possessor of the great. He who is mastered by the small can achieve no superlative victory.

Life is a kind of cooperative trust in which the whole is of the nature of, and dependent upon, the unit.

A successful business, a perfect machine, a glorious temple, or a beautiful character is evolved from the perfect adjustment of a multliplicity of parts.

The foolish man thinks that little faults, little indulgences, little sins, are of no consequence; he persuades himself that so long as he does not commit flagrant immoralities he is virtuous, and even holy; but he is thereby deprived of virtue, and holiness, and the world knows him accordingly; it does not reverence, adore, and love him; it passes him by; he is reckoned of no account; his influence is destroyed. The efforts of such a man to make the world virtuous, his exhortations to his fellow-men to abandon great vices, are empty of substance and barren of fruitage. The insignificance which he attaches to his small vices permeates his whole character and is the measure of his manhood: he is regarded as an insignificant man. The levity with which he commits his errors and publishes his weakness comes back to him in the form of neglect and loss of influence and respect: he is not sought after, for who will seek to be taught of folly? His work does not prosper, for who will lean upon a reed? His words fall upon deaf ears, for they are void of practice, wisdom, and experience, and who will go after an echo?

The wise man, or he who is becoming wise, sees the danger which lurks in those common personal faults which men mostly commit thoughtlessly and with impunity; he also sees the salvation which inheres in the abandonment of those faults, as well as in the practice of virtuous thoughts and acts which the majority disregard as unimportant, and in those quiet but momentous daily conquests over self which are hidden from other's eyes.

He who regards his molest delinquencies as of the gravest nature becomes a saint. He sees the far reaching influence, good or bad, which extends from his every thought and act, and how he himself is made or unmade by the soundness or unsoundness of those innumerable details of conduct which combine to form his character and life, and so he watches, guards, purifies, and perfects himself little by little and step by step.

As the ocean is composed of drops, the earth of grains, and the stars of points of light, so is life composed of thoughts and acts; without these, life would not be. Every man's life, therefore, is what his apparently detached thoughts and acts make it. There combination is himself. As the year consists, of a given number of sequential moments, so a man's character and life consists of a given number of sequential thoughts and deeds, and the finished whole will bear the impress of the parts.

"All sorts of things and weather
Must be taken in together,
To make up a year
And a sphere."

Little kindnesses, generosities, and sacrifices make up a kind and generous character. Little renounciations, endurances, and victories over self make up a strong and noble character. The truly honest man is honest in the minutest details of his life. The noble man is noble in every little thing he says and does.

It is a fatal delusion with men to think that life is detached from the momentary thought and act, and not to understand that the passing thought and deed is the foundation and substance of life. When this is fully understood all things are seen as sacred, and every act becomes religious. Truth is wrapped up in infinitesimal details. Thoroughness is genius.

"Possessions vanish, and opinions change,
And passions hold a fluctuating seat:
But, by the storms of circumstance unshaken,
And subject neither to eclipse nor wane,
Duty exists."

You do not live your life in the mass; you live it in the fragments and from these the mass emerges. You can will to live each fragment nobly if you choose, and, this being done, there can be no particle of baseness in the finished whole. The saying "Take care of the pence and the pounds will take care of themselves" is seen to be more than worldly-wise when applied spiritually, for, to take care of the present, passing act, knowing that by so doing the total sum and amount of life and character will be safely preserved, is to be divinely wise. Do not long to do great and laudable things; these will do themselves if you do your present task nobly. Do not chafe at the restrictions and limitations of your present duty but be nobly unselfish in the doing of it, putting aside discontent, listlessness, and the foolish contemplation of great deeds which lie beyond you— and lo! already the greatness for which you sighed begins to appear. There is no weakness like peevishness. Aspire to the attainment of inward nobility, not outward glory, and begin to attain it where you now are.

The irksomeness and sting which you feel to be in your task are in your mind only. Alter your attitude of mind towards it, and at once the crooked path is made straight, the unhappiness is turned into joy.

See that your every fleeting moment is strong, pure, and purposeful; put earnestness and unselfishness into every passing task and duty; make your every thought, word, and deed sweet and true; thus learning, by practice and experience, the inestimable value of the small things of life, you will gather, little by little, abundant and enduring blessedness.

Transcending Difficulties and Perplexities

"Man who man would be
Must rule the empire of himself; in it
Must be supreme, establishing his throne
On vanquished will, quelling the anarchy
Of hopes and fears, being himself alone."—Shelley

"Have you missed in your aim? Well, the mark is still shining.
Did you faint in the race? Well, take breath for the next."—Ellu Wheelar Wilcose.

To suggest that any degree of blessedness may be extracted from difficulties and perplexities will doubtless appear absurd to many; but truth is ever paradoxical, and the curses of the foolish are the blessings of the wise. Difficulties arise in ignorance and weakness, and they call for the attainment of knowledge and the acquisition of the strength.

As understanding is acquired by right living, difficulties become fewer, and perplexities gradually fade away, like the perishable mists which they are.

Your difficulty is not contained, primarily, in the situation which gave rise to it, but in the mental state with which you regard that situation and which you bring to bear upon it. That which is difficult to a child presents no difficulty to the matured mind of the man; and that which to the mind of an unintelligent man is surrounded with perplexity would afford no ground for perplexity to an intelligent man.

To the untutored and undeveloped mind of the child how great, and apparently insurmountable, appear the difficulties which are involved in the learning of some simple lesson. How many anxious and laborious hours and days, or even months, its solution costs; and, frequently, how many tears are shed in hopeless contemplation of the unmastered, and apparently insurmountable, wall of difficulty! Yet the difficulty is in the ignorance of the child only, and its conquest and solution is absolutely necessary for the development of intelligence and for the ultimate welfare, happiness, and usefulness of the child.

Even so is it with the difficulties of life with which older children are confronted, and which it is imperative, for their own growth and development, that they should solve and surmount; and each difficulty solved means so much more experience gained, so much more insight and wisdom acquired; it means a valuable lesson learned, with the added gladness and freedom of a task successfully accomplished.

What is the real nature of a difficulty? Is it not a situation which is not fully grasped and understood in all it bearings? As such, it calls for the development and exercise of a deeper insight and broader intelligence than has hitherto been exercised. It is an urgent necessity calling forth unused energy, and demanding the expression and employment of latent power and hidden resources. It is, therefore, a good angel, albeit disguised; a friend, a teacher; and, when calmly listened to and rightly understood, leads to larger blessedness and higher wisdom.

Without difficulties there could be no progress, no unfoldment, no evolution; universal stagnation would prevail, and humanity would perish of ennui.

Let a man rejoice when he is confronted with obstacles, for it means that he has reached the end of some particular line of indifference or folly, and is now called upon to summon up all his energy and intelligence in order to extricate himself, and to find a better way; that the powers within him are crying out for greater freedom, for enlarged exercise and scope.

No situation can be difficult of itself; it is the lack of insight into its intricacies, and the want of wisdom in dealing with it, which give rise to the difficulty. Immeasurable, therefore, is the gain of a difficulty transcended.

Difficulties do not spring into existence arbitrarily and accidentally; they have their causes, and are called forth by the law of evolution itself, by the growing necessities of the man's being. Herein resides their blessedness.

There are ways of conduct which end inevitably in complications and perplexities, and there are ways of conduct which lead, just as inevitably, out of troublesome complexities. Howsoever tightly a man may have bound himself round he can always unbind himself. Into whatsoever morasses of trouble and trackless wastes of perplexity he may have ignorantly wandered he can always find his way out again, can always recover the lost highway of uninvolved simplicity which leads, straight and clear, to the sunny city of wise and blessed action. But he will never do this by sitting down and weeping in despair, nor by complaining and worrying and aimlessly wishing he were differently situated. His dilemma calls for alertness, logical thought, and calm calculation. His position requires that he shall strongly command himself; that he shall think and search, and rouse himself to strenuous and unremitting exertion in order to regain himself. Worry and anxiety only serve to heighten the gloom and exaggerate the magnitude of the difficulty. If he will but quietly take himself to task, and retrace, in thought, the more or less intricate way by which he has come to his present position, he will soon perceive where he made mistakes; will discover those places where he took a false turn, and where a little

The Selected Teachings of James Allen

more thoughtfulness, judgement, economy, or self-denial would have saved him. He will see how, step by step, he has involved himself, and how a riper judgement and clearer wisdom would have enabled him to take an altogether different and truer course. Having proceeded thus far, and extracted from his past conduct this priceless grain of golden wisdom, his difficulty will already have assumed less impregnable proportions, and he will then be able to bring to bear upon it the searchlight of dispassionate thought, to thoroughly anatomize it, to comprehend it in all its details, and to perceive the relation which those details bear to the motive source of action and conduct within himself. This being done, the difficulty will have ceased, for the straight way out of it will plainly appear, and the man will thus have learned, for all time, his lesson; will have gained an item of wisdom and a measure of blessedness of which he can never again be deprived.

Just as there are ways of ignorance, selfishness, folly, and blindness which end in confusion and perplexity, so there are ways of knowledge, self-denial, wisdom, and insight which lead to pleasant and peaceful consummations. He who knows this will meet difficulties in a courageous spirit, and, in overcoming them, will evolve truth out of error, bliss out of pain, and peace out of perturbation.

No man can be confronted with a difficulty which he has not the strength to meet and subdue. Worry is not merely useless, it is folly, for it defeats that power and intelligence which is otherwise equal to the task. Every difficulty can be overcome if rightly dealt with; anxiety is, therefore, unnecessary. The task which cannot be overcome ceases to be a difficulty, and becomes an impossibility; and anxiety is still unnecessary, for there is only one way of dealing with an impossibility— namely, to submit to it. The inevitable is the best.

"Heartily know,
When half-gods go,
The gods arrive."

And just as domestic, social, and economic difficulties are born of ignorance and lead to riper knowledge, so every religious doubt, every mental-perplexity, every heart-beclouding shadow, presages greater spiritual gain, is prophetic of a brighter dawn of intelligence for him on whom it falls.

It is a great day in the life of a man (though at the time he knows it not) when bewildering perplexities concerning the mystery of life take possession of his mind, for it signifies that his era of dead indifference, of animal sloth, of mere vegetative happiness, has come to an end, and that henceforth he is to live as an aspiring, self-evolving being. No longer a mere human animal, he will now begin to live as a man, exerting all his mental energies to the solution of life's problems, to the answering of those haunting perplexities which are the sentinels of truth, and which stand at the gate and threshold of the Temple of Wisdom.

"He it is who, when great trials come,
Nor seeks nor shuns them, but doth calmly stay."

Nor will he ever rest again in selfish ease and listless ignorance; nor sleekly sate himself upon the swine's husks of fleshly pleasures; nor find a hiding-place from the ceaseless whisperings of his heart's dark and indefinable interrogatories. The divine within him has awakened; a sleeping god is shaking off the incoherent visions of the night, never again to slumber, never again to rest until his eyes rest upon the full, broad day of Truth.

It is impossible for such a man to hush, for any length of time, the call to higher purposes and achievements which is aroused within him, for the awakened faculties of his being will ceaselessly urge him on to the unraveling of his perplexities; for him there is no more peace in sin, no more rest in error, no final refuge but in Wisdom.

Great will be the blessedness of such a man when, conscious of the ignorance of which his doubts and perplexities are born, and acknowledging and understanding that ignorance, not striving to hide himself from it, he earnestly applies himself to its removal, seeks unremittingly, day after day, for that pathway of light which shall enable him to dispel all the dark shadows, dissolve his doubts, and find the solution to all his pressing problems. And as a child is glad when it has mastered a lesson long toiled over, just so a man's heart becomes light and free when he has satisfactorily met some worldly difficulty; even so, but to a far greater degree, is the heart of a man rendered joyous and peaceful when some vital and eternal question which has been long brooded over and grappled with is at last completely answered, and its darkness is for ever dispelled.

Do not regard your difficulties and perplexities as portentous of ill; by so doing you will make them ill; but regard them as prophetic of good, which, indeed, they are. Do not persuade yourself that you can evade them; you cannot. Do not try to run away from them; this is impossible, for wherever you go they will still be there with you— but meet them calmly and bravely; confront them with all the dispassion and dignity which you can command; weigh up their proportions; analyze them; grasp their details; measure their strength; understand them; attack them, and finally vanquish them. Thus will you develop strength and intelligence; thus will you enter one of those byways of blessedness which are hidden from the superficial gaze.

Burden-Dropping

"This to me is life;
That if life be a burden, I will join
To make it but the burden of a song."—Bailey

"Have you heard that it was good to gain the day?
I also say it is good to fall, battles are lost in the same
spirit in which they are won."—Walt Whitman

We hear and read much about burden-bearing, but of the better way of burden-dropping very little is heard or known. Yet why should you go about with an oppressive weight at your heart when you might relieve yourself of it and move amongst your fellows heart-free and cheerful? No man carries a load upon his back except to necessarily transfer something from one place to another; he does not saddle his shoulders with a perpetual burden, and then regard himself as a martyr for his pains; and why should you impose upon your mind a useless burden, and then add to its weight the miseries of self-condolence and self-pity? Why not abandon both your load and your misery, and thus add to the gladness of the world by first making yourself glad? No reason can justify, and no logic support, the ceaseless carrying of a grievous load. As in things material a load is only undertaken as a necessary means of transference, and is never a source of sorrow, so in things spiritual a burden should only be taken up as a means towards some good and necessary end, which, when attained, the burden is put aside; and the carrying of such a burden, far from being a source of grief would be a cause for rejoicing.

We say that bodily mortifications which some religious ascetics inflict upon themselves are unnecessary and vain; and are the mental mortifications which so many people inflict upon themselves less unnecessary and vain?

Where is the burden which should cause unhappiness or sorrow? It does not exist. If a thing is to be done let it be done cheerfully, and not with inward groanings and lamentations. It is of the highest wisdom to embrace necessity as a friend and guide. It is of the greatest folly to scowl upon necessity as an enemy, and to wish or try to overcome or avoid her. We meet our own at every turn, and duties only become oppressive loads when we refuse to recognize and embrace them. He who does any necessary thing in a niggardly and complaining spirit, hunting the while after unnecessary pleasures, lashes himself with the scorpions of misery and disappointment, and imposes upon himself a doubly-weighted burden of weariness and unrest under which he incessantly groans.

> "Wake thou, O self, to better things;
> To yonder heights uplift thy wings;
> Take up the psalm of life anew;
> Sing of the good, sing of the true;
> Sing of full victory o'er wrong;
> Make though a richer, sweeter song;
> Out of thy doubting, care and pain
> Weave thou a joyous, glad refrain;
> Out of thy thorns a crown weave thou
> Of rare rejoicing. Sing thou, now."

I will give my cheerful, unselfish, and undivided attention to the doing of all those things which enter into my compact with life, and, though I walk under colossal responsibilities, I shall be unconscious of any troublesome weight or grievous burden.

You say a certain thing (a duty, a companionship, or a social obligation) troubles you, is burdensome, and you resign yourself to oppression with the thought: "I have entered into this, and will go through with it, but it is a heavy and grievous work." But is the thing really burdensome, or is it your selfishness that is oppressing you? I tell you that that very thing which you regard as so imprisoning a restriction is the first gateway to your emancipation; that work which you regard as a perpetual curse contains for you the actual blessedness which you vainly persuade yourself lies in another and unapproachable direction. All things are mirrors in which you see yourself reflected, and the gloom which you perceive in your work is but a reflection of that mental state which you bring to it. Bring a right, an unselfish, state of heart to the thing, and lo! it is at once transformed, and becomes a means of strength and blessedness, reflecting back that which you have brought to it. If you bring a scowling face to your looking glass will you complain of the glass that it glowers upon you with a deformed visage, or will you put your face right, and so get back from the reflector a more pleasing countenance?

If it is right and necessary that a thing should be done then the doing of it is good, and it can only become burdensome in wishing not to do it. The selfish wish makes the thing appear evil. If it is neither right nor necessary that a thing should be done then the doing of it in order to gain some coveted pleasure is folly, which can only lead to burdensome issues.

The duty which you shirk is your reproving angel; the pleasure which you race after is your flattering enemy. Foolish man! when will you turn round and be wise?

It is the beneficence of the universe that it is everywhere, and at all times, urging its creatures to wisdom as it demands coherence of its atoms. That folly and selfishness entail suffering in ever-increasing degrees of intensity is preservative and good, for agony is the enemy of apathy and the herald of wisdom.

What is painful? What is grievous? What is burdensome? Passion is painful; folly is grievous; selfishness is burdensome.

"It is the dark idolatry of self
Which, when our thoughts and actions once are done,
Demands that man should weep, and bleed, and groan."

Eliminate passion, folly and selfishness from your mind and conduct and you will eliminate suffering from your life. Burden-dropping consists in abandoning the inward selfishness and putting pure love in its place. Go to your task with love in your heart and you will go to it light-hearted and cheerful.

The mind, through ignorance creates its own burdens and inflicts its own punishments. No one is doomed to carry any load. Sorrow is not arbitrarily imposed. These things are self-made. Reason is the rightful monarch of the mind, and anarchy reigns in his spiritual kingdom when his throne is usurped by passion. When love of pleasure is to the fore, heaviness and anguish compose the rear. You are free to choose. Even if you are bound by passion, and feel helpless, you have bound yourself, and are not helpless. Where you have bound you can unbind. You have come to your present state by degrees, and you can recover yourself by degrees, can reinstate reason and dethrone passion. The time to avoid evil is before pleasure is embraced, but, once embraced, its train of consequences should teach you wisdom. The time to decide is before responsibilities are adopted, but, once adopted, all selfish considerations, with their attendant grumblings, whinings, and complainings, should be religiously excluded from the heart. Responsibilities lose their weight when carried lovingly and wisely.

What heavy burden is a man weighted with which is not made heavier and more unendurable by weak thoughts of selfish desires? If your circumstances are "trying" it is because you need them and can evolve the strength to meet them. They are trying because there is some weak spot within you, and they will continue to be trying until that spot is eradicated. Be glad that you have the opportunity of becoming stronger and wiser. No circumstances can be trying to wisdom; nothing can weary love. Stop brooding over your own trying circumstances and contemplate the lives of some of those about you.

Here is a woman with a large family who has to make ends meet on a pound a week. She performs all her domestic duties, down to the washing, finds time to attend on sick neighbors, and manages to keep entirely out of the two common quagmires— debt and despondency. She is cheerful from morning to night, and never complains of her "trying circumstances." She is perennially cheerful because she is unselfish. She is happy in the thought that she is the means of happiness to others. Were she to brood upon the holidays, the pretty baubles, the lazy hours of which she is deprived; of the plays she cannot see, the music she cannot hear, the books she cannot read, the parties she cannot attend, the good she might do, the friendships she is debarred from forming; of the many pleasures which might only be hers if her circumstances were more favorable— if she brooded thus what a miserable creature she would be! How unbearably laborious her work would become! How every little domestic duty would hang like a millstone about her neck, dragging her down to the grave which, unless she altered her state of mind, she would quickly reach, killed by— selfishness! But, not living in vain desires for herself, she is relieved of all burdens, and is happy. Cheerfulness and unselfishness are sworn friends. Love knows no heavy toil.

Here is another woman, with a private income which is more than sufficient, combined with leisure and luxury, yet, because she is called upon to forfeit a portion of her time, pleasure, and money to discharge some obligation which she wishes to be rid of, and which should be to her a work of loving service, or fostering in her heart some ungratified desire, she is perpetually discontented and unhappy, and complains of "trying circumstances". Discontent and Selfishness are inseparable companions. Self-love knows no joyful labor.

Of the two sets of circumstances above depicted (and life is crowded with such contrasted instances) which are the "trying" conditions? Is it not true that neither of them are trying, and that both are blest or unblest in accordance with the measure of love or selfishness which is infused into them? Is not the root of the whole matter in the mind of the individual and not in the circumstance?

When a man, who has recently taken up the study of some branch of theology, religion, or "occultism," says: "If I had not burdened myself with a wife and family I could have done a great work; and had I known years ago what I know now I would never have married." I know that that man has not yet found the commonest and broadest way of wisdom (for there is no greater folly than regret), and that he is incapable of the great work which he is so ambitious to perform. If a man has such deep love for his fellow-men that he is anxious to do a great work for humanity he will manifest that surpassing love always and in the place where he now is. His home will be filled with it, and the beauty and sweetness and peace of his unselfish love will follow wherever he goes, making happy those about him and transmuting all things into good. The love that goes abroad to air itself, and is undiscoverable at home, is not love— it is vanity.

Have I not seen (Oh, pitiful sight!) the cheerless home and neglected children of the misguided missioner and religionist? It is on such self-delusion as this that self-pity and self-martyrdom ever wait, and its self-inflicted misery is regarded by the deluded one as a holy and religious burden which he or she is called upon to bear.

Only a great man can do a great work; and he will be great wherever he is, and will do his noble work under whatsoever conditions he may find himself when he has unfolded and revealed that work.

Thou who art so anxious to work for humanity, to help thy fellow-men, begin that work at home; help thyself, thy neighbor, thy wife, thy child. Do not be deluded; until thou doest, with utmost faithfulness, the nearer and the lesser thou canst not do the farther and greater.

If a man has lived many years of his life in lust and selfish pleasure it is in the order of things that his accumulated errors should at last weigh heavily upon him, as, until they are thus brought home to him, he will not abandon them, will not exert himself to find a better life; but whilst he regards his self-made, self-imposed burdens as "holy crosses" imposed upon him by the Supreme, or as marks of superior virtue, or as loads which Fate, circumstances, or other people have heaped undeservedly and unjustly upon him, he is but lengthening out his folly, increasing the weight of his burdens, and multiplying his pains and sorrows. Only when such a man wakes up to the truth that his burdens are of his own making, that they are the accumulated effects of his own acts, will he cease from unmanly self-pity and find the better way of burden-dropping; only when he opens his eyes to see that his every thought and act is another brick, another stone, built into the temple of his life will he develop the insight which will enable him to recognize his own unstable handiwork, the unflinching manliness to acknowledge it, and the courage to build more nobly and enduringly.

Painful burdens are necessary, but only so long as we lack love and wisdom.

The Temple of Blessedness lies beyond the outer courts of suffering and humiliation and to reach it the pilgrim must pass through the outer courts. For a time he will linger in the outer, but only so long as, through his own imperfect understanding, he mistakes it for the inner. While he pities himself and confounds suffering with holiness he will remain in suffering: but when, casting off the last unholy rag of self-pity, he perceives that suffering is a means and not an end, that it is a state self-originated and self-propagated, then, converted and right-minded, he will rapidly pass through the outer courts, and reach the inner abode of peace.

Suffering does not originate in the perfect but in the imperfect; it does not mark the complete but the incomplete; it can, therefore, be transcended. Its self-born cause can be found, investigated, comprehended, and for ever removed.

It is true therefore, that we must pass through agony to rest, through loneliness to peace; but let the sufferer not forget that it is a "passing through;" that the agony is a gateway and not a habitation; that the loneliness is a pathway and not a destination; and that a little farther on he will come to the painless and blissful repose.

Little by little is a burden accumulated; imperceptibly and by degrees is its weight increased. A thoughtless impulse, a gross self-indulgence, a blind passion yielded to and gratified again and again; an impure thought fostered, a cruel word uttered, a foolish thing done time after time, and at last the gathered weight of many follies becomes oppressive. At first, and for a time, the weight is not felt; but it is being added to day after day, and the time comes when the accumulated burden is felt in all its galling weight, when the bitter fruits of selfishness are gathered, and the heart is troubled with the weariness of life. When this period arrives let the sufferer look to himself; let him search for the blessed way of burden-dropping, finding which he will find wisdom to live better, purity to live sweeter, love to live nobler; will find, in the reversal of that conduct by which his burdens were accumulated, light-hearted nights and days, cheerful action, and unclouded joy.

> "Come out of the world— come above it—
> Up over its crosses and graves;
> Though the green earth is fair and I love it,
> We must love it as masters, not slaves,
> Come up where the dust never rises—
> But only the perfume of flowers—
> And your life shall be glad with surprises
> Of beautiful hours."

Hidden Sacrifices

"What need hath man
Of Eden passed, or Paradise to come,
When heaven is round us and within ourselves?"

"Lowliness is the base of every virtue:
Who goes the lowest, builds, doubt not, the safest."—Bailey.

"Truth is within ourselves; it takes no rise
From outward things, whate'er you may believe."—Browning

It is one of the paradoxes of Truth that we gain by giving up; we lose by greedily grasping. Every gain in virtue necessitates some loss in vice; every accession of holiness means some selfish pleasure yielded up; and every forward step on the path of Truth demands the forfeit of some self-assertive error.

He who would be clothed in new garments must first cast away the old, and he who would find the True must sacrifice the false. The gardener digs in the weeds in order that they may feed, with their decay, the plants which are good for food; and the Tree of Wisdom can only flourish on the compost of uprooted follies. Growth— gain— necessitates sacrifice— loss.

The true life, the blessed life, the life that is not tormented with passions and pains, is reached only through sacrifice, not necessarily the sacrifice of outward things, but the sacrifice of the inward errors and defilements, for it is these, and these only, which bring misery into life. It is not the good and true that needs to be sacrificed but the evil and false; therefore all sacrifice is ultimately gain, and there is no essential loss. Yet at first the loss seems great, and the sacrifice is painful, but this is because of the self-delusion and spiritual blindness which always accompany selfishness, and pain must always accompany the cutting away of some selfish portion of one's nature. When the drunkard resolves to sacrifice his lust for strong drink he passes through a period of great suffering, and he feels that he is forfeiting a great pleasure; but when his victory is complete, when the lust is dead, and his mind is calm and sober, then he knows that he has gained incalculably by the giving up of his selfish animal pleasure. What he has lost was evil and false and not worth keeping— nay, its keeping entailed continual misery— but what he has gained in character, in self-control, in soberness had greater peace of mind, is good and true, and it was necessary that he should acquire it.

So it is with all true sacrifice; it is at first, and until it is completed, painful, and this is why men shrink from it. They cannot see any purpose in abstaining from and overcoming selfish gratification, it seems to them like losing so much that is sweet; seems to them like courting misery, and giving up all happiness and pleasure. And this must be so; for if a man could know that by giving up his particular forms of selfishness his gain in happiness would be immeasurably greater, unselfishness (which is now so difficult of attainment) would then be rendered infinitely more difficult of achievement, for his desire for the greater gain— his selfishness— would thereby be greatly intensified.

No man can become unselfish, and thereby arrive at the highest bliss, until he is willing to lose, looking for neither gain nor reward: it is this state of mind which constitutes unselfishness. A man must be willing to humbly sacrifice his selfish habits and practices because they are untrue and unworthy, and for the happiness of those about him, without expecting any reward or looking for any good to accrue to himself; nay, he must be prepared to lose for himself, to forfeit pleasure and happiness, even life itself, if by so doing he can make the world more beautiful and happy. But does he lose? Does the miser lose when he gives up his lust for gold? Does the thief lose when he abandons stealing? Does the libertine lose when he sacrifices his unworthy pleasures? No man loses by the sacrifice of self, or some portion of self; nevertheless, he thinks he will lose by so doing, and because he so thinks he suffers and this is where the sacrifice comes in— this is where he gains by losing.

All true sacrifice is within; it is spiritual and hidden, and is prompted by deep humility of heart. Nothing but the sacrifice of self can avail, and to this must all men come sooner or later during their spiritual evolution. But in what does this self-abnegation consist? How is it practiced? Where is it sought and found? It consists in overcoming the daily proneness to selfish thoughts and acts; it is practiced in our common intercourse with others; and it is found in the hour of tumult and temptation.

There are hidden sacrifices of the heart which are infinitely blessed both to him that makes them and those for whom they are made, albeit their making costs much effort and some pain. Men are anxious to do some great thing, to perform some great sacrifice which lies beyond the necessities of their experience, while all the time, perhaps, they are neglecting the one thing needful, are blind to that sacrifice which by its very nearness is rendered imperative. Where lurks your besetting sin? Where lies your weakness? Where does temptation assail you most strongly? There shall you make your first sacrifice, and shall find thereby the way unto your peace. Perhaps it is anger or unkindness. Are you prepared to sacrifice the angry impulse and word, the unkind thought and deed? Are you prepared to silently endure abuse, attack, accusation, and unkindness, refusing to pay back these in their own coin? Nay, more, are you prepared to give in return for these dark follies kindness and loving protection? If so, then you are ready to make those hidden sacrifices which lead to beatific bliss.

If you are given to anger or unkindness offer it up. These hard, cruel, and wrong conditions of mind never brought you any good; they can never bring you anything but unrest, misery, and spiritual blindness. Nor can they ever bring to others anything but unhappiness. Perhaps you will say: "But he was unkind to me first; he treated me unjustly." Perhaps so, but what a poor excuse is this! What an unmanly and ineffectual refuge! For if his unkindness toward you is so wrong and hurtful yours to him must be equally so. Because another is unkind to you is no justification of your own unkindness, but is rather a call for the exercise of great kindness on your part. Can the pouring in of more water prevent a flood? Neither can unkindness lessen unkindness. Can fire quench fire? Neither can anger overcome anger.

Offer up all unkindness, all anger. "It takes two to make a quarrel;" don't be the "other one." If one is angry or unkind to you try to find out where you have acted wrongly; and, whether you have acted wrongly or not, do not throw back the angry word or unkind act. Remain silent, self-contained, and kindly disposed; and learn, by continual effort in right-doing, to have compassion upon the wrong-doer.

Perhaps you are habitually impatient and irritable. Know, then, the hidden sacrifice which it is needful that you should make. Give up your impatience. Overcome it there where it is wont to assert itself. Resolve that you will yield no longer to its tyrannical sway but will conquer it and cast it out. It is not worth keeping a single hour, nor would it dominate you for another moment if you were not laboring under the delusion that the follies and perversities of others render impatience on your part necessary. Whatever others may do or say, even though they may mock and taunt you, impatience is not only unnecessary, it can never do any other than aggravate the evil which it seeks to remove. Calm, strong, and deliberate action can accomplish much, but impatience and its accompanying irritability are always indications of weakness and inefficiency. And what do they bestow upon you? Do they bestow rest, peace, happiness, or bring these to those about you? Do they not, rather, make you and those about you wretched? But though your impatience may hurt others it certainly hurts and wounds and impoverishes yourself most of all.

Nor can the impatient man know aught of true blessedness, for he is a continual source of trouble and unrest to himself. The calm beauty and perpetual sweetness of patience are unknown to him, and peace cannot draw near to soothe and comfort him.

There is no blessedness anywhere until impatience is sacrificed; and its sacrifice means the development of endurance, the practice of forbearance, and the creation of a new and gentler habit of mind. When impatience and irritability are entirely put away, are finally offered up on the altar of unselfishness, then is realized and enjoyed the blessedness of a strong, quiet, and peaceful mind.

"Each hour we think
Of others more than self, that hour we live again,
And every lowly sacrifice we make
For other's good shall make life more than self,
And ope the windows of thy soul to light
From higher spheres. So hail thy lot with lot with joy."

Then there are little selfish indulgences, some of which appear harmless, and are commonly fostered; but no selfish indulgence can be harmless, and men and women do not know what they lose by repeatedly and habitually succumbing to effeminate and selfish gratifications. If the God in man is to rise strong and triumphant, the beast in man must perish. The pandering to the animal nature, even when it appears innocent and seems sweet, leads away from truth and blessedness. Each time you give way to the animal within you, and feed and gratify him, he waxes stronger and more rebellious, and takes firmer possession of your mind, which should be in the keeping of Truth. Not until a man has sacrifice some apparently trivial indulgence does he discover what strength, what joy, what poise of character and holy influence he has all along been losing by that gratification; not until a man sacrifices his hankering for pleasure does he enter into the fulness of abiding joy.

By his personal indulgences a man demeans himself, forfeits self-respect to the extent and frequency of his indulgence, and deprives himself of exemplary influence and the power to accomplish lasting good in his work in the world. He also, by allowing himself to be led by blind desire, increases his mental blindness, and fails of that ultimate clearness of vision, that clarified percipience which pierces to the heart of things and comprehends the real and the true. Animal indulgence is alien to the perception of Truth. By the sacrifice of his indulgences man rises above confusion and doubt, and arrives at the possession of insight and surety.

Sacrifice your cherished and coveted indulgence; fix your mind on something higher, nobler, and more enduring than ephemeral pleasure; live superior to the craving for sense-excitement, and you will live neither vainly nor uncertainly.

Very far-reaching in its effect upon others, and rich with the revelations of Truth for him who makes it, is the sacrifice of self-assertion— the giving up of all interference with the lives, views, or religion of other people, substituting for it an understanding love and sympathy. Self-assertion or opinionativeness is a form of egotism or selfishness most generally found in connection with intellectualism and dialectical skill. It is blindly presumptive and uncharitable, and, more often than not, is regarded as a virtue; but when once the mind has opened to perceive the way of gentleness and self-sacrificing love then the ignorance, deformity, and painful nature of self-assertion become apparent.

The victim of self-assertion, setting up his own opinions as the standard of right and the measure of judgment, regards all those as wrong whose lives and opinions run counter to his own, and, being eager to put others right, is thereby prevented from putting himself right. His attitude of mind brings about him opposition and contradiction from people who are anxious to put him right, and this wounds his vanity and makes him miserable, so that he lives in an almost continual fever of unhappy, resentful and uncharitable thoughts. There can be no peace for such a man, no true knowledge, and no advancement until he sacrifices his desire to bend others to his own way of thinking and acting. Nor can he understand the hearts of others, and enter lovingly into their strivings and aspirations. His mind is cramped and embittered, and he is shut out from all sweet sympathy and spiritual communion.

He who sacrifices the spirit of self-assertion, who in his daily contact with others put aside his prejudices and opinions, and strives both to learn from others and to understand them as they are, who allows to others perfect liberty (such as he exercises himself) to choose their own opinions, their own way in life— such a man will acquire a deeper insight, a broader charity, and a richer bliss than he has hitherto experienced, and will strike a byway of blessedness from which he has formerly shut out.

Then there is the sacrifice of greed and all greedy thoughts. The willingness that others should possess rather than we; the not-coveting of things for ourselves but rejoicing that they are possessed and enjoyed by others, that they bring happiness to others; the ceasing to claim one's "own", and the giving up to others, unselfishly and without malice, that which they exact. This attitude of mind is a source of deep peace and great spiritual strength. It is the sacrifice of self-interest.

Material possessions are temporary, and in this sense we cannot truly call them our own— they are merely in our keeping for a short time— but spiritual possessions are eternal and must ever remain with us. Unselfishness is a spiritual possession which is only secured by ceasing to covet material possessions and enjoyments, by ceasing to regard things as for our own special and exclusive pleasure, and by our readiness to yield them up for the good of others.

The unselfish man, even though he finds himself involved in riches, stands aloof, in his mind, from the idea of "exclusive possession", and so escapes the bitterness and fear and anxiety which ever accompany the covetous spirit. He does not regard any of his outward accretions as being too valuable to lose, but he regards the virtue of unselfishness as being too valuable to the world— to suffering humanity— to lose or cast away.

And who is the blessed man? He who is ever hankering after more possessions, thinking only of the personal pleasure he can get out of them? or he who is ever ready to give up what he has for the good and happiness of others? By greed happiness is destroyed; by not-greed happiness is restored.

Another hidden sacrifice, one of great spiritual beauty and of powerful efficacy in the healing of human sorrows, is the sacrifice of hatred— the giving up of all bitter thoughts against others, of all malice, dislike, and resentment. Bitter thoughts and blessedness cannot dwell together. Hatred is a fierce fire that scorches up, in the heart of him who harbors it, all the sweet flowers of peace and happiness, and makes a hell of every place where it comes.

Hatred has many names and many forms but only one essence— namely, burning thoughts of resentment against others. It is sometimes, by its blind votaries called by the name of religion, causing them to attack, slander, and persecute each other because they will not accept each other's views of life and death, thus filling the earth with miseries and tears.

All resentment, dislike, ill-thinking, and ill-speaking of others is hatred, and where there is hatred there is always unhappiness. No one has conquered hatred while thoughts of resentment towards others spring up in his mind. This sacrifice is not complete until a man can think kindly of those who try to do him wrong. Yet it must be made before true blessedness can be realized and known. Beyond the hard, cruel, steely gates of hatred waits the divine angel of love, ready to reveal herself to him who will subdue and sacrifice his hateful thoughts, and conduct him to his peace.

Whatever others may say of you, whatever they may do to you, never take offence. Do not return hatred with hatred. If another hates you perhaps you have, consciously or unconsciously, failed somewhere in your conduct, or there may be some misunderstanding which the exercise of a little gentleness and reason may remove; but, under all circumstances, "Father, forgive them" is infinitely better, sweeter, and nobler than "I will have nothing more to do with them." Hatred is so small and poor, so blind and wretched. Love is so great and rich, so far-seeing and blissful.

"The highest culture is to speak no ill:
The best reformer is the man whose eyes

Are quick to see all beauty and all worth;
And by his own discreet, well-ordered life
Alone reproves the erring."

Sacrifice all hatred, slay it upon the holy altar of devotion— devotion to others. Think no more of any injury to your own petty self, but see to it that henceforth you injure and wound no other. Open the flood gates of your heart for the inpouring of that sweet, great, beautiful love which embraces all with strong yet tender thoughts of protection and peace, leaving not one, nay, not even he who hates or despises or slanders you, out in the cold.

Then there is the hidden sacrifice of impure desires, of weak self-pity and degrading self-praise, of vanity and pride, for these are unblest attitudes of mind, deformities of heart. He who makes them, one by one, gradually subduing and overcoming them, will, according to the measure of his success, rise above weakness and suffering and sorrow, and will comprehend and enjoy the perfect and imperishable blessedness.

Now, all these hidden sacrifices which are here mentioned are pure, humble heart-offerings. They are made within; are offered up on the sacred, lonely, unseen altar of one's own heart. Not one of them can be made until the fault is first silently acknowledged and confessed. No man can sacrifice an error until he first of all confess (to himself) "I am in error;" when, yielding it up, he will perceive and receive the truth which his error formerly obscured.

"The kingdom of heaven cometh not by observation," and the silent sacrifice of self for the good of others, the daily giving up of one's egotistic tendencies, is not seen and rewarded of men, and brings no loud blazon of popularity and praise. It is hidden away from the eyes of all the world, nay, even from the gaze of those who are nearest to you, for no eyes of flesh can perceive its spiritual beauty. But think not that because it is unperceived it is therefore futile. Its blissful radiance is enjoyed by you, and its power for good over others is great and far-reaching, for though they cannot see it, nor, perhaps understand it, yet they are unconsciously influenced by it. They will not know what silent battles you are fighting, what eternal victories over self you are achieving, but, they will feel your altered attitude, your new mind, wrought of the fabric of love and loving thoughts, and will share somewhat in its happiness and bliss. They will know nothing of the frequent fierceness of the fight you are waging, of the wounds you receive and the healing balm you apply, of the anguish and the after-peace; but they will know that you have grown sweeter and gentler, stronger and more silently self-reliant, more patient and pure, and that they are rested and helped by your presence. What rewards can compare with this? Beside the fragrant offices of love the praises of men are gross and fulsome, and in the pure flame of a selfless heart the flatteries of the world are turned to ashes. Love is its own reward, its own joy, its own satisfaction; it is the final refuge and resting-place of passion-tortured souls.

The sacrifice of self, and the acquisition of the supreme knowledge and bliss which it confers, is not accomplished by one great and glorious act but by a series of lesser and successive sacrifices in the ordinary life of the world, by a succession of steps in the daily conquest of Truth over selfishness. He who each day accomplishes some victory over himself, who subdues and puts behind him some unkind thought, some impure desire, some tendency to sin, is everyday growing stronger, purer, and wiser, and every dawn finds him nearer to that final glory of Truth which each self-sacrificing act reveals in part.

Look not outside thee nor beyond thee for the light and blessedness of Truth, but look within; thou wilt find it within the narrow sphere of thy duty, even in the humble and hidden sacrifices of thine own heart.

Sympathy

"When thy gaze
Turns it on thine own soul, be most severe:
But when it falls upon a fellow-man
Let kindliness control it; and refrain
From that belittling censure that springs forth
From common lips like weeds from marshy soil."—Ella Wheeler Wilcox.

"I do not ask the wounded person how he feels,
I myself become the wounded person."——Walt Whitman.

We can only sympathize with others in so far as we have conquered ourselves. We cannot think and feel for others while we are engaged in condoling with and pitying ourselves; cannot deal tenderly and lovingly with others while we are anxious for our own pre-eminence or for the exclusive preservation of ourselves, our opinions, and our own generally. What is sympathy but thoughtfulness for others in the forgetfulness of self?

To sympathize with others we must first understand them, and to understand them we must put away all personal preconceptions concerning them, and must see them as they are. We must enter into their inner state and become one with them, looking through their mental eyes and comprehending the range of their experience. You cannot, of course, do this with a being whose wisdom and experience are greater than your own; nor can you do it with any if you regard yourself as being on a higher plane than others (for egotism and sympathy cannot dwell together), but you can practice it with all those who are involved in sins and sufferings from which you have successfully extricated yourself, and, though your sympathy cannot embrace and overshadow the man whose greatness is beyond you, yet you can place yourself in such an attitude towards him as to receive the protection of his larger sympathy and so make for yourself an easier way out of the sins and sufferings by which you are still enchained.

Prejudice and ill-will are complete barriers to the giving of sympathy, while pride and vanity are total barriers to its reception. You cannot sympathize with a person for whom you have conceived a hatred; you cannot enjoy the sympathy of one whom you envy. You cannot understand the person whom you dislike, or he for whom, through animal impulse, you have framed an ill-formed affection. You do not, cannot, see him as he is, but see only your own imperfect notions of him; see only a distorted image of him through the exaggerating medium of your ill-grounded opinions.

To see others as they are you must not allow impulsive likes and dislikes, powerful prejudices, or egotistic considerations to come between you and them. You must not resent their actions or condemn their beliefs and opinions. You must leave yourself entirely out, and must, for the time being, assume their position. Only in this way can you become en rapport with them, and so fathom their life, their experience, and understand it, and when a man is understood it becomes impossible to condemn him. Men misjudge, condemn, and avoid each other because they do not understand each other, and they do not understand each other because they have not overcome and purified themselves.

Life is growth, development, evolution, and there is no essential distinction between the sinner and the saint— there is only a difference in degree. The saint was once a sinner; the sinner will one day be a saint. The sinner is the child; the saint is the grown man. He who separates himself from sinners, regarding them as wicked men to be avoided, is like a man avoiding contact with little children because they are unwise, disobedient, and play with toys.

All life is one, but it has a variety of manifestations. The grown flower is not something distinct from the tree: it is a part of it; is only another form of leaf. Steam is not something apart from water: it is but another form of water. And in like manner good is transmuted evil: the saint is the sinner developed and transformed.

The sinner is one whose understanding is undeveloped, and he ignorantly chooses wrong modes of action. The saint is one whose understanding is ripened, and he wisely chooses right modes of action. The sinner condemns the sinner, condemnation being a wrong mode of action. The saint never condemns the sinner, remembering that he himself formerly occupied the same place, but thinks of him with deep sympathy, regarding him in the light of a younger brother or a friend, for sympathy is a right and enlightened mode of action.

The perfected saint, who gives sympathy to all, needs it of none, for he has transcended sin and suffering, and lives in the enjoyment of lasting bliss; but all who suffer need sympathy, and all who sin must suffer. When a man comes to understand that every sin, whether of thought or deed, receives its just quota of suffering he ceases to condemn and begins to sympathize, seeing the sufferings which sin entails; and he comes to such understanding by purifying himself.

As a man purges himself of passions, as he transmutes his selfish desires and puts under foot his egotistic tendencies, he sounds the depths of all human experiences— all sins and sufferings and sorrows, all motives and thoughts and deeds— and comprehends the moral law in its perfection. Complete self-conquest is perfect knowledge, perfect sympathy, and he who views men with the stainless vision of a pure heart views them with a pitying heart, sees them as a part of himself, not as something defiled and separate and distinct, but as his very self, sinning as he has sinned, suffering as he has suffered, sorrowing as he has sorrowed, yet, withal, glad in the knowledge that they will come, as he has come, to perfect peace at last.

The truly good and wise man cannot be a passionate partisan, but extends his sympathy to all, seeing no evil in others to be condemned and resisted, but seeing the sin which is pleasant to the sinner, and the after-sorrow and pain which the sinner does not see, and, when it overtakes him, does not understand.

A man's sympathy extends just so far as his wisdom reaches, and no further; and a man only grows wiser as he grows tenderer and more compassionate. To narrow one's sympathy is to narrow one's heart, and so to darken and embitter one's life. To extend and broaden one's sympathy is to enlighten and gladden one's life and to make plainer to others the way of light and gladness.

To sympathize with another is to receive his being into our own, to become one with him, for unselfish love indissolubly unites, and he whose sympathy reaches out to and embraces all humankind and all living creatures has realized his identity and oneness with all, and comprehends the universal Love and Law and Wisdom.

Man is shut out from Heaven and Peace and Truth only in so far as he shuts out others from his sympathy. Where his sympathy ends his darkness and torment and turmolis begin, for to shut others out from our love is to shut ourselves out from the blessedness of love, and to become cramped in the dark prison of self.

"Whoever walks a furlong without sympathy walks to his own funeral dressed in a shroud."

Only when one's sympathy is unlimited is the Eternal Light of Truth revealed; only in the Love that knows no restriction is the boundness bliss enjoyed.

Sympathy is bliss; in it is revealed the highest, purest blessedness. It is divine, for in its reciprocal light all thought of self is lost, and there remains only the pure joy of oneness with others, the ineffable communion of spiritual identity. Where a man ceases to sympathize he ceases to live, ceases to see and realize and know.

One cannot truly sympathize with others until all selfish considerations concerning them are put away, and he who does this and strives to see others as they are, strives to realize their particular sins, temptations, and sorrows, their beliefs, opinions, and prejudices, comes at last to see exactly where they stand in their spiritual evolution, comprehends the arc of their experience, and knows that they cannot for the present act otherwise than they do. He sees that their thoughts and acts are prompted by the extent of their knowledge, or their lack of knowledge, and that if they act blindly and foolishly it is because their knowledge and experience are immature, and they can only come to act more wisely by gradual growth into more enlightened states of mind. He also sees that though this growth can be encouraged, helped, and stimulated by the influence of a riper example, by seasonable words and well-timed instruction, it cannot be unnaturally forced; the flowers of love and wisdom must have time to grow, and the barren branches of hatred and folly cannot be all cut away at once.

Such a man finds the doorway into the inner world of those with whom he comes in contact, and he opens it and enters in and dwells with them in the hidden and sacred sanctuary of their being. And he finds nothing to hate, nothing to revile, nothing to condemn in that sacred place, but something to love and tend, and, in his own heart, room only for greater pity, greater patience, greater love.

He sees that he is one with them, that they are but another aspect of himself, that their natures are not different from his own, except in modification and degree, but are identical with it. If they are acting out certain sinful tendencies he has but to look within to find the same tendencies in himself, albeit, perhaps, restrained or purified; if they are manifesting certain holy and divine qualities he finds the same pure spirit within himself, though, perhaps, in a lesser degree of power and development.

"One touch of nature makes the whole world kin."

The sin of one is the sin of all; the virtue of one is the virtue of all. No man can be separate from another. There is no difference of nature but only difference of condition. If a man thinks he is separated from another by virtue of his superior holiness he is not so separated, and his darkness and delusion are very great. Humanity is one, and in the holy sanctuary of sympathy saint and sinner meet and unite.

It is said of Jesus that He took upon Himself the sins of the whole world— that is, He identified Himself with those sins, and did not regard Himself as essentially separate from sinners but as being of a like nature with them— and his realization of His oneness with all men was manifested in His life as profound sympathy with those who, for their deep sins, were avoided and cast off by others.

And who is it that is in the greatest need of sympathy? Not the saint, not the enlightened seer, not the perfect man. It is the sinner, the unenlightened man, the imperfect one; and the greater the sin the greater is the need. "I came not to call the righteous but sinners to repentance" is the statement of One who comprehended all human needs. The righteous man does not need your sympathy, but the unrighteous; he who, by his wrong-doing, is laying up for himself long periods of suffering and woe is in need of it.

The flagrantly unrighteous man is condemned, despised, and avoided by those who are living in a similar condition to himself, though for the time being, they may not be subject to his particular form of sin, for that withholding of sympathy and that mutual condemnation which are so rife is the commonest manifestation of that lack of understanding in which all sin takes its rise. While a man is involved in sin he will condemn others who are likewise involved, and the deeper and greater his sin the more severe will be his condemnation of others. It is only when a man begins to sorrow for his sin, and so to rise above it into the clearer light of purity and understanding, that he ceases from condemning others and learns to sympathize with them. But this ceaseless condemnation of each other by those who are involved in the fierce play of the passions must needs, be, for it one of the modes of operation of the Great Law which universally and eternally obtains, and the unrighteous one who falls under the condemnation of his fellows will the more rapidly reach a higher and nobler condition of heart and life if he humbly accepts the censure of others as the effect of his own sin, and resolves henceforward to refrain from all condemnation of others.

The truly good and wise man condemns none, having put away all blind passion and selfishness he lives in the calm regions of love and peace, and understands all modes of sin, with their consequent sufferings and sorrows. Enlightened and awakened, freed from all selfish bias, and seeing men as they are, his heart responds in holy sympathy with all. Should any condemn, abuse, or slander him he throws around them the kindly protection of his sympathy, seeing the ignorance which prompts them so to act, and knowing that they alone will suffer for their wrong acts.

Learn, by self-conquest and the acquisition of wisdom, to love him whom you now condemn, to sympathize with those who condemn you. Turn your eyes away from their condemnation and search your own heart, to find, perchance, some hard, unkind, or wrong thoughts which, when discovered and understood, you will condemn yourself.

Much that is commonly called sympathy is personal affection. To love them who love us is human bias and inclination; but to love them who do not love us is divine sympathy.

Sympathy is needed because of the prevalence of suffering, for there is no being or creature who has not suffered. Through suffering sympathy is evolved. Not in a year or a life or an age is the human heart purified and softened by suffering, but after many lives of intermittent pain, after many ages of ever recurring sorrow, man reaps the golden harvest of his experiences, and garners in the rich, ripe sheaves of love and wisdom. And then he understands, and understanding, he sympathizes.

All suffering is the result of ignorantly violated law, and after many repetitions of the same wrong act, and the same kind of suffering resulting from that act, knowledge of the law is acquired, and the higher state of obedience and wisdom is reached. Then there blossoms the pure and perfect flower of sympathy.

One aspect of sympathy is that of pity— pity for the distressed or pain-stricken, with a desire to alleviate or help them bear their sufferings. The world needs more of this divine quality. "For pity makes the world
Soft to the weak, and noble for the strong."

But it can only be developed by eradicating all hardness and unkindness, all accusation and resentment. He who, when he sees another suffering for his sin, hardens his heart and thinks or says: "It serves him right"- such a one cannot exercise pity nor apply its healing balm. Every time a man acts cruelly towards another (be it only a dumb creature), or refuses to bestow needed sympathy, he dwarfs himself, deprives himself of ineffable blessedness, and prepares himself for suffering.

Another form of sympathy is that of rejoicing with those who are more successful than ourselves, as though their success were our own. Blessed indeed is he who is free from all envy and malice, and can rejoice and be glad when he hears of the good fortune of those who regard him as an enemy.

The protecting of creatures weaker and more indefensible than oneself is another form in which this divine sympathy is manifested. The helpless frailty of the dumb creation calls for the exercise of the deepest sympathy. The glory of superior strength resides in its power to shield, not to destroy. Not by the callous of destruction of weaker things is life truly lived, but by their preservation: "All life Is linked and kin," and the lowest creature is not separated from the highest but by greater weakness, by lesser intelligence. When we pity and protect we reveal and enlarge the divine life and joy within ourselves. When we thoughtlessly or callously inflict suffering or destroy, then our divine life becomes obscured, and its joy fades and dies. Bodies may feed bodies, and passions, but man's divine nature is only nurtured, sustained, and developed by kindness, love, sympathy, and all pure and unselfish acts.

By bestowing sympathy on others we increase our own. Sympathy given can never be wasted. Even the meanest creature will respond to its heavenly touch, for it is the universal language which all creatures understand. I have recently heard a true story of a Dartmoor convict whose terms of incarceration in various convict stations extended to over forty years. As a criminal he was considered one of the most callous and hopelessly abandoned, and the warders found him almost intractable. But one day he caught a mouse— a weak, terrified, hunted thing like himself— and its helpless frailty, and the similarity of its condition with his own, appealed to him, and started into flame the divine spark of sympathy which smouldered in his crime-hardened heart, and which no human touch had ever wakened into life.

He kept the mouse in an old boot in his cell, fed, tended, and loved it, and in his love for the weak and helpless he forgot and lost his hatred for the strong. His heart and his hand were no longer against his fellows. He became tractable and obedient to the uttermost. The warders could not understand his change; it seemed to them little short of miraculous that this most hardened of all criminals should suddenly be transformed into the likeness of a gentle, obedient child. Even the expression of his features altered remarkably: a pleasing smile began to play around the mouth which had formerly been moved to nothing better than a cruel grin, and the implacable hardness of his eyes disappeared and gave place to a soft, deep, mellow light. The criminal was a criminal no longer; he was saved, converted; clothed, and in his right mind; restored to humaneness and to humanity, and set firmly on the pathway to divinity by pitying and caring for a defenseless creature. All this was made known to the warders shortly afterwards, when, on his discharge, he took the mouse away with him.

Thus sympathy bestowed increases its store in our own hearts, and enriches and fructifies our own life. Sympathy given is blessedness received; sympathy withheld is blessedness forfeited. In the measure that a man increases and enlarges his sympathy so much nearer does he approach the ideal life, the perfect blessedness; and when his heart has become so mellowed that no hard, bitter, or cruel thought can enter and detract from its permanent sweetness, then indeed is he richly and divinely blessed.

Forgiveness

"If men only understood
All the emptiness and acting
Of the sleeping and the waking
Of the souls they judge so blindly,
Of the hearts they pierce so unkindly,
They, with gentler words and feeling,
Would apply the balm of healing-
If they only understood."
"Kindness, nobler ever than revenge."—Shakespeare.

The remembering of injuries is spiritual darkness; the fostering of resentment is spiritual suicide. To resort to the spirit and practice of forgiveness is the beginning of enlightenment; it is also the beginning of peace and happiness. There is no rest for him who broods over slights and injuries and wrongs; no quiet repose of mind for him who feels that he has been unjustly treated, and who schemes how best to act for the discomfiture of his enemy.

How can happiness dwell in a heart that is so disturbed by ill-will? Do birds resort to a burning bush wherein to build and sing? Neither can happiness inhabit in that breast that is aflame with burning thoughts of resentment. Nor can wisdom come and dwell where such folly resides.

Revenge seems sweet only to the mind that is unacquainted with the spirit of forgiveness; but when the sweetness of forgiveness is tasted then the extreme bitterness of revenge is known. Revenge seems to lead to happiness to those who are involved in the darkness of passion; but when the violence of passion is abandoned, and the mildness of forgiveness is restored to, then it is seen that revenge leads to suffering.

Revenge is a virus which eats into the very vitals of the mind, and poisons the entire spiritual being. Resentment is a mental fever which burns up the wholesome energies of the mind, and "taking offence" is a form of moral sickness which saps the healthy flow of kindliness and good-will, and from which men and women should seek to be delivered. The unforgiving and resentful spirit is a source of great suffering and sorrow, and he who harbors and encourages it, who does not overcome and abandon it, forfeits much blessedness, and does not obtain any measure of true enlightenment. To be hard-hearted is to suffer, is to be deprived of light and comfort; to be tender-hearted is to be serenely glad, is to receive light and be well comforted. It will seem strange to many to be told that the hard-hearted and unforgiving suffer most; yet it is profoundly true, for not only do they, by the law of attraction, draw to themselves the revengeful passions in other people, but their hardness of heart itself is a continual source of suffering. Every time a man hardens his heart against a fellow-being he inflicts upon himself five kinds of suffering— namely, the suffering of loss of love; the suffering of lost communion and fellowship; the suffering of a troubled and confused mind; the suffering of wounded passion or pride; and the suffering of punishment inflicted by others. Every act of unforgiveness entails upon the doer of that act these five sufferings; whereas every act of forgiveness brings to the doer five kinds of blessedness— the blessedness of love; the blessedness of increased communion and fellowship; the blessedness of a calm and peaceful mind; the blessedness of passion stilled and pride overcome; and the blessedness and kindness and good-will bestowed by others.

Numbers of people are today suffering the fiery torments of an unforgiving spirit, and only when they make an effort to overcome that spirit can they know what a cruel and exacting taskmaster they are serving. Only those who have abandoned the service of such a master for that of the nobler master of forgiveness can realize and know how grievous a service is the one, how sweet the other.

Let a man contemplate the strife of the world: how individuals and communities, neighbors and nations, live in continual retaliations towards each other; let him realize the heartaches, the bitter tears, the grievous partings and misunderstandings— yea, even the blood-shed and woe which spring from that strife— and, thus realizing, he will never again yield to ignoble thoughts of resentment, never again take offence at the actions of others, never again live in unforgiveness towards any being.

"Have good-will
To all that lives, letting unkindness die
And greed and wrath; so that your lives be made
Like soft airs passing by."

When a man abandons retaliation for forgiveness he passes from darkness to light. So dark and ignorant is unforgiveness that no being who is at all wise or enlightened could descend to it; but its darkness is not understood and known until it is left behind, and the better and nobler course of conduct is sought and practiced. Man is blinded and deluded only by his own dark and sinful tendencies; and the giving up of all unforgiveness means the giving up of pride and certain forms of passion, the abandonment of the deeply-rooted idea of the importance of one-self and of the necessity for protecting and defending that self; and when that is done the higher life, greater wisdom, and pure enlightenment, which pride and passion completely obscured, are revealed in all their light and beauty.

Then there are petty offences, little spites and passing slights, which, while of a less serious nature than deep-seated hatreds and revenges, dwarf the character and cramp the soul. They are due to the sin of self and self-importance and thrive on vanity. Whosoever is blinded and deluded by vanity will continually see something in the actions and the attitudes of others towards him at which to take offence, and the more there is of vanity the more greatly will the imaginary slight or wrong be exaggerated. Moreover, to live in the frequent indulgence of petty resentments increase the spirit of hatred, and leads gradually downward to greater darkness, suffering, and self-delusion. Don't take offence or allow your feelings to be hurt, which means— get rid of pride and vanity. Don't give occasion for offence or hurt the feelings of others, which means— be gently considerate, forgiving, and charitable towards all.

The giving up— the total uprooting— of vanity and pride is a great task; but it is a blessed task, and it can be accomplished by constant practice in non-resentment and by meditating upon one's thoughts and actions so as to understand and purify them; and the spirit of forgiveness is perfected in one in the measure that pride and vanity are overcome and abandoned.

The not-taking-offence and the not-giving-offence go together. When a man ceases to resent the actions of others he is already acting kindly towards them, considering them before himself or his own defense. Such a man will be gently in what he says and does, will arouse love and kindness in others, and not stir them up to ill-will and strife. He will also be free from all fear concerning the actions of others towards him, for he who hurts none fears none. But the unforgiving man, he who is eager to "pay back" some real or imaginary slight or injury, will not be considerate towards others, for he considers himself first, and is continually making enemies; he also loves in the fear of others, thinking that they are trying to do towards him as he is doing towards them. He who contrives the hurt of others fears others.

That is a beautiful story of Prince Dhirgayu which was told by an ancient Indian teacher to his disciples in order to impress them with the truth of the ublime percept that "hatred ceases not by hatred at any time; hatred ceases by not-hatred." The story is as follows:—
Brahmadatta, a powerful king of Benares, made war upon Dirgheti, the king of Kosala, in order to annex his kingdom, which was much smaller than his own. Dirgheti, seeing that it was impossible for him to resist the greater power of bramhadatta, fled, and left his kingdom in his enemy's hands. For some time he wandered from place to place in disguise, and at last settled down with his queen in an artisan's cottage; and the queen gave birth to a son, whom they called Dirghayu.

Now, King Brahmadatta was anxious to discover the hiding-place of Dirgheti, in order to put to death the conquered king, for he thought,

"Seeing that I have deprived him of his kingdom he may someday treacherously kill me If I do not kill him."

But many years passed away, and Dirgheti devoted himself to the education of his son,. who by diligent application, became learned and skillful and wise.

And after a time Dirgheti's secret became known, and he, fearing that brahmadatta would discover him and slay all three, and thinking more of the life of his son than his own, sent away the prince. Soon after the exile king fell into the hands of Brahmadatta, and was, along with his queen, executed.

Now Brahmadatta thought: I have got rid of Dirgheti and his queen, but their son, Prince Dirghayu, lives, and he will be sure to contrive some means of effecting my assassination; yet he is unknown to any, and I have no means of discovering him." So the king lived in great fear and continual distress of mind.

Soon after the execution of his parents, Dirghayu, under an assumed name, sought employment in the king's stables, and was engaged by the master of elephants.

Dirghayu quickly endeared himself to all, and his superior abilities came at last under the notice of the king, who had the young man brought before him, and was so charmed with him that he employed him in his own castle, and he proved to be so able and diligent that the king shortly placed him in a position of great trust under himself.

one day the king went on a long hunting exception, and became separated from his retinue, Dirghayu alone remaining with him. And the king, being fatigued with his exertions, lay down, and slept with his head in Dirghayu's lap.

Then Dirghayu thought: This king has greatly wronged me. He robbed my father of his kingdom, and slew my parents, and he is now entirely in my power." And he drew his sword, thinking to slay Brahmadatta. But, remembering how his father had taught him never to seek revenge but to forgive to the uttermost, he sheathed his sword.

At last the king awoke out of a disturbed sleep, and the youth inquired of him why he looked so frightened. "My sleep", said the king "is always restless, for I frequently dream that I am in the power of young Dirghayu and that he is alone to slay me. While lying here I again dreamed that with greater vividness than ever before and it has filled me with dread and terror.

Then the youth, drawing his sword, said: "I am Prince Dirghayu, and you are in my power: the time of vengeance has arrived."

Then the king fell upon his knees and begged Dirghayu to spare his life. And Dirghayu said: "It is you, O King! who must spare my life. For many years you have wished to find me in order that you might kill me; and , now that you have found me, let me beg of you to grant me my life."

And there and then did Brahmadatta and Dirghayu grant each other life, took hands, and solemnly vowed never to harm each other. And so overcome was the king by the noble and forgiving spirit of Dirghayu that he gave him his daughter in marriage, and restored to him his father's kingdom.

Thus hatred ceases by not-hatred- by forgiveness, which is very beautiful, and is sweeter and more effective than revenge. It is the beginning of love, of that divine love that does not seek its own; and he who practices it, who perfects himself in it, comes at last to realize that blessed state wherein the torments of pride and vanity and hatred and retaliation are forever dispelled, and good-will and peace are unchanging and unlimited. In that state of calm, silent bliss, even forgiveness passes away, and is no longer needed, for he who has reached it sees no evil to resent but only ignorance and delusion on which to have compassion, and forgiveness is only needed so long as there is any tendency to resent, retaliate, and take offence. Equal love towards all is the perfect law, the perfect state in which all lesser states find their completion. Forgiveness is one of the doorways in the faultless temple of Love Divine.

Seeing No Evil

The solid, solid universe
Is pervious to love;
With bandaged eyes he never errs,
Around, below, above.
His blinding light
He flingeth white
On God's and Satan's brood,
And reconciles
By mystic wiles
The evil and the good."—Emerson

"If thou thinkest evil, be thou sure
Thine acts will bear the shadow of the stain;
And if they thought be perfect, then thy deed
Will be as of the perfect, true, and pure."—After Confucius

After much practice in forgiveness and having cultivated the spirit of forgiveness up to a certain point, knowledge of the actual nature of good and evil dawns upon the mind, and a man begins to understand how thoughts and motives are formed in the human heart, how they develop, and how take birth in the form of actions. This marks the opening of a new vision in the mind, the commencement of a nobler, higher, diviner life; for the man now begins to perceive that there is no necessity to resist or resent the actions of others towards him, whatever those actions may be, and that all along his resentment has been caused by his own ignorance, and that his own bitterness of spirit is wrong. Having arrived thus far he will take himself with some such questionings as these: "Why this continual retaliation and forgiveness ? Why this tormenting anger against another and then this repentance and forgiveness ? Is not forgiveness the taking back of one's anger, the giving up of one's resentment; and if anger and resentment are good and necessary why repent of them and give them up ? If it is so beautiful, so sweet, so peaceful to get rid of all feelings of bitterness and to utterly and wholly forgive, would it not be still more beautiful and sweet and peaceful never to grow bitter at all, never to know anger, never to resent as evil the action of another, but always to live in the experience of that pure, calm, blissful love which is known when an act of forgiveness is done, and all unruly passion towards another is put away ? If another has done me wrong is not my hatred towards him wrong, and can one wrong right another ? Moreover, has he by his wrong really injured me, or has he injured himself? Am I not injured by my own wrong rather than by his ? Why, then, do I grow angry? why do I resent, retaliate, and engage in bitter thoughts? Is it not because my pride is piqued or my vanity wounded or my selfishness thwarted ? Is not because my blind animal passions are aroused and allowed to subdue my better nature ? Seeing that I am hurt by another person's attitude towards me because of my own pride or vanity or ungoverned and unpurified passions, would it not be better to look to the wrong in myself rather than the wrong in another, to get rid of pride and vanity and passion, and so avoid being hurt at all ?

By such self-questionings and their elucidation in the light of mild thoughts and dispassionate conduct a man, gradually overcoming passion and rising out of the ignorance which gave rise to passion, will at last reach that blessed state in which he will cease to see evil in others, and will dwell in universal good-will and love and peace. Not that he will cease to see ignorance and folly; not that he will cease to see suffering and sorrow and misery; not that he will cease to distinguish between acts that are pure and impure, right and wrong, for, having put away passion and prejudice, he will see these things in the full, clear light of knowledge, and exactly as they are; but he will cease to see anything-any evil power- in another which can do him injury, which he must violently oppose and strive to crush, and against which he must guard himself. Having arrived at right understanding of evil by purging it away from his own heart he sees that it is a thing that does not call for hatred and fear and resentment but for consideration, compassion, and love.

Shakespeare through one of his characters says: "There is no darkness but ignorance." All evil is ignorance, is dense darkness of mind, and the removal of sin from one's mind is a coming out of darkness into spiritual light. Evil is the negation of good, just as darkness is the negation, or absence of light, and what is there in a negation to arouse anger or resentment ? When night settles down upon the world who is so foolish as to rail at the darkness? The enlightened man, likewise, does not accuse or condemn the spiritual darkness in men's hearts which is manifested in the form of sin, though by gentle reproof he may sometimes point out where the light lies.

Now the ignorance to which I refer as evil, or as the source of evil, is two-fold. There is wrong-doing which is committed without any knowledge of good and evil, and where there is no choice— this is unconscious wrong-doing. Then there is wrong-doing which is done in the knowledge that it ought not to be done— this is conscious wrong-doing; but both unconscious and conscious wrong-doing arise in ignorance-that is, ignorance of the real nature and painful consequences of the wrong-doing.

Why does a man continue to do certain things which he feels he ought not to do? If he knows that what he is doing is wrong where lies the ignorance?

He continues to do those things because his knowledge of them is incomplete. He only knows he ought not to do them by certain precepts without and qualms of conscience within, but he does not fully and completely understand what he is doing. He knows that certain acts bring him immediate pleasure, and so, in spite of the troubled conscience which follows that pleasure, he continues to commit them. He is convinced that the pleasure is good and desirable, and therefore to be enjoyed. He does not know that pleasure and pain are one, but thinks he can have the one without the other. He has no knowledge of the law which governs human actions, and never thinks of associating his sufferings with his own wrong-doing, but believes that they are caused by the wrong-doing of others or are the mysterious dispensations of Providence, and therefore not to be inquired into or understood. He is seeking happiness, and does those things which he believes will bring him most enjoyment, but he acts in entire ignorance of the hidden and inevitable consequences which attach to his actions.

Said a man to me once who was the victim of a bad habit: "I know the habit is a bad one, and that it does me more harm than good" I said: " If you know that what you are doing is bad and harmful why do you continue to do it?" And he replied: "Because it is pleasant, and I like it."

This man, of course, did not really know that his habit was bad. He had been told that it was, and he thought he knew or believed it was, but in reality he thought it was good, that it was conducive to his happiness and well-being, and therefore he continue to practice it. When a man knows by experience that a thing is bad, and that every time he does it he injuries body or mind, or both; when his knowledge of that thing is so complete that he is acquainted with its hole train of baneful effects, then he cannot only not do it any longer, he cannot even desire to do it, and even the pleasure that was formerly in that thing becomes painful. No man would put a venomous snake in his pocket because it is prettily colored. He knows that a deadly sting lurks in those beautiful markings. Nor, when a man knows the unavoidable pain and hurt which lie hidden in wrong thoughts and acts, does he continue to think and commit them. Even the immediate pleasure which formerly he greedily sought is gone from them; their surface attractiveness has vanished; he is no longer ignorant concerning their true nature; he sees them as they are.

I knew a young man who was in business, and although a member of a church, and occupying the position of voluntary religious instructor, he told me that it was absolutely necessary to practice lying and deception in business, otherwise sure and certain ruin would follow. He said he knew lying was wrong, but while he remained in business he must continue to do it. Upon questioning him I found, of course, that he had never tried truth and honesty in his business, had not even thought of trying the better way, so firmly convinced was he that it was not possible for him to know whether or not it would be productive or ruin. Now, did this young man know that lying was wrong? There was a perceptual sense only in which he knew, but there was a deeper and more real sense in which he did not know. He had been taught to regard lying as wrong, and his conscience bore out that teaching, but he believed that it brought to him profit, prosperity and happiness, and that honesty would bring him loss, poverty, and misery— in a word, he regarded lying, deep in his heart, as the right thing to do, and honesty as the wrong practice. He had no knowledge whatever of the real nature of the act of lying: how it is, on the instant of its committal, loss of character, loss of self-respect, loss of power, usefulness, and influence, and loss of blessedness; and how it unerringly leads to loss of reputation and loss of material profit and prosperity. Only when such a man begins to consider happiness of others, prefers to embrace the loss which he fears rather than clutch at the gain which he desires, will he obtain that real knowledge which lofty moral conduct alone can reveal; and then, experiencing the greater blessedness, he will see how, all along, he has been deceiving and defrauding himself rather than others, has been living in darkest ignorance and self-delusion.

These two common instances of wrong-doing will serve to illustrate and make plainer, to those of my readers who, while searching for Truth, are as yet doubtful, uncertain, and confused, the deep Truth that all sin, or evil, is a condition of ignorance and therefore to be dealt with in a loving and not a hateful spirit.

And as with bad habits and lying so with all sin— with lust, hatred, malice, envy, pride, vanity, self-indulgence and selfishness in all its forms; it is a state of spiritual darkness, the absence of the Light of Truth in the heart, the negation of knowledge.

Thus when, by overcoming the wrong condition in one's own heart, the nature of evil is fully realized and mere belief gives place to living knowledge, evil can no longer be hatefully condemned and violently resisted, and the wrong-doer is thought of with tender compassion.

And this brings us to another aspect of evil-namely, that of individual freedom; the right of every person to choose his own actions. Along with the seeing of evil in others is the desire to convert or coerce others into one's own ways of thinking and acting. Probably the commonest delusion in which men are involved is that of thinking that what they themselves believe and think and do is good, and all that is otherwise is evil, and therefore to be powerfully condemned and resisted. It is out of this delusion that all persecutions springs. There are Christians who regard all Atheists as men wholly evil, as given up to the service of an evil power; and there are Atheists who firmly believe that all Christians are doing the greatest harm to the whole human race by their "superstitious and false doctrines." The truth is that neither the Christian nor the Atheist is evil, nor in the service of evil, but each is choosing his own way, and is pursuing that course which he is convinced is right.

Let a man quietly contemplate the fact that numbers of followers of various religions the world over are, as they ever were, engaged in condemning each other as evil and wrong, and regarding themselves as good and right, and it will help him to realize how all evil is merely ignorance, spiritual darkness; and earnest meditation on that fact will be found to be one of the greatest aids in developing greater kindness, charity, insight and breadth of mind.

The truly wise and good man sees good in all, evil in none. He has abandoned the folly of wanting others to think and act as he thinks and acts, for he sees men are variously constituted, are at different points in their spiritual evolution, and must, of necessity, think and act differently. Having put away hatred, condemnation, egotism, and prejudice he has become enlightened, and sees that purity, love compassion, gentleness, patience, humility, and unselfishness are manifestations of light and knowledge; while impurity, hatred, cruelty, passion, darkness and ignorance; and that whether men are living in light or darkness they are one and all doing that which they think is necessary, are acting in accordance with their own measure of light or darkness. The wise man understands and understanding, he ceases from all bitterness and accusation.

Every man acts in accordance with his nature, with his own sense of right and wrong, and is surely gathering in the results of his own experience. There is one supreme right which every being possesses— to think and act as he chooses. If he chooses to think and act selfishly, thinking of his own immediate happiness only and not of that of others , then he will rapidly bring upon himself, by the action of the moral law of cause and effect, such afflictions as will cause him to pause and consider, and so find a better way. There is no teacher to compare with experience, no chastisement so corrective and purifying as that which men ignorantly inflict upon themselves. The selfish man is the ignorant man; he chooses his own way, but it is a way which leads to suffering, and through suffering to knowledge and bliss. The good man is the wise man; he likewise chooses his own way, but he chooses it in the full light of knowledge, having passed through the stages of ignorance and suffering, and arrived at knowledge and bliss.

A man begins to understand what "seeing no evil" is when, putting away all personal desires in his judgments of others, he considers them from their own standpoint, and judges their actions not from his own standard but from theirs. It is because men setup arbitrary standards of right and wrong, and are anxious that all should conform to their particular standard, that they see evil in each other. A man is only rightly judged when he is judged not from my standard or yours but from his own, and to deal with him thus is not judgment it is Love. It is only when we look through the eyes of Impersonal Love that we become enlightened, and see others as they really are; and a man is approaching that Love when he can say in his heart: "Who am I that I should judge another? Am I so pure and sinless that I arraign men and pass the judgment of evil upon them? Rather let me humble myself, and correct mine own errors, before assuming the position of supreme judge of those of other men."

It was said by one of old to those who were about to stone, as evil, a woman taken in the act of committing one of the darkest sins: "He that is without sin let him cast the first stone"; and though he who said it was without sin yet he took up no stone, nor passed any bitter judgment, but said, with infinite gentleness and compassion: "Neither do I condemn thee; go, and sin no more."

In the pure heart there is no room left where personal judgements and hatreds can find lodgement, for it is filled to overflowing with tenderness and love; it sees no evil; and only as men succeed in seeing no evil in others will they become free from sin and sorrow and suffering.

No man sees evil in himself or his own acts except the man who is becoming enlightened, and then he abandons those acts which he has come to see are wrong. Every man justifies himself in what he does, and, however evil others may regard his conduct, he himself thinks it to be good and necessary; If he did not he would not, could not do it. The angry man always justifies his anger; the covetous man his greed; the impure man his unchastity; the liar considers that his lying is altogether necessary; the slanderer believes that, in vilifying the characters of those whom he dislikes, and warning other people against their "evil" natures, he is doing well; the thief is convinced that stealing is the shortest and best way to plenty, prosperity, and happiness; and even the murderer thinks that there is a ground of justification for his deed.

Every man's deeds are in accordance with the measure of his own light or darkness, and no man can live higher than he is or act beyond the limits of his knowledge. Nevertheless, he can improve himself, and thereby gradually increase his light and extend the range of his knowledge. The angry man indulgence in raillery and abuse because his knowledge does not extend to forbearance and patience. Not having practiced gentleness, he does not understand it, and cannot choose it; nor can he know, by its comparison with the light of gentleness, the darkness of anger. It is the same with the liar, the slanderer, and the thief; he lives in this dark condition of mind and action because he is limited to it by his immature knowledge and experience, because never having lived in the higher conditions, he has no knowledge of them, and it is, to him, as if they were non-existent: "The light shineth in the darkness and the darkness comprehendenth it not. Nor can he understand even the conditions in which he is living, because, being dark, they are necessarily devoid of all knowledge.

When a man driven by repeated sufferings to at last reflect upon his conduct, comes to see that his anger or lying, or whatever ignorant condition he may have been living in, is productive only of trouble and sorrow then he abandons it, and commences to search for , and practice, the opposite and enlightened condition; and when he is firmly established in the better way, so that his knowledge of both conditions is complete, then he realizes in what great darkness he had formerly lived. This knowledge of good and evil by experience constitutes enlightenment.

When a man begins to look, as it were, through the eyes of others, and to measure them by their own standard and not by his, then he ceases from seeing of evil in others, for he knows that every man's perception and standard of good and evil is different; that there is no vice so low but some men regard it as good; no virtue so high but some men regard it as evil; and what a man regards as good that to him is good; what he regards as evil that to him is evil.

Nor will the purified man, who has ceased to see evil in others, have any desire to win men to his own ways or opinions, but will rather help them in their own particular groove, knowing that an enlarged experience only, and not merely change of opinion can lead to higher knowledge and greater blessedness.

It will be found that men see evil in those who differ from them, good in those who agree with them. The man who greatly loves himself and is enamored of his opinions will love all those who agree with him and will dislike all those who disagree with him. "If ye love them that love ye, what reward have ye...? Love your enemies, do good to them that hate you." Egotism and vanity make men blind. Men of opposing religious views hate and persecute each other; men of opposing political views fight and condemn each other. The partisan measures all men by his own standard, and sets up his judgements accordingly. So convinced is he that he is right and others wrong that he at last persuades himself that to inflict cruelty on others is both good and necessary in order to coerce them into his way of thinking and acting, and so bring them to the right— his right— against their own reason and will.

Men hate, condemn, resist and inflict suffering upon each other, not because they are intrinsically evil, not because they are deliberately "wicked" and are doing, in the full light of truth, what they know to be wrong, but because they regard such conduct as necessary and right. All men are intrinsically good, but some are wiser than others, are older in experience than others. I recently heard, in substance, the following conversation between two men whom I will call D- and E-. The third person referred to as X is a prominent politician:—

E. Every man reaps the result of his own thoughts and deeds, and suffers for his own wrong.

D. If that is so, and if no man can escape from the penalty of his evil deeds, what an inferno some of our men in power must be preparing for themselves.

E. Whether a man is in power or not, so long as he lives in ignorance and sin, he will reap sorrow and suffering.

D. Look, for instance, at X-, a man totally evil, given up entirely to selfishness and ambition; surely great torments are reserved for so unprincipled a man.

E. But how do you know he is so evil.

D. By his works, his fruits. When I see a man doing evil I know that he is evil; and I cannot even think of X- but I burn with righteous indignation. I am sometimes inclined to doubt that there is an overruling power for good when I see such a man in a position where he can do so much harm to others.

E. What evil is he committing?

D. His whole policy is evil. He will ruin the country if he remains in power.

E. But while there are large numbers of people who think of X- as you do there are also large numbers, equally intelligent, who look on him as good and able, who admire him for his excellent qualities, and regard his policy as beneficent and making for national progress. He owes his position to these people; are they also evil?

D. They are deceived and mislead. And this only makes— X's evil all the greater, in that he can so successfully employ his talents in deceiving others in order to gain his own selfish ends. I hate the man.

E. May it not be possible that you are deceived?

D. In what way?

E. Hatred is self-deception; love is self-enlightenment. No man can see either himself or others clearly until he ceases from hatred and practices love.

D. That sounds very beautiful, but it is impracticable. When I see a man doing evil to others, and deceiving and misleading them, I must hate him. It is right that I should do so. X- is without a spark of conscience.

E. X- may or may not be all you believe to be, but, even if he is, according to your own words, he should be pitied and not condemned.

D. How so?

E. You say he is without a conscience.

D. Entirely so.

E. Then he is a mental cripple. Do you hate the blind because they cannot see, that dumb because they cannot speak, or the deaf because they cannot hear ? When a captain has lost his rudder or broken his compass do you condemn him because he did not keep his ship off the rocks ? Do you hold him responsible for the loss of life? If a man is totally devoid of conscience he is without the means of moral guidance, and all his selfishness must, perforce, appear to him good and right and proper. X- may appear evil to you, but is he evil to himself? Does he regard his own conduct as evil?

D. Whether he regards himself as evil or not he is evil.

E. If I were to regard you as evil because of your hatred for X- should I be right?

D. No.

E. Why not?

D. Because in such a case hatred is necessary, justifiable and righteous. There is such a thing as righteous anger, righteous hatred.

E. Is there such a thing as righteous selfishness, righteous ambition, righteous evil ? I should be quite wrong in regarding you as evil, because you are doing what you are convinced is right, because you regard your hatred for X- as part of your duty as a man and a citizen; nevertheless, there is a better way than that of hatred, and it is the knowledge of this better way that prevents me from hating X- as you do, because however wrong his conduct might appear to me, it is not wrong to him nor to his supporters; moreover, all men reap as they sow.

D. What, then, is that better way?

E. It is the way of Love; the ceasing to regard others as evil. It is a blessed and peaceful state of heart.

D. Do you mean that there is a state which a man can reach wherein he will grow angry when he sees people doing evil?

E. No, I do not mean that, for while a man regards others as evil he will continue to grow angry with them; but I mean that a man can reach a state of calm insight and spotless love wherein he sees no evil to grow angry with, wherein he understands the various natures of men— how they are prompted to act, and how they reap, as the harvest of their own thoughts and deeds, the tares of sufferings and the corn of bliss. To reach that state is to regard all men with compassion and love.

D. The state that you picture is a very high one- it is, no doubt, a very holy and beautiful one- but it is a state that I should be sorry to reach; and I should pray to be preserved from a state of mind were I could not hate a man like X- with an intense hatred.

Thus by this conversation it will be seen that D- regarded his hatred as good. Even so all men regard that which they do as necessary to be done. The things which men habitually practice those things they believe in. When faith in a thing wholly ceases it ceases to be practiced.

D-'s individual liberty is equal to that of other men, and he has a right to hate another if he so wishes, nor will he abandon his hatred until he discovers, by the sorrow and unrest which it entails, how wrong and foolish and blind it is, and how, by its practice, he is injuring himself.

A great Teacher was once asked by one of His disciples to explain the distinction between good and evil, and holding His hand with the fingers pointing downward, He said: "Where is my hand pointing?"

And the disciple replied: "It is pointing downward."

Then, turning His hand upward, the Teacher asked: "Where now is my hand pointing?"

And the disciple answered: "It is pointing upward."

"That," said the Teacher, "is the distinction between evil and good."

By this simple illustration He indicated that evil is merely wrongly-directed energy, and good rightly-directed energy, and that the so-called evil man becomes good by reversing his conduct.

To understand the true nature of evil by living in the good is to cease to see other men as evil. Blessed is he who, turning from the evil in others exerts himself in the purification of his own heart. He shall one day become of "too pure eyes to behold evil."

Knowing the nature of evil, what does it behoove a man to do? It behooves him to live only in that which is good: therefore if a man condemn me, I will not condemn him in return; if he revile me I will give him kindness; if he slander me I will speak of his good qualities, if he hate me then he greatly needs, and shall receive, my love. With the impatient I will be patient; with the greedy I will be generous, and with the violent and quarrelsome I will be mild and peaceable. Seeing no evil, whom should I hate or who regard as mine enemy?

"Were mankind murderous or jealous upon you, my brother, my sister?
I'm so sorry for you. They are not murderous or jealous upon me;
All has been gentle with me, I keep no account with lamentation;
What have I to do with lamentation?"

He who sees men as evil imagines that behind those acts which are called "wicked" there is a corporate and substantial evil prompting those particular sins but he of stainless vision sees the deeds, themselves as the evil, and knows that there is no evil power, no evil soul or man behind those deeds. The substance of the universe is good; there is no substance of evil. Good alone is permanent; there is no fixed or permanent evil.

As brothers and sisters, born of the same parents and being of one house-hold, love each other through all vicissitudes, see no evil in each other, but overlook all errors, and cling together in the strong bonds of affection-even so the good man sees humanity as one spiritual family, born of the same Father-Mother, being of the same essence and making for the same goal, and he regards all men and women as his brothers and sisters, makes no divisions and distinctions, sees none as evil, but is at peace with all. Happy is he who attains to this blessed state.

Abiding Joy

"Serene will be our days and bright,
And happy will our nature be,
When love is an unerring light,
And joy its own security.—Wordsworth

Abiding joy! Is there such a thing ? Where is it? Who possesses it? Yea; there is such a thing. It is where there is no sin. It is possessed by the pure hearted.

As darkness is a passing shadow, and light is substance that remains, so sorrow is fleeting, but joy abides for ever. No true thing can pass away and become lost; no false thing can remain and be preserved. Sorrow is false, and it cannot live; joy is true, and it cannot die. Joy may become hidden for a time, but it can be always be recovered; sorrow may remain for a period, but it can be transcended and dispersed.

Do not think your sorrow will remain; it will pass away like a cloud. Do not believe that the torments of sin are ever your portion; they will vanish like a hideous nightmare. Awake! arise! Be holy and Joyful!

You are the creator of your own shadows; you desire and then you grieve; renounce and then you all rejoice.

You are not the impotent slave of sorrow; the Never-Ending Gladness awaits your Home-coming. You are not the helpless prisoner of the darkness and dreams of sin; even now the beautiful light of holiness shines upon your sleeping lids, ready to greet your awakening vision.

In the heavy, troubled sleep of sin and self the abiding joy is lost and forgotten; its undying music is no more heard, and the fragrance of its fadeless flowers no longer cheers the heart of the wayfarer.

But when sin and self are abandoned, when the clinging to things for personal pleasure is put away, then the shadows of grief disappear, and the heart is restored to its Imperishable Joy.

Joy comes and fills the self-emptied heart; it abides with the peaceful; its reign is with the pure.

Joy flees from the selfish; it deserts the quarrel-some; it is hidden from the impure.

Joy is as an angel so beautiful and delicate and chaste that she can only dwell with holiness. She cannot remain with selfishness; she is wedded to Love. Every man is truly happy in so far as he is unselfish; he is miserable in so far as he is selfish. All truly good men, and by good men I mean those who have fought victoriously the battle against self, are men of joy. How great is the jubilation of the saint ! No true teacher promises sorrow as the ultimate of life; he promises joy. He points to sorrow, but only as a process which sin has rendered necessary. Where self ends grief passes away. Joy is the companion of righteousness. In the divine life tender compassion fills the place where weeping sorrow sat. During the process of becoming unselfish there are periods of deep sorrow. Purification is necessarily severe. All becoming is painful. Abiding joy is its completion is realized only in the perfection of being, and this is:

"A state
Where all is lovelines, and power and love,
With all sublimest qualities of mind,
... Where all
Enjoy entire dominion o'er themselves.
Acts, feelings, thoughts, conditions, qualities."

Consider how a flower evolves and becomes; at first there is a little germ groping its way in the dark soil towards the upper light; then the plant appears, and leaf is added unto leaf; and finally the perfected flower appears, in the sweet perfume and chaste beauty of which all effort ceases.

So, with human life; at first the blind groping for the light in the dark soil of selfishness and ignorance; then the coming into the light, and the gradual overcoming of selfishness with its accompanying pain and sorrow; and finally the perfect flower of a pure, unselfish life, giving forth, without effort, the perfume of holiness and the beauty of joy.

The good, the pure, are the superlatively happy. However men may argumentatively deny or qualify this, humanity instinctively knows it to be true. Do not men everywhere picture their angels as the most joyful of beings? There are joyful angels in bodies of flesh; we meet them and pass on; and how many of those who come in contact with them are sufficiently pure to see vision within the form— to see the incorruptible angel in its common instrument of clay?

"They needs must grope who cannot see,
The blade before the ear must be;
The outward symbols disappear
From him whose inward sight is clear."

Yes; the pure are the joyful. We look almost in vain for any expressions of sorrow in the words of Jesus. The "Man of Sorrows" is only completed in the Man of Joy.

"I, Buddha, who wept with all my brother's tears,

Whose heart was broken by a whole world's woe,
Laugh and am glad, for there is Liberty!"

In sin, and in the struggle against sin, there is unrest and affliction, but in the perfection of Truth, in the path of Righteousness, there is abiding joy.

"Enter the Path! There spring the healing streams
Quenching all thirst! There bloom th' immortal flowers
Carpeting all the way with joy! There throng
Swiftest and sweetest hours!"

Tribulation lasts only so long as there remains some chaff of self which needs to be removed. The tribulum, or threshing-machine, ceases to work when all the grain is separated from chaff; and when the last impurities are blown away from the soul, tribulation has completed its work, and there is no more need for it; then abiding joy is realized.

All the saints and prophets and saviors of the race have proclaimed with rejoicing the "Gospel" or the "Good News." All men know what Good News is— An impending calamity avoided, a disease cured, friends arrived or returned in safety, difficulties overcome, success in some enterprise assured— but what is the "Good News" of the saintly ones? This: that there is peace for the troubled, healing for the afflicted, gladness for the grief-stricken, victory for the sinful, a homecoming for the wanderer, and joy for the sorrowing and broken-hearted. Not that these beautiful realities shall be in some future world, but they are here and now, that they are known and realized and enjoyed; and are, therefore, proclaimed that all may accept them who will break the galling bonds of self and rise into the glorious liberty of unselfish love.

Seek the highest Good, and as you find it, as you practice it and realize it, you will taste the deepest, sweetest joy. As you succeed in forgetting your own selfish desires in your thoughtfulness for others, in your care for others, in your service for others, just so far and no further will you find and realize the abiding joy in life.

Inside the gateway of unselfishness lies the Elysium of Abiding Joy, and whosoever will may enter in, whosoever doubts let him come and see.

And knowing this— that selfishness leads to misery, unselfishness to joy, not merely for one's self alone— for if this were all how unworthy could be our endeavors!— but for the whole world and because all with whom we live and come in contact will be the happier and truer for our unselfishness; because Humanity is one, and the joy of one is the joy of all— knowing this let us scatter flowers and not thorns in the common ways of life— yea, even in the highway of our enemies let us scatter the blossoms of unselfish love— so shall the pressure in their footprints fill the air with the perfume of holiness and gladden the world with the aroma of joy.

Silentness

"Be still! The crown of life is silentness.
Give thou a quiet hour to each long day,
Too much of time we spend in profitless
And foolish talk. Too little do we say.

"If thou wouldst gather words that shall avail,
Learning a wisdom worthy to express,
Leave for a while thy chat and empty tale-
Study the golden speech of silentness."—A.L.Salmon.

"Be still, my soul.
Rest awhile from the feverish activities in
which you lose yourself.
Be not afraid to be left alone with yourself
for one short hour."—Ernest Crosly.

In the words of a wise man there is great power, but his silence is more powerful still. The greatest men teach us most effectively when they are purposely silent. The silent attitude of the great man noted, perhaps, by one or two of his disciples only is recorded and preserved through the ages; while the obtrusive words of the merely clever talker, heard, perhaps, by thousands, and at once popularized, are neglected and forgotten in, at most, a few generations. The silence of Jesus, when asked by Pilate "What is Truth?" is the impressive, the awful silence of profound wisdom; it is pregnant with humility and reproof, and perpetually rebukes that shallowness that, illustrating the truth that "fools step in where angels fear to tread," would in terms of triteness parcel out the universe, or think to utter the be-all and the end-all of the mystery of things in some textual formula or theological platitude. When, plied with questions about Brahma (God) by the argumentative Brahmans, Buddha remained silent, he taught them better than they knew, and if by his silence he failed to satisfy the foolish he thereby profoundly instructed the wise. Why all this ceaseless talk about God, with its accompaniment of intolerance? Let men practice some measure of kindliness and good-will, and thereby acquaint themselves with the simple rudiments of wisdom. Why all these speculative arguments about the nature of God? Let us first understand somewhat of ourselves. There are no greater marks of folly and moral immaturity than irreverence and presumption; no greater manifestations of wisdom and moral maturity than reverence and humility. Lao-Tze, in his own life, exemplified his teaching that the wise man "teaches without words." Disciples were attracted to him by the power which ever accompanies a wise reserve. Living in comparative obscurity and silence, not courting the ear of men, and never going out to teach, men sought him out and learned of him wisdom.

The silent acts of the Great Ones are beacons to the wise, illuminating their pathway with no uncertain radiance, for he would attain to virtue and wisdom must learn, not only when to speak and what to say, but also when to remain silent and what not to say. The right control of the tongue is the beginning of wisdom; the right control of the mind is the consummation of wisdom. By curbing his tongue a man gains possession of his mind, and to have complete possession of one's mind is to be a Master of Silence.

The fool babbles, gossips, argues, and bandies words. He glories in the fact that he has had the last word and has silenced his opponent. He exults in his own folly, is ever on the defensive, and wastes his energies in unprofitable channels. He is like a gardener who continues to dig and plant in unproductive soil.

The wise man avoids idle words, gossip, vain argument, and self-defense. He is content to appear defeated; rejoices when he is defeated, knowing that, having found and removed another error in himself he has thereby become wiser. Blessed is he who does not strive for the last word!

"Backward I see in my own days where I sweated through
fog with linguists and contenders;
I have no mockings or arguments, I witness and wait "

Silence under provocation is the mark of a cultured and sympathetic soul. The thoughtless and unkind are stirred by every slight provocation, and will lose their mental balance by even the appearance of a personal encroachment. The self-possession of Jesus is not a miracle; it is the flower of culture, the diadem of wisdom. When we read of Jesus that "He answered never a word" and of Buddha that "He remained silent," we get a glimpse of the vast power of silence, of the silent majesty of true greatness.

The silent man is the powerful man. The victim of garrulity is devoid of influence; his spiritual energies are dissipated. Every mechanic knows that before a force can be utilized and definitely directed it must be conserved and stored; and the wise man is a spiritual mechanic who conserves the energies of his mind, holds them in masterful abeyance, ready at any moment to direct them, with effective purpose, to the accomplishment of some necessary work.

The true strength is in silentness. It is well said that "The dog that barks does not bite." The grim and rarely broken silence of the bull-dog is the necessary adjunct to that powerfully concentrated and effectual action for which the animal is known and feared. This, of course, is a lower form of silentness, but the principle is the same. The boaster fails; his mind is diverted from the main purpose; and his energies are frittered away upon self-glorification. His forces are divided between his task and the reward to himself, the greater portion going to feed the lust of reward. He is like an unskillful general who loses the battle through dividing his forces instead of concentrating them upon a point. Or he is like a careless engineer who leaves open the waste-valve of his engine and allows the steam to run down. The modest, silent, earnest man succeeds: freed from vanity, and avoiding the dissipation of self-glorification, all his powers are concentrated upon the successful performance of his task. Even while the other man is talking about his powers he is already about his work, and is so much nearer than the other to its completion. It is a law everywhere and always that energy distributed is subject unto energy conserved. The noisy and boasting Charles will ever be thrown by the quiet and modest Orlando.

It is a law universally applicable that quietness is strength. The business man who succeeds never talks about his plans, methods, and affairs, and should he, turned giddy by success, begin to do this he will then commence to fail. The man of great moral influence never talks about himself and his spiritual victories, for, should he do so, in that moment his moral power and influence would be gone, and, like Samson, he would be shorn of his strength. Success, worldly or spiritual, is the willing servant of strong, steady, silent, unflinching purpose. The most powerful disintegrating forces make no noise. The greatly-overcoming mind works silently.

If you would be strong, useful, and self-reliant learn the value and power of silentness. Do not talk about yourself. The world instinctively knows that the vain talker is weak and empty, and so it leaves him to his own vanity. Do not talk about what you are going to do but do it, and let your finished work speak for itself. Do not waste your forces in criticizing and disparaging the work of others but set about to do your own work thoroughly and well. The worst work with earnestness and sweetness behind it is altogether better than barking at others. While you are disparaging the work of others you are neglecting your own. If others are doing badly help and instruct them by doing better yourself. Neither abuse others nor account their abuse of any weight. When attacked remain silent: in this way you will conquer yourself, and will, without the use of words, teach others.

But the true silence is not merely a silent tongue; it is a silent mind. To merely hold one's tongue, and yet to carry about a disturbed and rankling mind, is no remedy for weakness and no source of power. Silentness, to be powerful, must envelop the whole mind, must permeate every chamber of the heart; it must be the silence of peace. To this broad, deep, abiding silentness a man attains only in the measure that he conquers himself. While passions, temptations, and sorrows disturb, the holier, profounder depths of silence are yet to be sounded. To smart under the words and actions of others means that you are yet weak, uncontrolled, unpurified. So rid your heart of the disturbing influences of vanity and pride and selfishness that no petty spite can reach you, no slander or abuse disturb your serene repose. As the storm rages ineffectually against a well-built house, while its occupant sits composed and happy by his fire side within, so no evil without can disturb or harm him who is well fortified with wisdom; self-governed and silent, he remains at peace within. To this great silence the self-conquered man attains.

"Envy and calumny, and hate and pain, And that unrest which men miscall delight, Can touch him not, nor torture him again "

There is no commoner error amongst men than that of supposing that nothing can be accomplished without much talking and much noise. The busy, shallow talker regards the quiet thinker or silent doer as a man wasted; he thinks silentness means "doing nothing, and that hurrying, bustling, and ceaseless talking means "doing much." He also confounds popularity with power. But the thinker and doer is the real and effectual worker. His work is at the root and core and substance of things, and as Nature silently, yet with hidden and wondrous alchemy, transmutes the rude elements of earth and air into tender leaves, beautiful flowers, delectable fruits,— yea into a myriad forms of beauty— even so does the silent purposeful worker transform the ways of men and the face of the world by the might and magic of his silently-directed energy. He wastes no time and force in tinkering with the ever-changing and artificial surface of things, but goes to the living vital center, and works therefrom and thereon; and in due season, perhaps when his perishable form is withdrawn from the world, the fruits of his obscure but imperishable labors come forth to gladden the world. But the words of the talker perish. The world reaps no harvest from the sowing of sound.

He who conserves his mental forces also conserves his physical forces. The strongly quiet, calm man lives to a greater age, and in the possession of better health than the hurrying, noisy man. Quiet, subdued mental harmony is conducive to physical harmony— health. The followers of George Fox are today the healthiest, longest-lived and most successful portion of the British community, and they live quiet, unostentatious, purposeful lives, avoiding all worldly excitements and unnecessary words. They are a silent people, all their meetings being conducted on the principle that "Silence is Power."

Silentness is powerful because it is the outcome of self-conquest, and the more successfully a man governs himself the more silent he becomes. As he succeeds in living to a purpose and not to the pleasures of self he withdraws himself from the outer discords of the world and reaches to the inward music of peace. Then when he speaks there is purpose and power behind his words, and when he maintains silence there is equal or even greater power therein. He does not utter that which is followed by pain and tears; does not do that which is productive of sorrow and remorse. But, saying and doing those things only which are ripe with thoughtfulness, his conscience is quiet, and all his days are blessed.

Solitude

"Why idly seek from outward things
The answer inward silence brings ?
Why climb the far-off hills with pain,
A nearer view of heaven to gain ?
In lowliest depths of bosky dells
The hermit Contemplation dwells,
Whence, piercing heaven, with screened sight,
He sees at noon the stars, whose light
Shall glorify the coming night."—Whittier

"In the still hour when passion is at rest
Gather up stores of wisdom in thy breast."—Wordsworth.

Man's essential being is inward, invisible, spiritual, and as such it derives its life, strength, from within, not from without. Outward things are channels through which its energies are expended, but for renewal it must fall back on the inward silence.

In so far as man strives to drown this silence in the noisy pleasures of the senses, and endeavors to live in the conflicts of outward things, just so much does he reap the experiences of pain and sorrow, which, becoming at last intolerable, drive him back to the feet of inward Comforter, to the shrine of the peaceful solitude within.

As the body cannot thrive on empty husks, neither can the spirit be sustained on empty pleasures. If not regularly fed the body loses its vitality, and, pained with hunger and thirst, cries out for food and drink. It is the same with the spirit: it must be regularly nourished in solitude on pure and holy thoughts or it will lose its freshness and strength, and will at last cry out in its painful and utter starvation. The yearning of an anguish-stricken soul for light and consolation is the cry of a spirit that is perishing of hunger and thirst. All pain and sorrow is spiritual starvation, and aspiration is the cry for food. It is the Prodigal Son who, perishing of hunger, turns his face longingly towards his Father's home.

The pure life of the spirit cannot be found; but is lost, in the life of the senses. The lower desires are ever clamorous for more, and they afford no rest. The outward world of pleasure, personal contact, and noisy activities is a sphere of wear and tear which necessitates the counterbalancing effect of solitude. Just as the body requires rest for the recuperation of its forces, so the spirit requires solitude for the renewal of its energies. Solitude is as indispensable to man's spiritual welfare as sleep is to his bodily well-being; and pure thought, or meditation, which is evoked in solitude, is to the spirit what activity is to the body. As the body breaks down when deprived of the needful rest and sleep, so do the spirits of men break down, being deprived of the necessary silence and solitude. Man, as a spiritual being, cannot be maintained in strength, uprightness, and peace except he periodically withdraw himself from the outer world of perishable things and reach inwardly towards the abiding and imperishable realities. The consolations of the creeds are derived from the solitude which those creeds enforce. The regular observance of the ceremonies of formal religion, attended, as they are, with concentrated silence and freedom from worldly distractions, compels men to do unconsciously that which they have not yet learned to do consciously— namely, to concentrate the mind periodically on the inward silence, and meditate, though very briefly, on high and holy things. The man who has not learned to control and purify his mind in seasons of chosen solitude, yet whose awakening aspirations grope for something higher and nobler than he yet possesses, feels the necessity for the aid of ceremonial religion; but he who has taken himself in hand with a view to self-conquest, who withdraws into solitude in order to grapple with his lower nature, and masterfully bend his mind in holy directions, requires no further aid from book or priest or Church. The Church does not exist for the pleasure of the saint but for the elevation of the sinner.

In solitude a man gathers strength to meet the difficulties and temptations of life, knowledge to understand and conquer them, and wisdom to transcend them. As a building is preserved and sustained by virtue of the foundation which is hidden and unobserved, so a man is maintained perpetually in strength and peace by virtue of his lonely hour of intense thought which no eye beholds.

It is in solitude only that a man can be truly revealed to himself, that he can come to understand his real nature, with all its powers and possibilities. The voice of the spirit is not heard in the hubbub of the world and amid the clamors of conflicting desires. There can be no spiritual growth without solitude.

There are those who shrink from too close a scrutiny of themselves, who dread too complete a self revelation, and who fear that solitude which would leave them alone with their own thoughts and call up before their mental vision the wraith of their desires. And so they go where the din of pleasure is loudest and where the reproving voice of Truth is drowned. But he who loves Truth, who desires and seeks wisdom, will be much alone. He will seek the fullest, clearest revelation of himself, will avoid the haunts of frivolity and noise, and will go where the sweet, tender voice of the spirit of Truth can speak within him and be heard.

Men go after much company and seek out new excitements, but they are not acquainted with peace; in diverse paths of pleasure they search for happiness but they do not come to rest; through diverse ways of laughter and feverish delirium they wander after gladness and life, but their tears are many and grievous, and they do not escape death.

Drifting upon the ocean of life in search of selfish indulgences men are caught in its storms and only after many tempests and much privation do they fly to the Rock of Refuge which rests in the deep silence of their own being.

While a man is absorbed in outward activities he is giving out his energies and is becoming spiritually weaker, and in order to retain his moral vigor he must resort to solitary meditation. So needful is this that he who neglects it loses or does not attain the right knowledge of life; nor does he comprehend and overcome those most deeply rooted and subtlest of sins which appear like virtues deceiving the elect, and to which all but the truly wise succumb.

"True dignity abides with him alone,
Who, in the silent hour of inward thought,
Can still suspect and still revere himself
In lowliness of heart."

He who lives, without ceasing in outward excitement lives most in disappointments and griefs. Where the sounds of pleasure are greatest heart-emptiness is the keenest and deepest. He, also, whose whole life, even if not one of lust for pleasure, is centered in outward works, who deals only with the changing panorama of visible things, never falling back, in solitude, upon the inner and invisible world of permanent being, such a man does not attain knowledge and wisdom, but remains empty; he cannot aid the world, cannot feed its aspirations, for he has no food to offer it, his spiritual store being empty. But he who courts solitude in order to search for the truth of things, who subdues his senses and makes quite his desires, such a man is daily attaining knowledge and wisdom; he becomes filled with the spirit of truth; he can aid the world, for his spiritual store is full, and is kept well replenished.

While a man is absorbed in the contemplation of inward realities he is receiving knowledge and power; he opens himself, like a flower, to the universal light of Truth, and receives and drinks in its life-imparting rays; he also goes to the eternal foundation of knowledge and quenches his thirst in its inspiring waters. Such a man gains, in one hour of concentrated thought, more essential knowledge than a whole year's reading could impart. Being is infinite and knowledge is illimitable and its source inexhaustible, and he who draws upon the innermost depths of his being drinks from the spring of divine wisdom which can never run dry, and quaffs the waters of immortality.

It is this habitual association with the deep realities of being, this continual drinking in of the Water of Life at its perennial source, that constitutes genius. The resources of genius are inexhaustible because they are drawn from the original and universal source, and for the same reason the works of genius are ever new and fresh. The more a genius gives out the fuller he becomes. With the accomplishment of every work his mind extends and expands, reaches out more vastly, and sees wider and ever wider ranges of power. The genius is inspired. He has bridged the gulf between the finite and infinite. He needs no secondary aids, but draws from that universal spring which is the source of every noble work. The difference between a genius and an ordinary man is this— the one lives in inward realities, the other in outward appearances; the one goes after pleasure, the other after wisdom; the one relies on books, the other relies upon his own being. Book-learning is good when its true place is understood, but is not the source of wisdom. The source of wisdom is in life itself, and is comprehended by effort, practice, and experience. Books give information but they cannot bestow knowledge; they can stimulate but cannot accomplish— you must put forth effort, and achieve for yourself. The man who relies entirely upon books, and does not go to the silent resources within himself, is superficial, and becomes rapidly exhausted. He is uninspired (though he may be extremely clever), for he soon reaches the end of his stock of information, and so becomes void and repetitious. His works lack the sweet spontaneity of life and ever-renewed freshness of inspiration. Such a man has cut himself off from the infinite supply and deals, not with life itself, but with dead or decaying appearances. Information is limited; knowledge is boundless.

The inspiration of genius and greatness is fostered, evolved, and finally completed in solitude. The most ordinary man who conceives a noble purpose, and, summoning all his energies and will, broods upon and ripens his purpose in solitude will accomplish his object and become a genius. The man who renounces the pleasure of the world, who avoids popularity and fame, and who works in obscurity and thinks in solitude for the accomplishment of a lofty ideal for the human race, becomes a seer and a prophet. He who silently sweetens his heart, who attunes his mind to that which is pure and beautiful and good, who in long hours of lonely contemplation strives to reach to the central an eternal heart of things, brings himself in touch with the inaudible harmonies of being, opens himself for the reception of the cosmic song, and becomes at last a singer and a poet.

And so with all genius: it is the child of solitude— a very simple-hearted child— wide-eyed and listening and beautiful, yet withal to the noise-enamored world an incomprehensible mystery, of which it is only now and then vouchsafed a glimpse from beyond the well-guarded Portals of Silence.

"In man's self arise August anticipations; symbols, types Of a dim splendor ever on before In that eternal circle life pursues." St. Paul, the cruel persecutor and blind bigot, after spending three years alone in the desert, comes forth a loving apostle and an inspired seer. Gautama Siddhartha, the man of the world, after six years (in the forest) of lonely struggle with his passions and intense meditation upon the deep mysteries of his nature, becomes Buddha, the enlightened one, the embodiment of calm, serene wisdom, to whom a heart-thirsty world turns to refreshing waters of immortality. Lao-tze, an ordinary citizen filling a worldly office, in his search for knowledge courts solitude, and discovers Tao, the Supreme Reason, by virtue of which he becomes a world-teacher. Jesus, the unlettered carpenter, after many years of solitary communion upon the mountains with the Unfailing Love and Wisdom, comes forth a blessed savior of mankind.

Even after they had attained, and had scaled the lofty heights of divine knowledge these Great Souls were much alone, and retired frequently for brief seasons of solitude. The greatest man will fall from his moral height and lose his influence if he neglects that renewal of power which can only be obtained in solitude. These Masters attained their power by consciously harmonizing their thoughts and lives with the creative energies within themselves, and by transcending individuality and sinking their petty personal will in the Universal Will they became Masters of Creative Thought, and stand as the loftiest instruments for the outworking of cosmic evolution.

And this is not miraculous, it is a matter of law; it is not mysterious except in so far as law is mysterious. Every man becomes a creative master in so far as he subordinate himself to the universally good and true. Every poet, painter, saint, and sage is the mouth-piece of the Eternal. The perfection of the message varies with the measure of individual selflessness. In so far as self intervenes the distinctness of the work and message becomes blurred. Perfect selflessness is the acme of genius, the consummation of power.

Such self-abnegation can only be begun, pursued, and completed in solitude. A man cannot gather together and concentrate his spiritual forces while he is engaged in spending those forces in worldly activities, and although after power is attained the balance of forces can be maintained under all circumstances, even in the midst of the antagonistic throng, such power is only secured after many years of frequent and habitual solitude.

Man's true Home is in the Great Silence— this is the source of all that is real and abiding within him; his present nature, however, is dual, and outer activities are necessary. Neither entire solitude nor entire action is the true life in the world, but that is the true life which gathers, in solitude, strength and wisdom to rightly perform the activities of life; and as a man returns to his home in the evening, weary with labor, for that sweet rest and refreshment which will prepare him for another day's toil, so must he would not break down in the labor of life come away form the noise and toil of the world's great workshop and rest for brief periods in his abiding Home in the Silence. He who does this, spending some portion of each day in sacred and purposeful solitude, will become strong and useful and blessed.

Solitude is for the strong, or for those who are ready to become strong. When a man is becoming great, he becomes solitary. He goes in solitude to seek, and that which he seeks, he finds, for there is a Way to all knowledge, all wisdom, all truth, all power. And the Way is for ever open, but it lies through soundless solitudes and the unexplored silences of man's being.

Standing Alone

"By all means use to be alone,
Salute thyself; see what thy soul doth wear."—George Herbert.

He that has light within his own clear breast
My sit in the center and enjoy bright day."—Milton.

In the life of blessedness self-reliance is of the utmost importance. If there is no peace there must be strength; if there is to be security there must be stability; if there is to be lasting joy there must be no leaning upon things which at any moment may be snatched away for ever.

A man does not commence to truly live until he finds an immovable center within himself on which to stand, by which to regulate his life, and from which to draw his peace. If he trusts to that which fluctuates he also will fluctuate; if he leans upon that which may be withdrawn he will fall and be bruised; if he looks for satisfaction in perishable accumulations he will starve for happiness in the midst of plenty.

Let a man learn to stand alone, looking to no one for support; expecting no favors, craving no personal advantages; not begging, nor complaining, not craving, nor regretting, but relying upon the truth within himself, deriving his satisfaction and comfort from the integrity of his own heart.

If a man can find no peace within himself where shall he find it? If he dreads to be alone with himself what steadfastness shall he find in company? If he can find no joy in communion with his own thoughts how shall he escape misery in his contact with others? The man who has yet found nothing within himself upon which to stand will nowhere find a place of constant rest.

Men everywhere are deluded by the superstition that their happiness rests with other people and with outward things, and, as a result, they live in continual disappointments, regrets, and lamentations. The man who does not look for happiness to any others or to external things, but finds within himself its inexhaustible source, will be self-contained and serene under all circumstances, and will never become the helpless victim of misery and grief. The man who looks to others for support, who measures his happiness by the conduct of others and not by his own, who depends upon their co-operation for his peace of mind— such a man has no spiritual foothold, his mind is tossed hither and thither with the continual changes going on around him, and he lives in that ceaseless ebb and flow of the spirits which is wretchedness and unrest. He is a spiritual cripple, and has yet to learn how to maintain his mental center of gravity, and so go without the aid of crutches.

As a child learns to walk in order to go about from place to place of itself strong and unaided, so should a man learn to stand alone, to judge and think and act for himself, and to choose, in the strength of his own mind, the oath-way which he shall walk.

Without is change and decay and insecurity, within is all surety and blessedness. The soul is sufficient of itself. Where the need is there is the abundant supply. Your eternal dwelling-place is within; go there and take possession of your mansion; there you are a king, elsewhere you are a vassal. Be contended that others shall manage or mismanage their own little kingdom, and see to it that you reign strongly over your own. Your entire well-being and the well-being of the whole world lies there. You have a conscience, follow it; you have a mind, clarify it; you have a judgment, use and improve it; you have a will, employ and strengthen it; you have knowledge, increase it; there is a light within your soul, watch it, tend it, encourage it, shield it from the winds of passion, and help it to burn with a steadier and ever steadier radiance. Leave the world and come back to yourself. Think as a man, act as a man, live as a man. Be rich in yourself, be complete in yourself. Find the abiding center within you and obey it. The earth is maintaining its orbit by its obedience to its center the sun. Obey the center of light that is within you; let others call it darkness if they will. You are responsible for yourself, are accountable to yourself, therefore rely upon yourself. If you fear yourself who will place confidence in you? If you are untrue to yourself where shall you find the sweet satisfaction of Truth?

The great man stands alone in the simple dignity of independent manhood; he pursues his own path fearlessly, and does not apologize or "beg leave." Criticism and applause are no more to him than the dust upon his coat, of which he shakes himself free. He is not guided by the changing opinions of men but guides himself by the light of his own mind. Other men barter away their manhood for messes of flattery or fashion.

Until you can stand alone, looking for guidance neither to spirits nor mortals, gods nor men, but guiding yourself by the light of the truth within you, you are not unfettered and free, not altogether blessed. But do not mistake pride for self-reliance. To attempt to stand upon the crumbling foundation of pride is to be already fallen. No man depends upon others more than the proud man. He drinks in their approbation and resents their censure. He mistakes flattery for sound judgment, and is most easily hurt or pleased by the opinions of others. His happiness is entirely in the hands of others. But the self-reliant man stands, not upon personal pride, but on an abiding law, principle, ideal, reality within himself. Upon this he poises himself, refusing to be swept from his strong foothold either by the waves of passion within or the storms of opinion without, but should he at any time lose his balance he quickly regains himself, and is fully restored. His happiness is entirely in his own hands.

Find your center of balance and succeed in standing alone, and, whatever your work in life may be, you will succeed; you will accomplish what you set your mind upon , for the truly self-reliant man is the invincible man. But though you do not rely upon others, learn of them. Never cease to increase in knowledge, and be ever ready to receive that which is good and useful. You can not have too much humility; the most self-reliant men are the most humble. "No aristocrat, no prince born to the purple, can begin to compare with the self-respect of the saint. Why is he lowly, but that he knows that he can well afford it, resting on the largeness of God in him." Learn of all men, and especially of the masters of Truth, but do not lose your hold upon the truth that the ultimate guidance is in yourself. A master can say : "Here is the path," but he can neither compel you to walk it nor walk it for you. You must put forth your own efforts , must achieve by your own strength, must make his truth your truth by your own unaided exertions; you must implicitly trust yourself.

"This thing is God— to be Man with thy might,
To grow great in the strength of thy spirit,
And live out thy life as the light."

You are to be master of yourself, lord over yourself, not fawning and imitating, but doing your work as a living, vital portion of the universe; giving love but not expecting it; giving sympathy but not craving for it; giving aid but not depending upon it. If men should censure your work, heed them not. It sufficeth that your work be true: rest you in this sufficiency. Do not ask : "Will my work please?" but : "Is it real?" If your work be true the criticism of men cannot touch it; if it be false their disapproval will not slay it quicker than it will die of itself. The words and acts of Truth cannot pass away until their work is fully accomplished; the words and acts of error cannot remain, for they have no work to do. Criticism and resentment are alike superfluous.

Free yourself from the self-imposed tyranny of slavish dependence, and stand alone, not as an isolated unit, but as a sympathetic portion of the whole. Find the Joy that results from well—earned freedom, the peace that flows from wise self-possession, the blessedness that inheres in native strength.

"Honor to him who, self-complete, if lone,
Carves to the grave one pathway all his own,
And heeding naught that men may think or say,
Asks but his soul if doubtful of the way."

Understanding The Simple Laws Of Life

"Watch narrowly
The demonstration of a truth, its birth,
And you trace back the effluence to its spring
And source within us."—Browning.

"More is the treasure of law than gems;
Sweeter than comb its sweetness. Its delights,
Delightful past compare."—The Light of Asia.

Walking those byways which I have so far pointed out, resting in their beauty and drinking in their blessedness, the pilgrim along life's broad highway will in due time come to one wherein his last burden will fall from him, where all his weariness will pass away, where he will drink of light-hearted liberty, and rest in perpetual peace. And this most blessed of spiritual byways, the richest source of strength and comfort, I call The Right Understanding of the Simple Laws of Life. He who comes to it leaves behind him all lack and longing, all doubt and perplexity, all sorrow and uncertainty. He lives in the fulness of satisfaction, in light and knowledge, in gladness and surety. He who comprehends the utter simplicity of life, who obeys its laws and does not step aside into the dark paths and complex mazes of selfish desire, stands where no harm can reach him, where no enemy can lay him low— and he doubts, desires, and sorrows no more. Doubt ends where reality begins; painful desire ceases where the fulness of joy is perpetual and complete; and when the Unfailing and Eternal Good is realized what room is there for sorrow?

Human life when rightly lived is simple with a beautiful simplicity, but it is not rightly lived while it is bound to a complexity of lusts, desires, and wants- these are not the real life but the burning fever and painful disease which originate in an unenlightened condition of mind. The curtailing of one's desires is the beginning of wisdom; their entire mastery its consummation. This is so because life is bounded by law, and ,being inseparable from law, life has no need that is not already supplied. Now lust, or desire, is not need, but a rebellious superfluity, and as such it leads to deprivation and misery. The prodigal son, while in his father's house, not only had all that he required, but was surrounded by a superabundance. Desire was not necessary, because all things were at hand; but when desire entered his heart he "went into a far country," and "began to be in want," and it was only when he became reduced to the utmost extremity of starvation that he turned with longing towards his father's home. This parable is symbolical of the evolution of the individual and the race. Man has come into such a complexity of cravings that he lives in continual discontent, dissatisfaction, want, and pain; and his only cure lies in a return to the Father's Home— that is, to actual living or being as distinguished from desiring. But a man does not do this until he is reduced to the last extremity of spiritual starvation ; he has then reaped the experience of pain and sorrow as the result of desire, and looks back with longing towards the true life of peace and plenty; and so he turns round, and begins his toilsome journey back towards his Home, towards that rich life of simple being wherein is emancipation from the thraldom and fever and hunger of desire, and this longing for the true life, for Truth, Reality, should not be confounded with desire: it is aspiration. Desire is the craving for possession: aspiration is the hunger of the heart for peace. The craving for things leads ever farther and farther from peace, and not only ends in deprivation but is, in itself, a state of perpetual want. Until it comes to an end rest, satisfaction , is an impossibility. The hunger for things can never be satisfied, but the hunger for peace can and the satisfaction of peace is found, is fully possessed, when all selfish desire is abandoned. Then there is fulness of joy, abounding plenty, and rich and complete blessedness. In this supremely blessed state life is comprehended in its perfect symmetry and simplicity and the acme of power and usefulness is attained. Then even the hunger for peace ceases, for peace becomes the normal condition, is fully possessed, constant and never-varying. Men, immersed in desire, ignorantly imagine that the conquest of desire, leads to inactivity, loss of power, and lifelessness. Instead , it leads to highly concentrated activity, to the full employment of power, and to a life so rich, so glorious, and so abundantly blessed as to be incomprehensible to those who hunger for pleasures and possessions. Of this life only can it be said:

> "Here are no sounds of discord— no profane
> Or senseless gossip of unworthy things—
> Only the songs of chisels and of pens,
> Of busy brushes, and ecstatic strains
> Of souls surcharged with music most divine
> Here is no idle sorrow, no poor grief
> For any day or object left behind—
> For time is counted precious, and herein
> Is such complete abandonment of Self
> That tears turn into rainbows, and enhance
> The beauty of the land where all is fair."

When a man is rescued from selfish desire his mind is unencumbered, and he is free to work for humanity. No longer racing after those gratifications which leave him hungry still, all his powers are at his immediate command. Seeking no rewards he can concentrate all his energies upon the faultless completion of his duties, and so accomplish all things and fulfill all righteousness.

The fully enlightened and fully blessed man is not prompted to action be desire but works from knowledge. The man of desire needs the promise of reward to urge him to action. He is as a child working for the possession of a toy. But the man of knowledge, living in the fulness of life and power, can at any moment bring his energies into requisition for the accomplishment of that which is necessary. He is, spiritually, a full-grown man; for him all rewards have ceased; to him all occurrences are good; he lives always in complete satisfaction. Such a man has attained to life, and his delight (and it is a sweet, perpetual, and never-failing delight) is in obedience to the simple demands of exact and never-failing law.

But this life of supreme blessedness is an end, and the pilgrim who is striving towards it, the prodigal returning to it, must travel thither, and employ means to get there. He must pass through the country of his animal desires, disentangling himself from their intricacies, simplifying them, overcoming them; this is the way, and he has no enemies but what spring within himself. At first the way seems hard because, blinded by desire, he does not perceive the simple structure of life, and its laws are hidden from him; but as he becomes more simple in his mind the direct laws of life become unfolded to his spiritual perception, and at once the point is reached where these laws begin to be understood and obeyed; then the way becomes plain and easy; there is no more uncertainty and darkness, but all is seen in the clear light of knowledge.

It will help to accelerate the progress of the searcher for the true and blessed life if we now turn to a consideration of some of these simple laws which are rigidly mathematical in their operations.

"The elementary laws never apologize."

All life is one, though it has a diversity of manifestations; all law is one, but it is applicable and operative in a variety of ways. There is not one law for matter and another for mind, not one for the material and visible and another for the spiritual and invisible; there is the same law throughout. There is not one kind of logic for the world and another for the spirit, but the same logic is applicable to both. Men faithfully, and with unerring worldly wisdom, observe certain laws or rules of action in material things, knowing that to ignore or disobey them would be great folly on their part, ending in disaster for themselves and confusion for society and the state, but they err in supposing and believing that the same rules do not apply in spiritual things, and thereby suffer for their ignorance and disobedience.

It is a law in worldly things that a man shall support himself, that he shall earn his living, and that "He that will not work, neither shall he eat." Men observe this law, recognizing its justice and goodness, and so earn the necessary material sustenance. But in spiritual things men, broadly speaking, deny and ignore the operation of this law. They think that, while it is absolutely just that a man should earn his material bread, and that the man who shirks this law should wander in rags ands want, it is right that they should beg for their spiritual bread, think it to be just that they should receive all spiritual blessings without either deserving or attempting to earn them. The result is that most men wander in spiritual beggary and want— that is, in suffering and sorrow— deprived of spiritual sustenance, of joy and knowledge and peace.

If you are in need of any worldly thing— food, clothing, furniture, or other necessary— you do not beg of the storekeeper to give it to you; you ask the price of it, pay for it with your money, and then it becomes your own. You recognize the perfect justice in giving an equivalent for what you receive, and would not wish it to be otherwise. The same just law prevails in spiritual things. If you are in need of any spiritual thing— joy, assurance, peace, or what else soever— you can only come into full possession of it by giving an equivalent; you must pay the price for it. As you must give a portion of your material substance for a worldly thing so you must give a portion of your immaterial substance for a spiritual thing. You must yield up some passion or lust or vanity or indulgence before the spiritual possession can be yours. The miser who clings to his money and will not give up any of it because of the pleasure which its possession affords him cannot have any of the material comforts of life. He lives in continual want and discomfort in spite of all his wealth. The man who will not give up his passions, who clings to anger, unkindness, sensuality, pride, vanity, self-indulgence, for the momentary pleasure which their gratification affords him is a spiritual miser; he cannot have any spiritual comforts, and suffers continual spiritual want and uneasiness in spite of the wealth of worldly pleasures which he fondly hugs and refuses to give up.

The man who is wise in worldly things neither begs nor steals, but labors and purchases, and the world honors him for his uprightness. The man who is wise in spiritual things neither begs nor steals, but labors in his own inner world, and purchases his spiritual possessions. Him the whole universe honors for his righteousness.

It is another law in worldly things that a man who engages himself to another in any form of employment shall be content with the wages upon which he agreed. If at the end of his week's work, and on receiving his wages, he were to ask his employer for a larger sum, pleading that, though he could not justly claim it and did not really deserve it, yet he expected it, he would not only not receive the larger sum but would, doubtless, be discharged from his post. Yet in spiritual things men do not think it to be either foolish or selfish to ask for those blessings— spiritual wages— upon which they never agreed, for which they never labored, and which they do not deserve. Every man gets from the law of the universe that upon which he agrees and for which he works— no more, no less; and he is continually entering into agreements with the Supreme Law— the Master of the universe. For every thought and act which he gives he receives its just equivalent; for all work done in the form of deeds he receives the wages due to him. Knowing this, the enlightened man is always content, always satisfied, and in perfect peace, knowing that whatever he receives (be it that men call misfortune or good fortune) he has earned. The Great Law never cheats any man of his just due, but it says to the railer and the complainer "Friend didst thou not agree with me for a penny a day?"

Again, if a man would grow rich in worldly goods he must economize, and husband his financial resources until he has accumulated sufficient capital to invest in some branch of industry; then he must judiciously invest his little store of capital, neither holding it too tightly nor letting it go carelessly. He thus increases both in worldly wisdom and worldly riches. The idle spendthrift cannot grow rich; he is wasteful and riotous. He who would grow rich in spiritual things must also economize, and husband his mental resources. He must curb his tongue and his impulses, not wasting his energy in idle gossip, vain argument, or excesses of temper. In this way he will accumulate a little store of wisdom which is his spiritual capital, and this he must send out into the world for the good of others, and the more he uses it the richer will he become. Thus does a man increase in both heavenly wisdom and heavenly riches. The man who follows his blind impulses and desires and does not control and govern his mind is a spiritual spendthrift. He can never become rich in divine things.

It is a physical law that if we would reach the summit of a mountain we must climb thither. The path must be sought and then carefully followed, and the climber must not give up and go back because of the labor involved and the difficulties to be overcome, nor on account of aching climbs, otherwise his object cannot be accomplished. And this law is also spiritual. He who would reach the high altitudes of moral or intellectual grandeur must climb thither by his own efforts. He must seek out the pathway and then assiduously follow it, not giving up and turning back, but surmounting all difficulties, and enduring for a time trials, temptations, and heartaches, and at last he will stand upon the glorious summit of moral perfection, the world of passion, temptation, and sorrow beneath his feet, and the boundless heavens of dignity stretching vast and silent above his head.

If a man would reach a distant city, or any place of destination, he must travel thither. There is no law by which he can be instantly transported there. He can only get there by putting forth the necessary exertion. If he walks he will put forth great exertion, but it will cost him nothing in money; if he drives or takes train, there will be less actual labor, but he must pay in money for which he has labored. To reach any place requires labor; this cannot be avoided; it is law. Equally so spiritually. He who would reach any spiritual destination, such as purity, compassion, wisdom, or peace, must travel thither, and must labor to get there. There is no law by which he can suddenly be transported to any of these beautiful spiritual cities. He must find the most direct route and then put forth the necessary labor, and at last he will come to the end of his journey.

These are but a few of the many laws, or manifestations of the One Great Law, which are to be understood, applied and obeyed before the full manhood and maturity of spiritual life and blessedness can be attained. There is no worldly or physical law which is not operative, with equal exactness, in the spiritual realm— that is, the inner and invisible world of man's beings. Just as physical things are the shadows and types, of spiritual realities so worldly wisdom is the reflected image of Divine Wisdom. All those simple operations of human life in worldly things which men never question, but follow and obey implicitly because of their obvious plainness and exactness, obtain in spiritual things with the same unerring accuracy; and when this is understood, and these laws are as implicitly obeyed in spiritual as in worldly matters, then has a man reached the firm standing-ground of exact knowledge; his sorrows are at an end, and he can doubt no more.

Life is uninvolved, uncompromising justice; its operations are simple, invincible logic. Law reigns for ever, and the heart of law is love. Favoritism and caprice are the reverse of both law and love. The universe has no favorites; it is supremely just, and gives to every man his rightful earnings. All is good because all his according to law, and because all his according to law, man can find the right way in life, and, having found it, can rejoice and be glad. The Father of Jesus is the Unfailing Good which is embodied in the law of things. "No evil can happen to a good man either in life or death." Jesus recognized the good in his own fate, and exonerated all his persecutors from blame. "No man," he declared, "taketh my life from me, but I lay it down of myself." That is, he himself had brought about his own end.

He who has, by simplifying his life and purifying his mind, arrived at an understanding of the beautiful simplicity of being, perceives the unvarying operation of law in all things, and knows the result of all his thoughts and deeds upon himself and the world— knows what effects are bound up with the mental causes which he sets in motion. He then thinks and does only those thoughts and deeds that are blessed in their inception, blessed in their growth, and blessed in their completion. Humbly accepting the lawful results of all the deeds done when in a state of ignorance, he neither complains nor fears nor questions, but is at rest in obedience, is perfectly blessed in his knowledge of the Good Law.

"The tissue of our life to be
We weave with colors all our own,
And in the field of Destiny
We reap as we have sown.

"And if we reap as we have sown,
And take the dole we deal,
The law of pain is love alone,
The wounding is to heal."

Happy Endings

"Such is the Law which moves to righteousness,
Which none at last can turn aside or stay;
The heart of it is Love, the end of it
Is peace and consummation sweet. Obey."—The Light of Asia.

"So, haply, when thy task shall end,
The wrong shall lose itself in right,
And all thy week-day Sabbaths blend
With the long Sabbath of the Light!"—Whittier

Life has many happy endings, because it has much that is noble and pure and beautiful. Although there is much sin and ignorance in the world, many tears, and much pain and sorrow, there is also much purity and knowledge, many smiles, and much healing and gladness. No pure thought, no unselfish deed can fall short of its felicitous result, and every such result is a happy consummation.

A pleasant home is a happy ending; a successful life is a happy ending; a task well and faithfully done is a happy ending; to be surrounded by kind friends is a happy ending. A quarrel put away, grudges wiped out, unkind words confessed and forgiven, friend restored to friend— all these are happy endings. To find that which one has long and tediously sought; to be restored from tears to gladness; to awaken in the bright sunlight out of the painful nightmare of sin, to strike, after much searching, the Heavenly Way in life— these are, indeed, blessed consummations.

He who looks for, finds, and enters the byways which I have indicated will come to this one without seeking it, for his whole life will be filled with happy endings. He who begins right and continues right does not need to desire and search for felicitous results; they are already at hand; they follow as consequences; they are the certainties, the realities of life.

There are happy endings which belong solely to the material world; these are transient, and they pass away. These are happy endings which belong to the spiritual world; these are eternal, and they do not pass away. Sweet are companionships, pleasures, and material comforts, but they change and fade away. Sweeter still are Purity, Wisdom, and the knowledge of Truth, and these never change nor fade away. Wherever a man goes in this world he can take his worldly possessions with him; but soon he must part company with them, and if he stands upon these alone, deriving all his happiness from them, he will come to a spiritual ending of great emptiness and want. But he has attained to the possession of spiritual things can never be deprived of his source of happiness: he will never have to part company with it, and wherever he goes in the whole universe he will carry his possession with him. His spiritual end will be the fulness of joy.

Happy in the Eternal Happiness is he who has come to that Life from which the thought of self is abolished. Already, even now and in this life, he has entered the Kingdom of Heaven, Nirvana, Paradise, the New Jerusalem, the Olympus of Jupiter, the Valhalla of the Gods. He knows the Final Unity of Life, the Great Reality of which these fleeting and changing names are but feeble utterances. He is at rest on the bosom of the Infinite.

Sweet is the rest and deep the bliss of him who has freed his heart from its lusts and hatreds and dark desires; and he who, without any shadow of bitterness or selfishness resting upon him, and looking out upon the world with boundless compassion and love, can breathe, in his inmost heart, the blessing:

Peace unto all living things,

making no exceptions or distinctions— such a man has reached that happy ending which can never be taken away, for this is the perfection of life, the fulness of peace, the consummation of perfect blessedness.

The Path of Prosperity

Forward

I looked around upon the world, and saw that it was shadowed by sorrow and scorched by the fierce fires of suffering. And I looked for the cause. I looked around, but could not find it; I looked in books, but could not find it; I looked within, and found there both the cause and the self-made nature of that cause. I looked again, and deeper, and found the remedy.

I found one Law, the Law of Love; one Life, the Life of adjustment to that Law; one Truth, the truth of a conquered mind and a quiet and obedient heart. And I dreamed of writing a book which should help men and women, whether rich or poor, learned or unlearned, worldly or unworldly, to find within themselves the source of all success, all happiness, all accomplishment, all truth. And the dream remained with me, and at last became substantial; and now I send it forth into the world on its mission of healing and blessedness, knowing that it cannot fail to reach the homes and hearts of those who are waiting and ready to receive it. —James Allen

The Lesson of Evil

Unrest and pain and sorrow are the shadows of life. There is no heart in all the world that has not felt the sting of pain, no mind has not been tossed upon the dark waters of trouble, no eye that has not wept the hot blinding tears of unspeakable anguish.

There is no household where the Great Destroyers, disease and death, have not entered, severing heart from heart, and casting over all the dark pall of sorrow. In the strong, and apparently indestructible meshes of evil all are more or less fast caught, and pain, unhappiness, and misfortune wait upon mankind.

With the object of escaping, or in some way mitigating this overshadowing gloom, men and women rush blindly into innumerable devices, pathways by which they fondly hope to enter into a happiness which will not pass away.

Such are the drunkard and the harlot, who revel in sensual excitements; such is the exclusive aesthete, who shuts himself out from the sorrows of the world, and surrounds himself with enervating luxuries; such is he who thirsts for wealth or fame, and subordinates all things to the achievement of that object; and such are they who seek consolation in the performance of religious rites.

And to all the happiness sought seems to come, and the soul, for a time, is lulled into a sweet security, and an intoxicating forgetfulness of the existence of evil; but the day of disease comes at last, or some great sorrow, temptation, or misfortune breaks suddenly in on the unfortified soul, and the fabric of its fancied happiness is torn to shreds.

So over the head of every personal joy hangs the Damocletian sword of pain, ready, at any moment, to fall and crush the soul of him who is unprotected by knowledge.

The child cries to be a man or woman; the man and woman sigh for the lost felicity of childhood. The poor man chafes under the chains of poverty by which he is bound, and the rich man often lives in fear of poverty, or scours the world in search of an elusive shadow he calls happiness.

Sometimes the soul feels that it has found a secure peace and happiness in adopting a certain religion, in embracing an intellectual philosophy, or in building up an intellectual or artistic ideal; but some overpowering temptation proves the religion to be inadequate or insufficient; the theoretical philosophy is found to be a useless prop; or in a moment, the idealistic statue upon which the devotee has for years been laboring, is shattered into fragments at his feet.

Is there, then, no way of escape from pain and sorrow? Are there no means by which bonds of evil may be broken? Is permanent happiness, secure prosperity, and abiding peace a foolish dream?

No, there is a way, and I speak it with gladness, by which evil can be slain for ever; there is a process by which disease, poverty, or any adverse condition or circumstance can be put on one side never to return; there is a method by which a permanent prosperity can be secured, free from all fear of the return of adversity, and there is a practice by which unbroken and unending peace and bliss can be partaken of and realized.

And the beginning of the way which leads to this glorious realization is the acquirement of a right understanding of the nature of evil.

It is not sufficient to deny or ignore evil; it must be understood. It is not enough to pray to God to remove the evil; you must find out why it is there, and what lesson it has for you.

It is of no avail to fret and fume and chafe at the chains which bind you; you must know why and how you are bound. Therefore, reader, you must get outside yourself, and must begin to examine and understand yourself.

You must cease to be a disobedient child in the school of experience and must begin to learn, with humility and patience, the lessons that are set for your edification and ultimate perfection; for evil, when rightly understood, is found to be, not an unlimited power or principle in the universe, but a passing phase of human experience, and it therefore becomes a teacher to those who are willing to learn.

Evil is not an abstract some thing outside yourself; it is an experience in your own heart, and by patiently examining and rectifying your heart you will be gradually led into the discovery of the origin and nature of evil, which will necessarily be followed by its complete eradication.

All evil is corrective and remedial, and is therefore not permanent. It is rooted in ignorance, ignorance of the true nature and relation of things, and so long as we remain in that state of ignorance, we remain subject to evil.

There is no evil in the universe which is not the result of ignorance, and which would not, if we were ready and willing to learn its lesson, lead us to higher wisdom, and then vanish away. But men remain in evil, and it does not pass away because men are not willing or prepared to learn the lesson which it came to teach them.

I knew a child who, every night when its mother took it to bed, cried to be allowed to play with the candle; and one night, when the mother was off guard for a moment, the child took hold of the candle; the inevitable result followed, and the child never wished to play with the candle again.

By its one foolish act it learned, and learned perfectly the lesson of obedience, and entered into the knowledge that fire burns. And, this incident is a complete illustration of the nature, meaning, and ultimate result of all sin and evil.

As the child suffered through its own ignorance of the real nature of fire, so older children suffer through their ignorance of the real nature of the things which they weep for and strive after, and which harm them when they are secured; the only difference being that in the latter case the ignorance and evil are more deeply rooted and obscure.

Evil has always been symbolized by darkness, and Good by light, and hidden within the symbol is contained the perfect interpretation, the reality; for, just as light always floods the universe, and darkness is only a mere speck or shadow cast by a small body intercepting a few rays of the illimitable light, so the Light of the Supreme Good is the positive and life-giving power which floods the universe, and evil the insignificant shadow cast by the self that intercepts and shuts off the illuminating rays which strive for entrance.

When night folds the world in its black impenetrable mantle, no matter how dense the darkness, it covers but the small space of half our little planet, while the whole universe is ablaze with living light, and every soul knows that it will awake in the light in the morning.

Know, then, that when the dark night of sorrow, pain, or misfortune settles down upon your soul, and you stumble along with weary and uncertain steps, that you are merely intercepting your own personal desires between yourself and the boundless light of joy and bliss, and the dark shadow that covers you is cast by none and nothing but yourself.

And just as the darkness without is but a negative shadow, an unreality which comes from nowhere, goes to nowhere, and has no abiding dwelling place, so the darkness within is equally a negative shadow passing over the evolving and Light-born soul.

"But," I fancy I hear someone say, "why pass through the darkness of evil at all?" Because, by ignorance, you have chosen to do so, and because, by doing so, you may understand both good and evil, and may the more appreciate the light by having passed through the darkness.

As evil is the direct outcome of ignorance, so, when the lessons of evil are fully learned, ignorance passes away, and wisdom takes its place. But as a disobedient child refuses to learn its lessons at school, so it is possible to refuse to learn the lessons of experience, and thus to remain in continual darkness, and to suffer continually recurring punishments in the form of disease, disappointment, and sorrow.

He, therefore, who would shake himself free of the evil which encompasses him, must be willing and ready to learn, and must be prepared to undergo that disciplinary process without which no grain of wisdom or abiding happiness and peace can be secured.

A man may shut himself up in a dark room, and deny that the light exists, but it is everywhere without, and darkness exists only in his own little room.

So you may shut out the light of Truth, or you may begin to pull down the walls of prejudice, self-seeking and error which you have built around yourself, and so let in the glorious and omnipresent Light.

By earnest self-examination strive to realize, and not merely hold as a theory, that evil is a passing phase, a self-created shadow; that all your pains, sorrows and misfortunes have come to you by a process of undeviating and absolutely perfect law; have come to you because you deserve and require them, and that by first enduring, and then understanding them, you may be made stronger, wiser, nobler.

When you have fully entered into this realization, you will be in a position to could your own circumstances, to transmute all evil into good and to weave, with a master hand, the fabric of your destiny.

What of the night, O Watchman! see'st thou yet
The glimmering dawn upon the mountain heights,
The golden Herald of the Light of lights,
Are his fair feet upon the hilltops set?

Cometh he yet to chase away the gloom,
And with it all the demons of the Night?
Strike yet his darting rays upon thy sight?
Hear'st thou his voice, the sound of error's doom?

The Morning cometh, lover of the Light;
Even now He gilds with gold the mountain's brow,
Dimly I see the path whereon even now
His shining feet are set toward the Night.

Darkness shall pass away, and all the things
That love the darkness, and that hate the Light
Shall disappear for ever with the Night:
Rejoice! for thus the speeding Herald sings.

The World a Reflex of Mental States

What you are, so is your world. Everything in the universe is resolved into your own inward experience. It matters little what is without, for it is all a reflection of your own state of consciousness.

It matters everything what you are within, for everything without will be mirrored and colored accordingly.

All that you positively know is contained in your own experience; all that you ever will know must pass through the gateway of experience, and so become part of yourself.

Your own thoughts, desires, and aspirations comprise your world, and, to you, all that there is in the universe of beauty and joy and bliss, or of ugliness and sorrow and pain, is contained within yourself.

By your own thoughts you make or mar your life, your world, your universe, As you build within by the power of thought, so will your outward life and circumstances shape themselves accordingly.

'Whatsoever you harbor in the inmost chambers of your heart will, sooner or later by the inevitable law of reaction, shape itself in your outward life.

The soul that is impure, sordid and selfish, is gravitating with unerring precision toward misfortune and catastrophe; the soul that is pure, unselfish, and noble is gravitating with equal precision toward happiness and prosperity.

Every soul attracts its own, and nothing can possibly come to it that does not belong to it. To realize this is to recognize the universality of Divine Law.

The incidents of every human life, which both make and mar, are drawn to it by the quality and power of its own inner thought-life. Every soul is a complex combination of gathered experiences and thoughts, and the body is but an improvised vehicle for its manifestation.

What, therefore, your thoughts are, that is your real self; and the world around, both animate and inanimate, wears the aspect with which your thoughts clothe it. "All that we are is the result of what we have thought.

It is founded on our thoughts; it is made up of our thoughts." Thus said Buddha, and it therefore follows that if a man is happy, it is because he dwells in happy thoughts; if miserable, because he dwells in despondent and debilitating thoughts,

Whether one be fearful or fearless, foolish or wise, troubled or serene, within that soul lies the cause of its own state or states, and never without. And now I seem to hear a chorus of voices exclaim, "But do you really mean to say that outward circumstances do not affect our minds?" I do not say that, but I say this, and know it to be an infallible truth, that circumstances can only affect you in so far as you allow them to do so.

You are swayed by circumstances because you have not a right understanding of the nature, use, and power of thought.

You believe (and upon this little word belief hang all our sorrows and joys) that outward things have the power to make or mar your life; by so doing you submit to those outward things, confess that you are their slave, and they your unconditional master; by so doing, you invest them with a power which they do not, of themselves, possess, and you succumb, in reality, not to the mere circumstances, but to the gloom or gladness, the fear or hope, the strength or weakness, which your thought-sphere has thrown around them.

I knew two men who, at an early age, lost the hard-earned savings of years. One was very deeply troubled, and gave way to chagrin, worry, and despondency.

The other, on reading in his morning paper that the bank in which his money was deposited had hopelessly failed, and that he had lost all, quietly and firmly remarked, "Well, it's gone, and trouble and worry won't bring it back, but hard work will."

He went to work with renewed vigor, and rapidly became prosperous, while the former man, continuing to mourn the loss of his money, and to grumble at his "bad luck," remained the sport and tool of adverse circumstances, in reality of his own weak and slavish thoughts.

The loss of money was a curse to the one because he clothed the event with dark and dreary thoughts; it was a blessing to the other, because he threw around it thoughts of strength, of hope, and renewed endeavor.

If circumstances had the power to bless or harm, they would bless and harm all men alike, but the fact that the same circumstances will be alike good and bad to different souls proves that the good or bad is not in the circumstance, but only in the mind of him that encounters it.

When you begin to realize this you will begin to control your thoughts, to regulate and discipline your mind, and to rebuild the inward temple of your soul, eliminating all useless and superfluous material, and incorporating into your being thoughts alone of joy and serenity, of strength and life, of compassion and love, of beauty and immortality; and as you do this you will become joyful and serene, strong and healthy, compassionate and loving, and beautiful with the beauty of immortality.

And as we clothe events with the drapery of our own thoughts, so likewise do we clothe the objects of the visible world around us, and where one sees harmony and beauty, another sees revolting ugliness.

An enthusiastic naturalist was one day roaming the country lanes in pursuit of his hobby, and during his rambles came upon a pool of brackish water near a farmyard.

As he proceeded to fill a small bottle with the water for the purpose of examination under the microscope, he dilated, with more enthusiasm than discretion, to an uncultivated son of the plough who stood close by, upon the hidden and innumerable wonders contained in the pool, and concluded by saying, "Yes, my friend, within this pool is contained a hundred, nay, a million universes, had we but the sense or the instrument by which we could apprehend them." And the unsophisticated one ponderously remarked, " I know the water be full o' tadpoles, but they be easy to catch."

Where the naturalist, his mind stored with the knowledge of natural facts, saw beauty, harmony, and hidden glory, the mind unenlightened upon those things saw only an offensive mud-puddle.

The wild flower which the casual wayfarer thoughtlessly tramples upon is, to the spiritual eye of the poet, an angelic messenger from the invisible.

To the many, the ocean is but a dreary expanse of water on which ships sail and are sometimes wrecked; to the soul of the musician it is a living thing, and he hears, in all its changing moods, divine harmonies.

Where the ordinary mind sees disaster and confusion, the mind of the philosopher sees the most perfect sequence of cause and effect, and where the materialist sees nothing but endless death, the mystic sees pulsating and eternal life.

And as we clothe both events and objects with our own thoughts, so likewise do we clothe the souls of others in the garments of our thoughts.

The suspicious believe everybody to be suspicious; the Liar feels secure in the thought that he is not so foolish as to believe that there is such a phenomenon as a strictly truthful person; the envious see envy in every soul; the miser thinks everybody is eager to get his money; he who has subordinated conscience in the making of his wealth, sleeps with a revolver under his pillow, wrapped in the delusion that the world is full of conscienceless people who are eager to rob him, and the abandoned sensualist looks upon the saint as a hypocrite.

On the other hand, those who dwell in loving thoughts, see that in all which calls forth their love and sympathy; the trusting and honest are not troubled by suspicions; the good-natured and charitable who rejoice at the good fortune of others, scarcely know what envy means; and he who has realized the Divine within himself recognizes it in all beings, even in the beasts.

And men and women are confirmed in their mental outlook because of the fact that, by the law of cause and effect, they attract to themselves that which they send forth, and so come in contact with people similar to themselves. The old adage, "Birds of a feather flock together," has a deeper significance than is generally attached to it, for in the thought-world as in the world of matter, each clings to its kind.

>   Do you wish for kindness? Be kind.
>   Do you ask for truth? Be true.
>   What you give of yourself you find;
>   Your world is a reflex of you.

If you are one of those who are praying for, and looking forward to, a happier world beyond the grave, here is a message of gladness for you, you may enter into and realize that happy world now; it fills the whole universe, and it is within you, waiting for you to find, acknowledge, and possess. Said one who knew the inner laws of Being,"
When men shall say I go here, or I go there, go not after them; the kingdom of God is within you."
What you have to do is to believe this, simply believe it with a mind unshadowed by doubt, and then meditate upon it till you understand it.
You will then begin to purify and to build your inner world, and as you proceed, passing from revelation to revelation, from realization to realization, you will discover the utter powerlessness of outward things beside the magic potency of a self-governed soul.

>   If thou would'st right the world,
>   And banish all its evils and its woes,
>   Make its wild places bloom,
>   And its drear deserts blossom as the rose,—
>   Then right thyself.
>
>   If thou would'st turn the world
>   From its long, lone captivity in sin,
>   Restore all broken hearts,
>   Slay grief, and let sweet consolation in,—
>   Turn thou thyself.
>
>   If thou would'st cure the world
>   Of its long sickness, end its grief and pain;
>   Bring in all-healing joy,
>   And give to the afflicted rest again,—
>   Then cure thyself.
>
>   If thou would'st wake the world
>   Out of its dream of death and dark'ning strife,
>   Bring it to Love and Peace,
>   And Light and brightness of immortal Life,—

Wake thou thyself.

The Way out of Undesirable Conditions

Having seen and realized that evil is but a passing shadow thrown, by the intercepting self, across the transcendent Form of the Eternal Good, and that the world is a mirror in which each sees a reflection of himself, we now ascend, by firm and easy steps, to that plane of perception whereon is seen and realized the Vision of the Law.

With this realization comes the knowledge that everything is included in a ceaseless interaction of cause and effect, and that nothing can possibly be divorced from law.

From the most trivial thought, word, or act of man, up to the groupings of the celestial bodies, law reigns supreme. No arbitrary condition can, even for one moment, exist, for such a condition would be a denial and an annihilation of law.

Every condition of life is, therefore, bound up in an orderly and harmonious sequence, and the secret and cause of every condition is contained within itself, The law, "Whatsoever a man sows that shall he also reap," is inscribed in flaming letters upon the portal of Eternity, and none can deny it, none can cheat it, none can escape it.

He who puts his hand in the fire must suffer the burning until such time as it has worked itself out, and neither curses nor prayers can avail to alter it.

And precisely the same law governs the realm of mind. Hatred, anger, jealousy, envy, lust, covetousness, all these are fires which bum, and whoever even so much as touches them must suffer the torments of burning.

All these conditions of mind are rightly called "evil," for they are the efforts of the soul to subvert, in its ignorance, the law, an they, therefore, lead to chaos and confusion within, and are sooner or later actualized in the outward circumstances as disease, failure, and misfortune, coupled with grief, pain, and despair.

Whereas love, gentleness, good-will, purity, are cooling airs which breathe peace upon the soul that woes them, and, being in harmony with the Eternal Law, they become actualized in the form of health, peaceful surroundings, and undeviating success and good fortune.

A thorough understanding of this Great Law which permeates the universe leads to the acquirement of that state of mind known as obedience.

To know that justice, harmony, and love are supreme in the universe is likewise to know that all adverse and painful conditions are the result of our own disobedience to that Law.

Such knowledge leads to strength and power, and it is upon such knowledge alone that a true life and an enduring success and happiness can be built.

To be patient under all circumstances, and to accept all conditions as necessary factors in your training, is to rise superior to all painful conditions, and to overcome them with an overcoming which is sure, and which leaves no fear of their return, for by the power of obedience to law they are utterly slain.

Such an obedient one is working in harmony with the law, has in fact, identified himself with the law, and whatsoever he conquers he conquers for ever, whatsoever he builds can never be destroyed.

The cause of all power, as of all weakness, is within; the secret of all happiness as of all misery is likewise within.

There is no progress apart from unfoldment within, and no sure foothold of prosperity or peace except by orderly advancement in knowledge.

You say you are chained by circumstances; you cry out for better opportunities, for a wider scope, for improved physical conditions, and perhaps you inwardly curse the fate that binds you hand and foot.

It is for you that I write; it is to you that I speak. Listen, and let my words burn themselves into your heart, for that which I say to you is truth:

You may bring about that improved condition in your outward life which you desire, if you will unswervingly resolve to improve your inner life.

I know this pathway looks barren at its commencement (truth always does, it is only error and delusion which are at first inviting and fascinating,) but if you undertake to walk it; if you perseveringly discipline your mind, eradicating your weaknesses, and allowing your soul-forces and spiritual powers to unfold themselves, you will be astonished at the magical changes which will be brought about in your outward life.

As you proceed, golden opportunities will be strewn across your path, and the power and judgment to properly utilize them will spring up within you. Genial friends will come unbidden to you; sympathetic souls will be drawn to you as the needle is to the magnet; and books and all outward aids that you require will come to you unsought.

Perhaps the chains of poverty hang heavily upon you, and you are friendless and alone, and you long with an intense longing that your load may be lightened; but the load continues, and you seem to be enveloped in an ever-increasing darkness.

Perhaps you complain, you bewail your lot; you blame your birth, your parents, your employer, or the unjust Powers who have bestowed upon you so undeservedly poverty and hardship, and upon another affluence and ease.

Cease your complaining and fretting; none of these things which you blame are the cause of your poverty; the cause is within yourself, and where the cause is, there is the remedy.

The very fact that you are a complainer, shows that you deserve your lot; shows that you lack that faith which is the ground of all effort and progress.

There is no room for a complainer in a universe of law, and worry is soul-suicide. By your very attitude of mind you are strengthening the chains which bind you, and are drawing about you the darkness by which you are enveloped, Alter your outlook upon life, and your outward life will alter.

Build yourself up in the faith and knowledge, and make yourself worthy of better surroundings and wider opportunities. Be sure, first of all, that you are making the best of what you have.

Do not delude yourself into supposing that you can step into greater advantages whilst overlooking smaller ones, for if you could, the advantage would be impermanent and you would quickly fall back again in order to learn the lesson which you had neglected.

As the child at school must master one standard before passing onto the next, so, before you can have that greater good which you so desire, must you faithfully employ that which you already possess.

The parable of the talents is a beautiful story illustrative of this truth, for does it not plainly show that if we misuse, neglect, or degrade that which we possess, be it ever so mean and insignificant, even that little will be taken from us, for, by our conduct we show that we are unworthy of it.

Perhaps you are living in a small cottage, and are surrounded by unhealthy and vicious influences.

You desire a larger and more sanitary residence. Then you must fit yourself for such a residence by first of all making your cottage as far as possible a little paradise.

Keep it spotlessly clean. Make it look as pretty and sweet as your limited means will allow. Cook your plain food with all care, and arrange your humble table as tastefully as you possibly can.

If you cannot afford a carpet, let your rooms be carpeted with smiles and welcomes, fastened down with the nails of kind words driven in with the hammer of patience. Such a carpet will not fade in the sun, and constant use will never wear it away.

By so ennobling your present surroundings you will rise above them, and above the need of them, and at the right time you will pass on into the better house and surroundings which have all along been waiting for you, and which you have fitted yourself to occupy.

Perhaps you desire more time for thought and effort, and feel that your hours of labor are too hard and long. Then see to it that you are utilizing to the fullest possible extent what little spare time you have.

It is useless to desire more time, if you are already wasting what little you have; for you would only grow more indolent and indifferent.

Even poverty and lack of time and leisure are not the evils that you imagine they are, and if they hinder you in your progress, it is because you have clothed them in your own weaknesses, and the evil that you see in them is really in yourself.

Endeavor to fully and completely realize that in so far as you shape and could your mind, you are the maker of your destiny, and as, by the transmuting power of self-discipline you realize this more and more, you will come to see that these so-called evils may be converted into blessings.

You will then utilize your poverty for the cultivation of patience, hope and courage; and your lack of time in the gaining of promptness of action and decision of mind, by seizing the precious moments as they present themselves for your acceptance.

As in the rankest soil the most beautiful flowers are grown, so in the dark soil of poverty the choicest flowers of humanity have developed and bloomed.

Where there are difficulties to cope with, and unsatisfactory conditions to overcome, there virtue most flourishes and manifests its glory.

It may be that you are in the employ of a tyrannous master or mistress, and you feel that you are harshly treated. Look upon this also as necessary to your training. Return your employer's unkindness with gentleness and forgiveness.

Practice unceasingly patience and self-control. Turn the disadvantage to account by utilizing it for the gaining of mental and spiritual strength, and by your silent example and influence you will thus be teaching your employer, will be helping him to grow ashamed of his conduct, and will, at the same time, be lifting yourself up to that height of spiritual attainment by which you will be enabled to step into new and more congenial surroundings at the time when they are presented to you.

Do not complain that you are a slave, but lift yourself up, by noble conduct, above the plane of slavery. Before complaining that you are a slave to another, be sure that you are not a slave to self.

Look within; look searchingly, and have no mercy upon yourself. You will find there, perchance, slavish thoughts, slavish desires, and in your daily life and conduct slavish habits.

Conquer these; cease to be a slave to self, and no man will have the power to enslave you. As you overcome self, you will overcome all adverse conditions, and every difficulty will fall before you.

Do not complain that you are oppressed by the rich. Are you sure that if you gained riches you would not be an oppressor yourself?

Remember that there is the Eternal Law which is absolutely just, and that he who oppresses today must himself be oppressed tomorrow; and from this there is no way of escape.

And perhaps you, yesterday (in some former existence) were rich and an oppressor, and that you are now merely paying off the debt which you owe to the Great Law. Practice, therefore, fortitude and faith.

Dwell constantly in mind upon the Eternal justice, the Eternal Good. Endeavor to lift yourself above the personal and the transitory into the impersonal and permanent.

Shake off the delusion that you are being injured or oppressed by another, and try to realize, by a profounder comprehension of your inner life, and the laws which govern that life, that you are only really injured by what is within you. There is no practice more degrading, debasing, and soul-destroying than that of self-pity.

Cast it out from you. While such a canker is feeding upon your heart you can never expect to grow into a fuller life.

Cease from the condemnation of others, and begin to condemn yourself. Condone none of your acts, desires or thoughts that will not bear comparison with spotless purity, or endure the light of sinless good.

By so doing you will be building your house upon the rock of the Eternal, and all that is required for your happiness and well-being will come to you in its own time.

There is positively no way of permanently rising above poverty, or any undesirable condition, except by eradicating those selfish and negative conditions within, of which these are the reflection, and by virtue of which they continue.

The way to true riches is to enrich the soul by the acquisition of virtue. Outside of real heart-virtue there is neither prosperity nor power, but only the appearances of these. I am aware that men make money who have acquired no measure of virtue, and have little desire to do so; but such money does not constitute true riches, and its possession is transitory and feverish.

Here is David's testimony:— For I was envious at the foolish when I saw the prosperity of the wicked.. .. .. . Their eyes stand out with fatness; they have more than heart could wish. . . —Verily I have cleansed my heart in vain, and washed my hands in innocence... When I thought to know this it was too painful for me; until I went into the sanctuary of God, then understood I their end."

The prosperity of the wicked was a great trial to David until he went into the sanctuary of God, and then he knew their end.

You likewise may go into that sanctuary. It is within you. It is that state of consciousness which remains when all that is sordid, and personal, and impermanent is risen above, and universal and eternal principles are realized.

That is the God state of consciousness; it is the sanctuary of the Most High. When by long strife and self-discipline, you have succeeded in entering the door of that holy Temple, you will perceive, with unobstructed vision, the end and fruit of all human thought and endeavor, both good and evil.

You will then no longer relax your faith when you see the immoral man accumulating outward riches, for you will know, that he must come again to poverty and degradation.

The rich man who is barren of virtue is, in reality, poor, and as surely, as the waters of the river are drifting to the ocean, so surely is he, in the midst of all his riches, drifting towards poverty and misfortune; and though he die rich, yet must he return to reap the bitter fruit of all of his immorality.

And though he become rich many times, yet as many times must he be thrown back into poverty, until, by long experience and suffering he conquers the poverty within.

But the man who is outwardly poor, yet rich in virtue, is truly rich, and, in the midst of all his poverty he is surely traveling towards prosperity; and abounding joy and bliss await his coming. If you would become truly and permanently prosperous, you must first become virtuous.

It is therefore unwise to aim directly at prosperity, to make it the one object of life, to reach out greedily for it, To do this is to ultimately defeat yourself.

But rather aim at self-perfection, make useful and unselfish service the object of your life, and ever reach out hands of faith towards the supreme and unalterable Good.

You say you desire wealth, not for your own sake, but in order to do good with it, and to bless others. If this is your real motive in desiring wealth, then wealth will come to you; for you are strong and unselfish indeed if, in the midst of riches, you are willing to look upon yourself as steward and not as owner.

But examine well your motive, for in the majority of instances where money is desired for the admitted object of blessing others, the real underlying motive is a love of popularity, and a desire to pose as a philanthropist or reformer.

If you are not doing good with what little you have, depend upon it the more money you got the more selfish you would become, and all the good you appeared to do with your money, if you attempted to do any, would be so much insinuating self-laudation.

If your real desire is to do good, there is no need to wait for money before you do it; you can do it now, this very moment, and just where you are. If you are really so unselfish as you believe yourself to be, you will show it by sacrificing yourself for others now.

No matter how poor you are, there is room for self-sacrifice, for did not the widow put her all into the treasury?

The heart that truly desires to do good does not wait for money before doing it, but comes to the altar of sacrifice and, leaving there the unworthy elements of self, goes out and breathes upon neighbor and stranger, friend and enemy alike the breath of blessedness.

As the effect is related to the cause, so is prosperity and power related to the inward good and poverty and weakness to the inward evil.

Money does not constitute true wealth, nor position, nor power, and to rely upon it alone is to stand upon a slippery place.

Your true wealth is your stock of virtue, and your true power the uses to which you put it. Rectify your heart, and you will rectify your life.

Lust, hatred, anger, vanity, pride, covetousness, self-indulgence, self-seeking, obstinacy,— all these are poverty and weakness; whereas love, purity, gentleness, meekness, compassion, generosity, self-forgetfulness, and self-renunciation,— all these are wealth and power.

As the elements of poverty and weakness are overcome, an irresistible and all-conquering power is evolved from within, and he who succeeds in establishing himself in the highest virtue, brings the whole world to his feet.

But the rich, as well as the poor, have their undesirable conditions, and are frequently farther removed from happiness than the poor. And here we see how happiness depends, not upon outward aids or possessions, but upon the inward life.

Perhaps you are an employer, and you have endless trouble with those whom you employ, and when you do get good and faithful servants they quickly leave you. As a result you are beginning to lose, or have completely lost, your faith in human nature.

You try to remedy matters by giving better wages, and by allowing certain liberties, yet matters remain unaltered. Let me advise you.

The secret of all your trouble is not in your servants, it is in yourself; and if you look within, with a humble and sincere desire to discover and eradicate your error, you will, sooner or later, find the origin of all your unhappiness.

It may be some selfish desire, or lurking suspicion, or unkind attitude of mind which sends out its poison upon those about you, and reacts upon yourself, even though you may not show it in your manner or speech.

Think of your servants with kindness, consider of them that extremity of service which you yourself would not care to perform were you in their place.

Rare and beautiful is that humility of soul by which a servant entirely forgets himself in his master's good; but far rarer, and beautiful with a divine beauty, is that nobility of soul by which a man, forgetting his own happiness, seeks the happiness of those who are under his authority, and who depend upon him for their bodily sustenance.

And such a man's happiness is increased tenfold, nor does he need to complain of those whom he employs. Said a well known and extensive employer of labor, who never needs to dismiss an employee: "I have always had the happiest relations with my workpeople.

If you ask me how it is to be accounted for, I can only say that it has been my aim from the first to do to them as I would wish to be done by." Herein lies the secret by which all desirable conditions are secured, and all that are undesirable are overcome.

Do you say that you are lonely and unloved, and have "not a friend in the world"? Then, I pray you, for the sake of your own happiness, blame nobody but yourself.

Be friendly towards others, and friends will soon flock round you. Make yourself pure and lovable, and you will be loved by all. Whatever conditions are rendering your life burdensome, you may pass out of and beyond them by developing and utilizing within you the transforming power of self-purification and self-conquest.

Be it the poverty which galls (and remember that the poverty upon which I have been dilating is that poverty which is a source of misery, and not that voluntary poverty which is the glory of emancipated souls), or the riches which burden, or the many misfortunes, griefs, and annoyances which form the dark background in the web of life, you may overcome them by overcoming the selfish elements within which give them life.

It matters not that by the unfailing Law, there are past thoughts and acts to work out and to atone for, as, by the same law, we are setting in motion, during every moment of our life, fresh thoughts and acts, and we have the power to make them good or ill.

Nor does it follow that if a man (reaping what he has sown) must lose money or forfeit position, that he must also lose his fortitude or forfeit his uprightness, and it is in these that his wealth and power and happiness are to be found.

He who clings to self is his own enemy and is surrounded by enemies. He who relinquishes self is his own savior, and is surrounded by friends like a protecting belt. Before the divine radiance of a pure heart all darkness vanishes and all clouds melt away, and he who has conquered self has conquered the universe.

Come, then, out of your poverty; come out of your pain; come out of your troubles, and sighings, and complainings, and heartaches, and loneliness by coming out of yourself.

Let the old tattered garment of your petty selfishness fall from you, and put on the new garment of universal Love. You will then realize the inward heaven, and it will be reflected in all your outward life.

He who sets his foot firmly upon the
Path of self-conquest, who walks, aided
By the staff of Faith, the highway of
Self-sacrifice, will assuredly achieve the
Highest prosperity, and will reap
Abounding and enduring joy and bliss.

To them that seek the highest good
All things subserve the wisest ends;
Nought comes as ill, and wisdom lends
Wings to all shapes of evil brood.

The dark'ning sorrow veils a Star
That waits to shine with gladsome light;
Hell waits on heaven; and after night
Comes golden glory from afar.

Defeats are steps by which we climb
With purer aim to nobler ends;
Loss leads to gain, and joy attends
True footsteps up the hills of time.

Pain leads to paths of holy bliss,
To thoughts and words and deeds divine—,
And clouds that gloom and rays that shine,
Along life's upward highway kiss.

Misfortune does but cloud the way
Whose end and summit in the sky
Of bright success, sunkiss'd and high,
Awaits our seeking and our stay.

The heavy pall of doubts and fears
That clouds the Valley of our hopes,
The shades with which the spirit copes,
The bitter harvesting of tears,

The heartaches, miseries, and griefs,
The bruisings born of broken ties,
All these are steps by which we rise
To living ways of sound beliefs.

Love, pitying, watchful, runs to meet
The Pilgrim from the Land of Fate;
All glory and all good await
The coming of obedient feet.

The Silent Power of Thought; Controlling and Directing One's Forces

The most powerful forces in the universe are the silent forces; and in accordance with the intensity of its power does a force become beneficent when rightly directed, and destructive when wrongly employed.

This is a common knowledge in regard to the mechanical forces, such as steam, electricity, etc., but few have yet learned to apply this knowledge to the realm of mind, where the thought-forces (most powerful of all) are continually being generated and sent forth as currents of salvation or destruction.

At this stage of his evolution, man has entered into the possession of these forces, and the whole trend of his present advancement is their complete subjugation. All the wisdom possible to man on this material earth is to be found only in complete self-mastery, and the command, "Love your enemies," resolves itself into an exhortation to enter here and now, into the possession of that sublime wisdom by taking hold of, mastering and transmuting, those mind forces to which man is now slavishly subject, and by which he is helplessly borne, like a straw on the stream, upon the currents of selfishness.

The Hebrew prophets, with their perfect knowledge of the Supreme Law, always related outward events to inward thought, and associated national disaster or success with the thoughts and desires that dominated the nation at the time.

The knowledge of the causal power of thought is the basis of all their prophecies, as it is the basis of all real wisdom and power. National events are simply the working out of the psychic forces of the nation.

Wars, plagues, and famines are the meeting and clashing of wrongly-directed thought-forces, the culminating points at which destruction steps in as the agent of the Law.

It is foolish to ascribe war to the influence of one man, or to one body of men. It is the crowning horror of national selfishness. It is the silent and conquering thought-forces which bring all things into manifestation.

The universe grew out of thought. Matter in its last analysis is found to be merely objectivized thought. All men's accomplishments were first wrought out in thought, and then objectivized.

The author, the inventor, the architect, first builds up his work in thought, and having perfected it in all its parts as a complete and harmonious whole upon the thought-plane. he then commences to materialize it, to bring it down to the material or sense-plane.

When the thought-forces are directed in harmony with the over-ruling Law, they are up-building and preservative, but when subverted they become disintegrating and self-destructive.

To adjust all your thoughts to a perfect and unswerving faith in the omnipotence and supremacy of Good, is to co-operate with that Good, and to realize within yourself the solution and destruction of all evil. Believe and ye shall live.

And here we have the true meaning of salvation; salvation from the darkness and negation of evil, by entering into, and realizing the living light of the Eternal Good.

Where there is fear, worry, anxiety, doubt, trouble, chagrin, or disappointment, there is ignorance and lack of faith.

All these conditions of mind are the direct outcome of selfishness, and are based upon an inherent belief in the power and supremacy of evil; they therefore constitute practical atheism; and to live in, and become subject to, these negative and soul-destroying conditions of mind is the only real atheism.

It is salvation from such conditions that the race needs, and let no man boast of salvation whilst he is their helpless and obedient slave. To fear or to worry is as sinful as to curse, for how can one fear or worry if he intrinsically believes in the Eternal justice, the Omnipotent Good, the Boundless Love? To fear, to worry, to doubt, is to deny, to disbelieve.

It is from such states of mind that all weakness and failure proceed, for they represent the annulling and disintegrating of the positive thought-forces which would otherwise speed to their object with power, and bring about their own beneficent results.

To overcome these negative conditions is to enter into a life of power, is to cease to be a slave, and to become a master, and there is only one way by which they can be overcome, and that is by steady and persistent growth in inward knowledge.

To mentally deny evil is not sufficient; it must, by daily practice, be risen above and understood. To mentally affirm the good is inadequate; it must, by unswerving endeavor, be entered into and comprehended.

The intelligent practice of self-control, quickly leads to a knowledge of one's interior thought-forces, and, later on, to the acquisition of that power by which they are rightly employed and directed.

In the measure that you master self, that you control your mental forces instead of being controlled by them, in just such measure will you master affairs and outward circumstances.

Show me a man under whose touch everything crumbles away, and who cannot retain success even when it is placed in his hands, and I will show you a man who dwells continually in those conditions of mind which are the very negation of power.

To be for ever wallowing in the bogs of doubt, to be drawn continually into the quicksands of fear, or blown ceaselessly about by the winds of anxiety, is to be a slave, and to live the life of a slave, even though success and influence be for ever knocking at your door seeking for admittance.

Such a man, being without faith and without self-government, is incapable of the right government of his affairs, and is a slave to circumstances; in reality a slave to himself. Such are taught by affliction, and ultimately pass from weakness to strength by the stress of bitter experience. Faith and purpose constitute the motive-power of life.

There is nothing that a strong faith and an unflinching purpose may not accomplish. By the daily exercise of silent faith, the thought-forces are gathered together, and by the daily strengthening of silent purpose, those forces are directed toward the object of accomplishment.

Whatever your position in life may be, before you can hope to enter into any measure of success, usefulness, and power, you must learn how to focus your thought-forces by cultivating calmness and repose. It may be that you are a business man, and you are suddenly confronted with some overwhelming difficulty or probable disaster. You grow fearful and anxious, and are at your wit's end.

To persist in such a state of mind would be fatal, for when anxiety steps in, correct judgment passes out. Now if you will take advantage of a quiet hour or two in the early morning or at night, and go away to some solitary spot, or to some room in your house where you know you will be absolutely free from intrusion, and, having seated yourself in an easy attitude, you forcibly direct your mind right away from the object of anxiety by dwelling upon something in your life that is pleasing and blissgiving, a calm, reposeful strength will gradually steal into your mind, and your anxiety will pass away.

Upon the instant that you find your mind reverting to the lower plane of worry bring it back again, and reestablish it on the plane of peace and strength.

When this is fully accomplished, you may then concentrate your whole mind upon the solution of your difficulty, and what was intricate and insurmountable to you in your hour of anxiety will be made plain and easy, and you will see, with that clear vision and perfect judgment which belong only to a calm and untroubled mind, the right course to pursue and the proper end to be brought about.

It may be that you will have to try day after day before you will be able to perfectly calm your mind, but if you persevere you will certainly accomplish it. And the course which is presented to you in that hour of calmness must be carried out.

Doubtless when you are again involved in the business of the day, and worries again creep in and begin to dominate you, you will begin to think that the course is a wrong or foolish one, but do not heed such suggestions.

Be guided absolutely and entirely by the vision of calmness, and not by the shadows of anxiety. The hour of calmness is the hour of illumination and correct judgment.

By such a course of mental discipline the scattered thought-forces are reunited, and directed, like the rays of the search-light, upon the problem at issue, with the result that it gives way before them.

There is no difficulty, however great, but will yield before a calm and powerful concentration of thought, and no legitimate object but may be speedily actualized by the intelligent use and direction of one's soul-forces.

Not until you have gone deeply and searchingly into your inner nature, and have overcome many enemies that lurk there, can you have any approximate conception of the subtle power of thought, of its inseparable relation to outward and material things, or of its magical potency, when rightly poised and directed, in readjusting and transforming the life-conditions.

Every thought you think is a force sent out, and in accordance with its nature and intensity will it go out to seek a lodgment in minds receptive to it, and will react upon yourself for good or evil. There is ceaseless reciprocity between mind and mind, and a continual interchange of thought-forces.

Selfish and disturbing thoughts are so many malignant and destructive forces, messengers of evil, sent out to stimulate and augment the evil in other minds, which in turn send them back upon you with added power.

While thoughts that are calm, pure, and unselfish are so many angelic messengers sent out into the world with health, healing, and blessedness upon their wings, counteracting the evil forces; pouring the oil of joy upon the troubled waters of anxiety and sorrow, and restoring to broken hearts their heritage of immortality.

Think good thoughts, and they will quickly become actualized in your outward life in the form of good conditions. Control your soul-forces, and you will be able to shape your outward life as you will. The difference between a savior and a sinner is this, that the one has a perfect control of all the forces within him; the other is dominated and controlled by them.

There is absolutely no other way to true power and abiding peace, but by self-control, self-government, self-purification. To be at the mercy of your disposition is to be impotent, unhappy, and of little real use in the world.

The conquest of your petty likes and dislikes, your capricious loves and hates, your fits of anger, suspicion, jealousy, and all the changing moods to which you are more or less helplessly subject, this is the task you have before you if you would weave into the web of life the golden threads of happiness and prosperity. In so far as you are enslaved by the changing moods within you, will you need to depend upon others and upon outward aids as you walk through life.

If you would walk firmly and securely, and would accomplish any achievement, you must learn to rise above and control all such disturbing and retarding vibrations.

You must daily practice the habit of putting your mind at rest, "going into the silence," as it is commonly called. This is a method of replacing a troubled thought with one of peace, a thought of weakness with one of strength.

Until you succeed in doing this you cannot hope to direct your mental forces upon the problems and pursuits of life with any appreciable measure of success. It is a process of diverting one's scattered forces into one powerful channel.

Just as a useless marsh may be converted into a field of golden corn or a fruitful garden by draining and directing the scattered and harmful streams into one well-cut channel, so, he who acquires calmness, and subdues and directs the thought-currents within himself, saves his soul, and fructifies his heart and life.

As you succeed in gaining mastery over your impulses and thoughts you will begin to feel, growing up within you, a new and silent power, and a settled feeling of composure and strength will remain with you.

Your latent powers will begin to unfold themselves, and whereas formerly your efforts were weak and ineffectual, you will now be able to work with that calm confidence which commands success.

And along with this new power and strength, there will be awakened within you that interior Illumination known as "intuition," and you will walk no longer in darkness and speculation, but in light and certainty.

With the development of this soul-vision, judgment and mental penetration will be incalculably increased, and there will evolve within you that prophetic vision by the aid of which you will be able to sense coming events, and to forecast, with remarkable accuracy, the result of your efforts.

And in just the measure that you alter from within will your outlook upon life alter; and as you alter your mental attitude towards others they will alter in their attitude and conduct toward you.

As you rise above the lower, debilitating, and destructive thoughtforces, you will come in contact with the positive, strengthening, and up-building currents generated by strong, pure, and noble minds, your happiness will be immeasurably intensified, and you will begin to realize the joy, strength, and power, which are born only of selfmastery.

And this joy, strength, and power will be continually radiating from you, and without any effort on your part, nay, though you are utterly unconscious of it, strong people will be drawn toward you, influence will be put into your hands, and in accordance with your altered thought-world will outward events shape themselves.

"A man's foes are they of his own household," and he who would be useful, strong, and happy, must cease to be a passive receptacle for the negative, beggardly, and impure streams of thought; and as a wise householder commands his servants and invites his guests, so must he learn to command his desires, and to say, with authority, what thoughts he shall admit into the mansion of his soul.

Even a very partial success in self-mastery adds greatly to one's power and he who succeeds in perfecting this divine accomplishment, enters into possession of undreamed-of wisdom and inward strength and peace, and realizes that all the forces of the universe aid and protect his footsteps who is master of his own soul.

> Would you scale the highest heaven,
> Would you pierce the lowest hell,
> Live in dreams of constant beauty,
>
> Or in basest thinkings dwell.
> For your thoughts are heaven above you,
> And your thoughts are hell below,
> Bliss is not, except in thinking,
> Torment nought but thought can know.
>
> Worlds would vanish but for thinking;
> Glory is not but in dreams;
> And the Drama of the ages
> From the Thought Eternal streams.
>
> Dignity and shame and sorrow,
> Pain and anguish, love and hate
> Are but maskings of the mighty
> Pulsing Thought that governs Fate.
>
> As the colors of the rainbow
> Makes the one uncolored beam,
> So the universal changes
> Make the One Eternal Dream.
>
> And the Dream is all within you,
> And the Dreamer waiteth long
> For the Morning to awake him
> To the living thought and strong.

That shall make the ideal real,
Make to vanish dreams of hell
In the highest, holiest heaven
Where the pure and perfect dwell.

Evil is the thought that thinks it;
Good, the thought that makes it so
Light and darkness, sin and pureness
Likewise out of thinking grow.

Dwell in thought upon the Grandest,
And the Grandest you shall see ;
Fix your mind upon the Highest,
And the Highest you shall be.

The Secret of Health, Success, and Power

We all remember with what intense delight, as children, we listened to the never-tiring fairy-tale. How eagerly we followed the fluctuating fortunes of the good boy or girl, ever protected, in the hour of crisis, from the evil machinations of the scheming witch, the cruel giant, or the wicked king.

And our little hearts never faltered for the fate of the hero or heroine, nor did we doubt their ultimate triumph over all their enemies, for we knew that the fairies were infallible, and that they would never desert those who had consecrated themselves to the good and the true.

And what unspeakable joy pulsated within us when the Fairy-Queen, bringing all her magic to bear at the critical moment, scattered all the darkness and trouble, and granted them the complete satisfaction of all their hopes, and they were "happy ever after."

With the accumulating years, and an ever-increasing intimacy with the so-called " realities" of life, our beautiful fairy-world became obliterated, and its wonderful inhabitants were relegated, in the archives of memory, to the shadowy and unreal.

And we thought we were wise and strong in thus leaving for ever the land of childish dreams, but as we re-become little children in the wondrous world of wisdom, we shall return again to the inspiring dreams of childhood and find that they are, after all, realities.

The fairy-folk, so small and nearly always invisible, yet possessed of an all-conquering and magical power, who bestow upon the good, health, wealth, and happiness, along with all the gifts of nature in lavish profusion, start again into reality and become immortalized in the soul-realm of him who, by growth in wisdom, has entered into a knowledge of the power of thought, and the laws which govern the inner world of being.

To him the fairies live again as thought-people, thought-messengers, thought-powers working in harmony with the over-ruling Good. And they who, day by day, endeavor to harmonize their hearts with the heart of the Supreme Good, do in reality acquire true health, wealth, and happiness.

There is no protection to compare with goodness, and by "goodness" I do not mean a mere outward conformity to the rules of morality; I mean pure thought, noble aspiration, unselfish love, and freedom from vainglory.

To dwell continually in good thoughts, is to throw around oneself a psychic atmosphere of sweetness and power which leaves its impress upon all who come in contact with it.

As the rising sun puts to rout the helpless shadows, so are all the impotent forces of evil put to flight by the searching rays of positive thought which shine forth from a heart made strong in purity and faith.

Where there is sterling faith and uncompromising purity there is health, there is success, there is power. In such a one, disease, failure, and disaster can find no lodgment, for there is nothing on which they can feed.

Even physical conditions are largely determined by mental states, and to this truth the scientific world is rapidly being drawn.

The old, materialistic belief that a man is what his body makes him, is rapidly passing away, and is being replaced by the inspiring belief that man is superior to his body, and that his body is what he makes it by the power of thought.

Men everywhere are ceasing to believe that a man is despairing because he is dyspeptic, and are coming to understand that he is dyspeptic because he is despairing, and in the near future, the fact that all disease has its origin in the mind will become common knowledge.

There is no evil in the universe but has its root and origin in the mind, and sin, sickness, sorrow, and affliction do not, in reality, belong to the universal order, are not inherent in the nature of things, but are the direct outcome of our ignorance of the right relations of things.

According to tradition, there once lived, in India, a school of philosophers who led a life of such absolute purity and simplicity that they commonly reached the age of one hundred and fifty years, and to fall sick was looked upon by them as an unpardonable disgrace, for it was considered to indicate a violation of law.

The sooner we realize and acknowledge that sickness, far from being the arbitrary visitation of an offended God, or the test of an unwise Providence, is the result of our own error or sin, the sooner shall we enter upon the highway of health.

Disease comes to those who attract it, to those whose minds and bodies are receptive to it, and flees from those whose strong, pure, and positive thought-sphere generates healing and life-giving currents.

If you are given to anger, worry, jealousy, greed, or any other inharmonious state of mind, and expect perfect physical health, you are expecting the impossible, for you are continually sowing the seeds of disease in your mind.

Such conditions of mind are carefully shunned by the wise man, for he knows them to be far more dangerous than a bad drain or an infected house.

If you would be free from all physical aches and pains, and would enjoy perfect physical harmony, then put your mind in order, and harmonize your thoughts. Think joyful thoughts; think loving thoughts; let the elixir of goodwill course through your veins, and you will need no other medicine. Put away your jealousies, your suspicions, your worries, your hatreds, your selfish indulgences, and you will put away your dyspepsia, your biliousness, your nervousness and aching joints.

If you will persist in clinging to these debilitating and demoralizing habits of mind, then do not complain when your body is laid low with sickness. The following story illustrates the close relation that exists between habits of mind and bodily conditions.

A certain man was afflicted with a painful disease, and he tried one physician after another, but all to no purpose. He then visited towns which were famous for their curative waters, and after having bathed in them all, his disease was more painful than ever.

One night he dreamed that a Presence came to him and said, "Brother, hast thou tried all the means of cure?" and he replied, "I have tried all." "Nay," said the Presence, "Come with me, and I will show thee a healing bath which has escaped thy notice."

The afflicted man followed, and the Presence led him to a clear pool of water, and said, "Plunge thyself in this water and thou shalt surely recover," and thereupon vanished.

The man plunged into the water, and on coming out, lo! his disease had left him, and at the same moment he saw written above the pool the word "Renounce." Upon waking, the fall meaning of his dream flashed across his mind, and looking within he discovered that he had, all along, been a victim to a sinful indulgence, and he vowed that he would renounce it for ever.

He carried out his vow, and from that day his affliction began to leave him, and in a short time he was completely restored to health. Many people complain that they have broken down through over-work. In the majority of such cases the breakdown is more frequently the result of foolishly wasted energy.

If you would secure health you must learn to work without friction. To become anxious or excited, or to worry over needless details is to invite a breakdown.

Work, whether of brain or body, is beneficial and health-giving, and the man who can work with a steady and calm persistency, freed from all anxiety and worry, and with his mind utterly oblivious to all but the work he has in hand, will not only accomplish far more than the man who is always hurried and anxious, but he will retain his health, a boon which the other quickly forfeits.

True health and true success go together, for they are inseparably intertwined in the thought-realm. As mental harmony produces bodily health, so it also leads to a harmonious sequence in the actual working out of one's plans.

Order your thoughts and you will order your life. Pour the oil of tranquility upon the turbulent waters of the passions and prejudices, and the tempests of misfortune, howsoever they may threaten, will be powerless to wreck the barque of your soul, as it threads its way across the ocean of life.

And if that barque be piloted by a cheerful and never-failing faith its course will be doubly sure, and many perils will pass it by which would other-wise attack it.

By the power of faith every enduring work is accomplished. Faith in the Supreme; faith in the over-ruling Law; faith in your work, and in your power to accomplish that work, —here is the rock upon which you must build if you would achieve, if you would stand and not fall.

To follow, under all circumstances, the highest promptings within you; to be always true to the divine self; to rely upon the inward Light, the inward Voice, and to pursue your purpose with a fearless and restful heart, believing that the future will yield unto you the meed of every thought and effort; knowing that the laws of the universe can never fail, and that your own will come back to you with mathematical exactitude, this is faith and the living of faith.

By the power of such a faith the dark waters of uncertainty are divided, every mountain of difficulty crumbles away, and the believing soul passes on unharmed.

Strive, O reader! to acquire, above everything, the priceless possession of this dauntless faith, for it is the talisman of happiness, of success, of peace, of power, of all that makes life great and superior to suffering.

Build upon such a faith, and you build upon the Rock of the Eternal, and with the materials of the Eternal, and the structure that you erect will never be dissolved, for it will transcend all the accumulations of material luxuries and riches, the end of which is dust.

Whether you are hurled into the depths of sorrow or lifted upon the heights of joy, ever retain your hold upon this faith, ever return to it as your rock of refuge, and keep your feet firmly planted upon its immortal and immovable base.

Centered in such a faith, you will become possessed of such a spiritual strength as will shatter, like so many toys of glass, all the forces of evil that are hurled against you, and you will achieve a success such as the mere striver after worldly gain can never know or even dream of. "If ye have faith, and doubt not, ye shall not only do this, . . . but if ye shall say unto this mountain, be thou removed and be thou cast into the sea, it shall be done."

There are those today, men and women tabernacle in flesh and blood, who have realized this faith, who live in it and by it day by day, and who, having put it to the uttermost test, have entered into the possession of its glory and peace.

Such have sent out the word of command, and the mountains of sorrow and disappointment, of mental weariness and physical pain have passed from them, and have been cast into the sea of oblivion.

If you will become possessed of this faith you will not need to trouble about your success or failure, and success will come.

You will not need to become anxious about results, but will work joyfully and peacefully, knowing that right thoughts and right efforts will inevitably bring about right results.

I know a lady who has entered into many blissful satisfactions, and recently a friend remarked to her, "Oh, how fortunate you are! You only have to wish for a thing, and it comes to you."

And it did, indeed, appear so on the surface; but in reality all the blessedness that has entered into this woman's life is the direct outcome of the inward state of blessedness which she has, throughout life, been cultivating and training toward perfection.

Mere wishing brings nothing but disappointment; it is living that tells.

The foolish wish and grumble; the wise, work and wait. And this woman had worked; worked without and within, but especially within upon heart and soul; and with the invisible hands of the spirit she had built up, with the precious stones of faith, hope, joy, devotion, and love, a fair temple of light, whose glorifying radiance was ever round about her.

It beamed in her eye; it shone through her countenance; it vibrated in her voice; and all who came into her presence felt its captivating spell.

And as with her, so with you. Your success, your failure, your influence, your whole life you carry about with you, for your dominant trends of thought are the determining factors in your destiny.

Send forth loving, stainless, and happy thoughts, and blessings will fall into your hands, and your table will be spread with the cloth of peace.

Send forth hateful, impure, and unhappy thoughts, and curses will rain down upon you, and fear and unrest will wait upon your pillow. You are the unconditional maker of your fate, be that fate what it may.

Every moment you are sending forth from you the influences which will make or mar your life.

Let your heart grow large and loving and unselfish, and great and lasting will be your influence and success, even though you make little money.

Confine it within the narrow limits of self-interest, and even though you become a millionaire your influence and success, at the final reckoning will be found to be utterly insignificant. Cultivate, then, this pure and unselfish spirit, and combine with purity and faith, singleness of purpose, and you are evolving from within the elements, not only of abounding health and enduring success, but of greatness and power.

If your present position is distasteful to you, and your heart is not in your work, nevertheless perform your duties with scrupulous diligence, and whilst resting your mind in the idea that the better position and greater opportunities are waiting for you, ever keep an active mental outlook for budding possibilities, so that when the critical moment arrives, and the new channel presents itself, you will step into it with your mind fully prepared for the undertaking, and with that intelligence and foresight which is born of mental discipline.

Whatever your task may be, concentrate your whole mind upon it, throw into it all the energy of which you are capable. The faultless completion of small tasks leads inevitably to larger tasks. See to it that you rise by steady climbing, and you will never fall. And herein lies the secret of true power.

Learn, by constant practice, how to husband your resources, and to concentrate them, at any moment, upon a given point. The foolish waste all their mental and spiritual energy in frivolity, foolish chatter, or selfish argument, not to mention wasteful physical excesses.

If you would acquire overcoming power you must cultivate poise and passivity. You must be able to stand alone. All power is associated with immovability. The mountain, the massive rock, the storm-tried oak, all speak to us of power, because of their combined solitary grandeur and defiant fixity; while the shifting sand, the yielding twig, and the waving reed speak to us of weakness, because they are movable and nonresistant, and are utterly useless when detached from their fellows.

He is the man of power who, when all his fellows are swayed by some emotion or passion, remains calm and unmoved. He only is fitted to command and control who has succeeded in commanding and controlling himself.

The hysterical, the fearful, the thoughtless and frivolous, let such seek company, or they will fall for lack of support; but the calm, the fearless, the thoughtful, and let such seek the solitude of the forest, the desert, and the mountain-top, and to their power more power will be added, and they will more and more successfully stem the psychic currents and whirlpools which engulf mankind.

Passion is not power; it is the abuse of power, the dispersion of power. Passion is like a furious storm which beats fiercely and wildly upon the embattled rock whilst power is like the rock itself, which remains silent and unmoved through it all.

That was a manifestation of true power when Martin Luther, wearied with the persuasions of his fearful friends, who were doubtful as to his safety should he go to Worms, replied, "If there were as many devils in Worms as there are tiles on the housetops I would go."

And when Benjamin Disraeli broke down in his first Parliamentary speech, and brought upon himself the derision of the House, that was an exhibition of germinal power when he exclaimed, "The day will come when you will consider it an honor to listen to me."

When that young man, whom I knew, passing through continual reverses and misfortunes, was mocked by his friends and told to desist from further effort, and he replied, "The time is not far distant when you will marvel at my good fortune and success," he showed that he was possessed of that silent and irresistible power which has taken him over innumerable difficulties, and crowned his life with success.

If you have not this power, you may acquire it by practice, and the beginning of power is likewise the beginning of wisdom. You must commence by overcoming those purposeless trivialities to which you have hitherto been a willing victim.

Boisterous and uncontrolled laughter, slander and idle talk, and joking merely to raise a laugh, all these things must be put on one side as so much waste of valuable energy.

St. Paul never showed his wonderful insight into the hidden laws of human progress to greater advantage than when he warned the Ephesians against "Foolish talking and jesting which is not convenient," for to dwell habitually in such practices is to destroy all spiritual power and life.

As you succeed in rendering yourself impervious to such mental dissipations you will begin to understand what true power is, and you will then commence to grapple with the more powerful desires and appetites which hold your soul in bondage, and bar the way to power, and your further progress will then be made clear.

Above all be of single aim; have a legitimate and useful purpose, and devote yourself unreservedly to it. Let nothing draw you aside ; remember that the double-minded man is unstable in all his ways.

Be eager to learn, but slow to beg. Have a thorough understanding of your work, and let it be your own; and as you proceed, ever following the inward Guide, the infallible Voice, you will pass on from victory to victory, and will rise step by step to higher resting-places, and your ever-broadening outlook will gradually reveal to you the essential beauty and purpose of life.

Self-purified, health will be yours; faith-protected, success will be yours; self-governed, power will be yours, and all that you do will prosper, for, ceasing to be a disjointed unit, self-enslaved, you will be in harmony with the Great Law, working no longer against, but with, the Universal Life, the Eternal Good.

And what health you gain it will remain with you; what success you achieve will be beyond all human computation, and will never pass away; and what influence and power you wield will continue to increase throughout the ages, for it will be a part of that unchangeable Principle which supports the universe.

This, then, is the secret of health, —a pure heart and a well-ordered mind ; this is the secret of success, —an unfaltering faith, and a wisely directed purpose; and to rein in, with unfaltering will, the dark steed of desire, this is the secret of power.

All ways are waiting for my feet to tread,
The light and dark, the living and the dead,
The broad and narrow way, the high and low,
The good and bad, and with quick step or slow,
I now may enter any way I will,
And find, by walking, which is good, which ill.

And all good things my wandering feet await,
If I but come, with vow inviolate,
Unto the narrow, high and holy way
Of heart-born purity, and therein stay;
Walking, secure from him who taunts and scorns,
To flowery meads, across the path of thorns.

And I may stand where health, success, and power
Await my coming, if, each fleeting hour,
I cling to love and patience; and abide
With stainlessness; and never step aside
From high integrity ; so shall I see
At last the land of immortality.

And I may seek and find; I may achieve,
I may not claim, but, losing, may retrieve.
The law bends not for me, but I must bend
Unto the law, if I would reach the end
Of my afflictions, if I would restore
My soul to Light and Life, and weep no more.

Not mine the arrogant and selfish claim
To all good things; be mine the lowly aim
To seek and find, to know and comprehend,
And wisdom-ward all holy footsteps wend,
Nothing is mine to claim or to command,
But all is mine to know and understand

The Secret of Abounding Happiness

Great is the thirst for happiness, and equally great is the lack of happiness. The majority of the poor long for riches, believing that their possession would bring them supreme and lasting happiness.

Many who are rich, having gratified every desire and whim, suffer from ennui and repletion, and are farther from the possession of happiness even than the very poor.

If we reflect upon this state of things it will ultimately lead us to a knowledge of the all important truth that happiness is not derived from mere outward possessions, nor misery from the lack of them; for if this were so, we should find the poor always miserable, and the rich always happy, whereas the reverse is frequently the case.

Some of the most wretched people whom I have known were those who were surrounded with riches and luxury, whilst some of the brightest and happiest people I have met were possessed of only the barest necessities of life.

Many men who have accumulated riches have confessed that the selfish gratification which followed the acquisition of riches has robbed life of its sweetness, and that they were never so happy as when they were poor.

What, then, is happiness, and how is it to be secured? Is it a figment, a delusion, and is suffering alone perennial? We shall find, after earnest observation and reflection, that all, except those who have entered the way of wisdom, believe that happiness is only to be obtained by the gratification of desire.

It is this belief, rooted in the soil of ignorance, and continually watered by selfish cravings, that is the cause of all the misery in the world.

And I do not limit the word desire to the grosser animal cravings; it extends to the higher psychic realm, where far more powerful, subtle, and insidious cravings hold in bondage the intellectual and refined, depriving them of all that beauty, harmony, and purity of soul whose expression is happiness.

Most people will admit that selfishness is the cause of all the unhappiness in the world, but they fall under the soul-destroying delusion that it is somebody else's selfishness, and not their own.

When you are willing to admit that all your unhappiness is the result of your own selfishness you will not be far from the gates of Paradise; but so long as you are convinced that it is the selfishness of others that is robbing you of joy, so long will you remain a prisoner in your self-created purgatory.

Happiness is that inward state of perfect satisfaction which is joy and peace, and from which all desire is eliminated. The satisfaction which results from gratified desire is brief and illusionary, and is always followed by an increased demand for gratification.

Desire is as insatiable as the ocean, and clamors louder and louder as its demands are attended to.

It claims ever-increasing service from its deluded devotees, until at last they are struck down with physical or mental anguish, and are hurled into the purifying fires of suffering. Desire is the region of hell, and all torments are centered there.

The giving up of desire is the realization of heaven, and all delights await the pilgrim there,

> I sent my soul through the invisible,
> Some letter of that after life to spell,
> And by-and-by my soul returned to me,
> And whispered, I myself am heaven and hell,"

Heaven and hell are inward states. Sink into self and all its gratifications, and you sink into hell; rise above self into that state of consciousness which is the utter denial and forgetfulness of self, and you enter heaven.

Self is blind, without judgment, not possessed of true knowledge, and always leads to suffering. Correct perception, unbiased judgment, and true knowledge belong only to the divine state, and only in so far as you realize this divine consciousness can you know what real happiness is.

So long as you persist in selfishly seeking for your own personal happiness, so long will happiness elude you, and you will be sowing the seeds of wretchedness.

In so far as you succeed in losing yourself in the service of others, in that measure will happiness come to you, and you will reap a harvest of bliss.

> It is in loving, not in being loved,
> The heart is blessed;
> It is in giving, not in seeking gifts,
> We find our quest.

> Whatever be thy longing or thy need,
> That do thou give;
> So shall thy soul be fed, and thou indeed
> Shalt truly live.

Cling to self, and you cling to sorrow, relinquish self, and you enter into peace. To seek selfishly is not only to lose happiness, but even that which we believe to be the source of happiness. See how the glutton is continually looking about for a new delicacy wherewith to stimulate his deadened appetite; and how, bloated, burdened, and diseased, scarcely any food at last is eaten with pleasure.

Whereas, he who has mastered his appetite, and not only does not seek, but never thinks of gustatory pleasure, finds delight in the most frugal meal. The angel-form of happiness, which men, looking through the eyes of self, imagine they see in gratified desire, when clasped is always found to be the skeleton of misery. Truly, "He that seeketh his life shall lose it, and he that loseth his life shall find it."

Abiding happiness will come to you when, ceasing to selfishly cling, you are willing to give up. When you are willing to lose, unreservedly, that impermanent thing which is so dear to you, and which, whether you cling to it or not, will one day be snatched from you, then you will find that that which seemed to you like a painful loss, turns out to be a supreme gain.

To give up in order to gain, than this there is no greater delusion, nor no more prolific source of misery; but to be willing to yield up and to suffer loss, this is indeed the Way of Life.

How is it possible to find real happiness by centering ourselves in those things which, by their very nature, must pass away? Abiding and real happiness can only be found by centering ourselves in that which is permanent.

Rise, therefore, above the clinging to and the craving for impermanent things, and you will then enter into a consciousness of the Eternal, and as, rising above self, and by growing more and more into the spirit of purity, self-sacrifice and universal Love, you become centered in that consciousness, you will realize that happiness which has no reaction, and which can never be taken from you.

The heart that has reached utter self-forgetfulness in its love for others has not only become possessed of the highest happiness but has entered into immortality, for it has realized the Divine.

Look back upon your life, and you will find that the moments of supremest happiness were those in which you uttered some word, or performed some act, of compassion or self-denying love. Spiritually, happiness and harmony are, synonymous.

Harmony is one phase of the Great Law whose spiritual expression is love. All selfishness is discord, and to be selfish is to be out of harmony with the Divine order.

As we realize that all-embracing love which is the negation of self, we put ourselves in harmony with the divine music, the universal song, and that ineffable melody which is true happiness becomes our own.

Men and women are rushing hither and thither in the blind search for happiness, and cannot find it; nor ever will until they recognize that happiness is already within them and round about them, filling the universe, and that they, in their selfish searching are shutting themselves out from it.

> I followed happiness to make her mine,
> Past towering oak and swinging ivy vine.
> She fled, I chased, o'er slanting hill and dale,
> O'er fields and meadows, in the purpling vale;
> Pursuing rapidly o'er dashing stream.
> I scaled the dizzy cliffs where eagles scream;
> I traversed swiftly every land and sea,
> But always happiness eluded me.
>
> Exhausted, fainting, I pursued no more,
> But sank to rest upon a barren shore.
> One came and asked for food, and one for alms
> I placed the bread and gold in bony palms.
> One came for sympathy, and one for rest;
> I shared with every needy one my best;
> When, lo! sweet Happiness, with form divine,
> Stood by me, whispering softly, 'I am thine'.

These beautiful lines of Burleigh's express the secret of all abounding happiness. Sacrifice the personal and transient, and you rise at once into the impersonal and permanent.

Give up that narrow cramped self that seeks to render all things subservient to its own petty interests, and you will enter into the company of the angels, into the very heart and essence of universal Love.

Forget yourself entirely in the sorrows of others and in ministering to others, and divine happiness will emancipate you from all sorrow and suffering.

"Taking the first step with a good thought, the second with a good word, and the third with a good deed, I entered Paradise." And you also may enter into Paradise by pursuing the same course. It is not beyond, it is here. It is realized only by the unselfish.

It is known in its fullness only to the pure in heart. If you have not realized this unbounded happiness you may begin to actualize it by ever holding before you the lofty ideal of unselfish love, and aspiring towards it.

Aspiration or prayer is desire turned upward. It is the soul turning toward its Divine source, where alone permanent satisfaction can be found. By aspiration the destructive forces of desire are transmuted into divine and all-preserving energy.

To aspire is to make an effort to shake off the trammels of desire; it is the prodigal made wise by loneliness and suffering, returning to his Father's Mansion.

As you rise above the sordid self; as you break, one after another, the chains that bind you, will you realize the joy of giving, as distinguished from the misery of grasping - giving of your substance; giving of your intellect; giving of the love and light that is growing within you.

You will then understand that it is indeed "more blessed to give than to receive."

But the giving must be of the heart without any taint of self, without desire for reward. The gift of pure love is always attended with bliss.

If, after you have given, you are wounded because you are not thanked or flattered, or your name put in the paper, know then that your gift was prompted by vanity and not by love, and you were merely giving in order to get; were not really giving, but grasping.

Lose yourself in the welfare of others; forget yourself in all that you do; this is the secret of abounding happiness.

Ever be on the watch to guard against selfishness, and learn faithfully the divine lessons of inward sacrifice; so shall you climb the highest heights of happiness, and shall remain in the never clouded sunshine of universal joy, clothed in the shining garment of immortality.

Are you searching for the happiness that does not fade away?
Are you looking for the joy that lives, and leaves no grievous day?
Are you panting for the waterbrooks of Love, and Life, and Peace?
Then let all dark desires depart, and selfish seeking cease.
Are you lingering in the paths of pain, grief-haunted, stricken sore?
Are you wandering in the ways that wound your weary feet the more?
Are you sighing for the Resting-Place where tears and sorrows cease?
Then sacrifice your selfish heart and find the Heart of Peace.

The Realization of Prosperity

It is granted only to the heart that abounds with integrity, trust, generosity and love to realize true prosperity. The heart that is not possessed of these qualities cannot know prosperity, for prosperity, like happiness, is not an outward possession, but an inward realization.

The greedy man may become a millionaire, but he will always be wretched, and mean, and poor, and will even consider himself outwardly poor so long as there is a man in the world who is richer than himself, whilst the upright, the open-handed and loving will realize a full and rich prosperity, even though their outward possessions may be small.

He is poor who is dissatisfied; he is rich who is contented with what he has, and he is richer who is generous with what he has.

When we contemplate the fact that the universe is abounding in all good things, material as well as spiritual, and compare it with man's blind eagerness to secure a few gold coins, or a few acres of dirt, it is then that we realize how dark and ignorant selfishness is; it is then that we know that self-seeking is self-destruction.

Nature gives all, without reservation, and loses nothing; man, grasping all, loses everything.

If you would realize true prosperity do not settle down, as many have done, into the belief that if you do right everything will go wrong. Do not allow the word "competition" to shake your faith in the supremacy of righteousness.

I care not what men may say about the "laws of competition," for do I not know the unchangeable Law, which shall one day put them all to rout, and which puts them to rout even now in the heart and life of the righteous man?

And knowing this Law I can contemplate all dishonesty with undisturbed repose, for I know where certain destruction awaits it.

Under all circumstances do that which you believe to be right, and trust the Law; trust the Divine Power that is imminent in the universe, and it will never desert you, and you will always be protected.

By such a trust all your losses will be converted into gains, and all curses which threaten will be transmuted into blessings. Never let go of integrity, generosity, and love, for these, coupled with energy, will lift you into the truly prosperous state.

Do not believe the world when it tells you that you must always attend to "number one" first, and to others afterwards. To do this is not to think of others at all, but only of one's own comforts.

To those who practice this the day will come when they will be deserted by all, and when they cry out in their loneliness and anguish there will be no one to hear and help them. To consider one's self before all others is to cramp and warp and hinder every noble and divine impulse.

Let your soul expand, let your heart reach out to others in loving and generous warmth, and great and lasting will be your joy, and all prosperity will come to you. Those who have wandered from the highway of righteousness guard themselves against competition; those who always pursue the right need not to trouble about such defense.

This is no empty statement, There are men today who, by the power of integrity and faith, have defied all competition, and who, without swerving in the least from their methods, when competed with, have risen steadily into prosperity, whilst those who tried to undermine them have fallen back defeated.

To possess those inward qualities which constitute goodness is to be armored against all the powers of evil, and to be doubly protected in every time of trial; and to build' oneself up in those qualities is to build up a success which cannot be shaken, and to enter into a prosperity which will endure forever.

The White Robe of the Heart Invisible
Is stained with sin and sorrow, grief and pain,
And all repentant pools and springs of prayer
Shall not avail to wash it white again.

While in the path of ignorance I walk,
The stains of error will not cease to cling
Defilements mark the crooked path of self,
Where anguish lurks and disappointments sting.

Knowledge and wisdom only can avail
To purify and make my garment clean,
For therein lie love's waters ; therein rests
Peace undisturbed, eternal, and serene.

Sin and repentance is the path of pain,
Knowledge and wisdom is the path of Peace
By the near way of practice I will find
Where bliss begins, how pains and sorrows cease.

Self shall depart, and Truth shall take its place
The Changeless One, the Indivisible
Shall take up His abode in me, and cleanse
The White Robe of the Heart Invisible.

www.ingramcontent.com/pod-product-compliance
Lightning Source LLC
LaVergne TN
LVHW011911080426
835508LV00007BA/342